❧ *Asinaria* ❧

Publication of this volume has been made possible in part through the generous support and enduring vision of Warren G. Moon.

⇒ *Asinaria* ⇐

The One about the Asses

Plautus

TRANSLATED WITH COMMENTARY
BY JOHN HENDERSON

THE UNIVERSITY OF WISCONSIN PRESS

The University of Wisconsin Press
1930 Monroe Street
Madison, Wisconsin 53711

www.wisc.edu/wisconsinpress/

3 Henrietta Street
London WC2E 8LU, England

5   4   3   2   1

Printed in the United States of America

Library of Congress Cataloging-in-Publication Data
Plautus, Titus Maccius.
[Asinaria. English & Latin]
Asinaria : the one about the asses / Plautus ; translated and with commentary
by John Henderson.
p. cm. — (Wisconsin studies in classics)
Text in Latin with English translation; introductory material and commentary in English.
Includes bibliographical references and indexes.
ISBN 0-299-21990-9 (cloth : alk. paper)—ISBN 0-299-21994-1 (pbk. : alk. paper)
1. Plautus, Titus Maccius. Asinaria. I. Henderson, John, 1948– .
II. Title. III. Series.
PA6568.A7   2006
872′.01—dc22   2006007519

Contents

Preface

She has her husband back, but he is no great prize.

Niall Slater

The tattered outlaw of the earth, | of ancient crooked will:
Starve, scourge, deride me: I am dumb, | I keep my secret still.

G. K. Chesterton, "The Donkey" (1920)

Res ridicula est. This play endured much comical misrepresentation and suffered farcical underappreciation in twentieth-century reception (p. **224** **n.5**). I should like to recommend its "wit and fun"; and proclaim to one and all: "it's a gas" (13–14). *The One about the Asses* is full of Rome: slavery and sex slavery; money and family structure; masculinity and social standing; senility and partying; jokes, lies, and idiocy. This is Latin behaving badly, and Plautus isn't a pushover to read (pp. **105–16**). But—especially if you have the sort of mind that will let you hear a donkey hee-haw as in *Don Quixote*—you'll go a bundle on the nonstop silliness. So, as the prologue yells, LISTEN, as naughty Rome gets its kicks—and gives itself a kick in the *Asinaria*.

We don't know the date of first production, but it must have been shown, in a temporary auditorium, to the people of Rome at some state festival provided by elected magistrates of the Republic at its zenith in the late third or early second centuries BCE (p. **127**). It then became classic theatre, revived and eventually edited for reading in and after school from the mid-first century BCE onwards. Like all Plautus' surviving score of verse comedies, it is written in a colourful splash of colloquial mixed with parodic Latin, from a couple of centuries before the rest of the Roman verse we read today was first composed (pp. **117–20**). A *special* language, then, and special play *of* language, but "Plautin" doesn't have to be daunting, particularly if you don't mind me supplying a guide to rare vocabulary and unfamiliar language (pp. 105–16)—and "normalizing" the spelling.

For the *text*, I list divergences from the long standard old stand-by, W. M. Lindsay's *Oxford Classical Text* (1904), where more than orthography is involved: pp. 121–2. Of course I'm dissing the paradosis, but we could never come anywhere close to *just* what Plautus may have written, and in practice this play is virtually unaffected by which, by whose, edition. For *all* matters of transmission, including spelling, I am fortunate to be able to refer you to R. M. Danese's *Sarsina/Urbino Text* (2004), which appeared after my work was completed. This amply conservative text is based on fresh, and definitive, collation of all the MSS, and will provide the *bedrock* for all future editions of the play (see the exact, and perfectly simultaneous, twin reviews, carefully noting all the misprints and slips, by Fontaine [2005] and Walker [2005], and the list of my divergences from Danese—again suppressing minimalia: p. 122). But here and now accessibility just *has* to take precedence.

The *metrical* scheme is mostly regular, and easy to grasp: I give a brief run down, in the modern—"syllabic"—style (pp. 117–19), and key the text so that the notation provided will keep the verse rhythm running "for you" (p. 2). Plautus *does* write in a brash poetic/unpoetic ("poetic") mode, which charges along noisily and heftily, taking charge of raw topics and risible relationships with a swagger in its step, and a lurching bravura all its own: well worth the rude ride.

Let me finally confirm, this playtime is, it boasts at once, "on the short side," as well (*breue est*, 8: under 1,000 lines). I.e., worth all the time you got.

In fact, I'm convinced there is nothing at all to stop us playing *Asinaria* for all it's worth: the "family plot" allows for every register of comedy, from crude farce to complex play within the leading roles (p. 221 n.20). The stand-out central scenes starring the pair of thinking and motoring slaves give us plenty to think about human relations in the intimacy of the classical household (chapters 3, 5, 9). Above all, they dish out humour. Cruel, brave, acute, stupid, basic, tantalizing, relentless, improvisational, knockabout, punning . . . humour. The verbal repartee supports a series of energetic bodily figures that lay bare the axioms of social status for all to beware. Sure, the play's Father makes a complete mug of himself by getting *far* too involved with his son's adventures in love, in the sex trade; until Mother has to shoo him back home (chapter 7). But all through, to right and to left, on stage and off it, where you most expect and least suspect, this play guarantees, you will keep finding yourself running into asses, asses, and (yes) more asses (pp. **xiv, 194, 236 n.12**).

If you'll let me be your "Donkey-Driver" (*asinarius*: p. **211**), I recommend that you read the play first time *in chunks* (see contents, pp. **v–vi**). Let my Prologue introduce you to Plautus' Prologue (pp. **xi–xiv**). Use and abuse my text and translation, and the help with Plautus' Latin (language and vocabulary) I supply for each scene (pp. **105–16**). Then see what you think about *my* thoughts on each major episode (chapters 1 through 7). Once you've read through the play, it will be time to reprise and reflect on the whole show, and I provide three further discussions for that stage (chapters 8 through 10). The first sets out *Asinaria's* dramaturgy of "Space, move-ment, verse." The second returns to the play's classic highpoint, focusing on the play's dominant imagery: "Beastly lives." In the third, I tune in to how this comedy tells us we should *listen*: "A right earful." To bring down the curtain, a minimal Epilogue sees off Plautus' (pp. **213–15**).

I'm presuming that it's a good idea to get *into* comedy when writing about it, otherwise how will anyone know it *is* comic? I think it best to stick to the play before us, in order to find out if it's worth booking tickets for any oth-ers: naturally, plenty of formulae, routines, conventions, and their deviation, inversion, mutation, and hybridization, are at work in generating *this* par-ticular entertainment; but the general structures shuffled to make this the-atre are familiar enough to all of us through their re-cycling in modern ad-aptation, re-cycling, and revival—the question that matters here is whether *this* play holds up, deserves your attention, trounces the competition.

The erudiated mix of slang and jive in my translation is meant to trip the "Plautus effect," which hits on out-and-out abuse of norms and normality with full-on assault from stuff and nonsense. In particular, a scattering of mid-Atlantic misfit between my worst samples of staged Anglo- and my best bites of media-American English stands (in) for the defamiliarizing turn in Plautin that sets out to resist appropriation from any naturalizing critique, no matter how plebeian, vulgarian, or populist: these items are explained in with the line-by-line notes on "Plautin": (pp. **105–16**). What farce can contrive to tell society about itself this way can be priceless—or so the thought-bubble will be saying in *my* cartoon.

I am, as ever, grateful to all the characters in and out of Cambridge with whom I (should) have studied Plautus over the years. This is, in my view, the most poorly served oeuvre in all Roman poetry. Let me acknowledge, however, that my ears were re-opened by Kathy McCarthy, *Slaves, Masters and the Art of Plautine Comedy* (2000), whose powerful construal happens to underplay *Asinaria*. Same goes for the supple and mature enquiry of William Fitzgerald, *Slavery and the Roman Literary Imagination* (2000). I found indispensable comments in Ussing (1875), 1:347–435 and notes in Gray (1894), and the tradition is faithfully decocted in Bertini (1968). Adrian Gratwick (1993) has revolutionized both the understanding and the presentation of Plautine verse. Without Malcolm Willcock, I'd be plain lost. Audiences at Duke University and at Harvard heard draft papers (my thanks to Micaela Janan and Peter and Maura Burian, and to Richard Thomas, for taking such good care of me, as superpower plunged us to war); more friends, but especially William Fitzgerald, Emily Gowers, Sharon James, Kathy McCarthy, Carole Newlands, Vicky Rimell, Patricia Rosenmeyer, Alison Sharrock, the press's ebullient referees, Sheila Moermond, copyeditor John Tiedemann, and my editor, Adam Mehring, all helped to make this book as well; other important contributions to the enjoyment and understanding of the play are recorded in the notes, usually with a leg-pull thrown in. All blunders are down to *this* asinigo.

The jacket shows us the actress "Mlle Lange (as Danae)" in all her glory. Before her turkey-cock lover, and firebrand lust, lurks the telltale roll emblazoned *ASINARIA*. She had played Élise in Molière's Plautine *l'Avare* in Paris in 1790, and this Vanitas is Girodet's comic revenge for spurning his previous portrayal of her as Venus: Anne-Louis Girodet de Roussy-Trioson (1799), oil on canvas, 65 by 54 cm, reproduced by kind permission of the Minnesota Institute of Arts. My thanks to DeAnn M. Dankowski for her generous help.

Prologue

1–15 The Prologue tells all | there's nothing to tell, so listen

"I'm a person as much as you," so the actor playing the slave playing the slave overseer tells the actor playing the straight-up role of free trader stranger-in-town.[1] "P'raps, and yet—," comes the rebuff, polite prudence to the end, "—A man's a wolf, not a man, to a man who don't know what he's like" (= humanity estranged: *homo*, 490 ~ 493, *homo homini, non homo*, 495).[2] The horseplay ends with wife-and-mother scolding naughty paterfamilias back home, for revenge with kisses (= bilge-water stench) and dinner on the table (= trouble, and so to bed: 893–940). The cast invite us to beg off the (castratory) husband-beating with a rousing score on the clapometer; and, curtains (= cut-off: 942–7). The stand-out moment of donkey business came a good deal earlier, in the cameo, one of Plautus' greatest, which had young master-lover-son stop and pick up a piggy-back passenger: the ringmaster Cunning Slave wants a ride, and gets one (= one of Plautus' daftest: 699–710).[3]

The businesslike Prologue gave spectators due notice, loud and clear, that today's *plot* "takes no time at all," it won't take a moment, and in fact—it doesn't (8, *sane breuest*)! Instead, in less time than it takes to say "~~plot~~," attention fastens on the *name* of the play, backed with a promise of "wit-n-fun—this one is a gas" (6–12; 13–14).

Such preliminaries need kid us not. They generally put in play tasters of what's to come, if only we knew it. On this occasion, as often, the tightly structured composition tips us the wink for the direction we should be looking—or rather, *listening*. A cruel gag (from the anarchic satirist Peter Cook) once ran:

And now, for those who are hard of hearing—LISTEN!

But Plautus' prologue beams up ears to hear for one and all. First off, the hope is—"Do it, if you will"—that the production will "turn out well, for me and for all you." Last up, farce does its will, telling that the writer "turned the play," out of Greek, for "such is his will, if you allow it. . . . Give it up real good for me, so for you"—the hope is—"Mars [Roman god of war, and *father* of Romulus, founder of Rome] will give his backing, *on a par* with his past record" (12–15).[4]

Prologue's "entrée, his will," was to "say," it is to "say" (and, as he says, he "says" he "said so," too), that "the play's changed its name from the Greek name of the play," ΌΝΑΓΟΣ, *The Donkey-driver*, to *ASINARIA—The One about Donkey-driver* or *The One about Donkey*[s] (6–12). Now this is fun. But is it fun and dandy because it's fussy fuss about nothing? Of course it is. Minutiae *are* fun, especially when they take over the whole of this amplified programme and yet *seem* to make such infinitesimal difference, any which way you look at it (see n. and p. 211).[5]

But (I said) our ears are meant to be flapping. Prologue already made a crier do his thing,

[SHHH! BRAY SILENCE!],

before sitting him down, with a reminder to claim a double fee: for noise *and* for silence. In a flash, the human otophone's rude proclamation made the whole of Rome into one acoustically amplified auditorium. From this moment on, who is there at the *Asinaria* that does not have ass's ears? "Me and you," Prologue began, "me so you," he bowed out, ". . . backing . . . on a par" (2 ~ 14–15). Point is, the tale is well and truly pinned to the donkey before the start, and just as the entire "troupe" on this stage will take some beating, so we otosclerotic spectators must pin back our ears and take what we have coming, to a man. No troop of monkeys, but a herd (this *should* be a "pace")—of donkeys (*grex*, 3).[6]

So much for the public address system. Brought to us in a neat, over-neat, rhetorical ring that gives nothing away and enjoys itself telling us so. The presenter, uptightass Prologue, stuffs in the deictic "shifters" (here-now-this-I/we/you):

hoc, 1; *huic*, 3; *huc*, 6

nunciam, 1; | *face nunciam . . .* , | *age nunc*, 3–4; | *nunc . . .* , | *nunc*, 6, 9;
    nunc, 15

nomen huius fabulae |, *. . . huic nomen . . . fabulae* |, 7, 10; *hac comoedia* |,
    13

mihi atque uobis, 2; *mihi . . .* , *uobis*, 6, 9; *uos*, 12; *mihi* | *ut uos*, 14–15.

In calling for his "turn" by insisting on presencing the act of utterance, he's doing his own heralding:

quid processerim . . . et quid uoluerim, | *dicam*, 6–7
quod me dixi uelle uobis dicere, | *dicam*, 9–10.

So here he is, now, in our face—and busy: the rhetorical thread runs bright and taut through the crier's inset and the writer's shift of title, between the ring of opening and closing "hopes":

agite ~ face . . . , *age ~ date*, 1, 4–5, 14
si-uultis ~ uolt . . . si per uos licet, 1, 12
uultis ~ uoluerim ~ uelle ~ uolt, 1, 6, 9, 12
mihi atque uobis res uortat bene ~ uortit ~ res . . . , *benigne . . . mihi* | *ut uos*,
    2, 11, 14–15.

Busily refusing to tell us, but busy filling us in.

If we only knew the upshot . . . —but that would stop us wondering, seeing if we can figure out *Asinaria* as we go. (Retrospect and re-run will feature, all in good time: chapters 8–10. Just before the Epilogue signs off: pp. **213–15**.) A decent playwright knows that teasing hints are what you *really* want from a preface. A good bet for now will be *not* to invest *too* much in the storyline, let alone the characters. Rather, cue "downgrading of plot" (= Prologue and Epilogue, chapter 1), and "insisting on payment—take the money," "parity," and "terms and conditions"—you can't say fairer than that (= chapters 2 and 3). "Fun" is promised—and, trust me, promises will make the fun fun (= esp. chapters 3, 5, 9). We will be "over-hearing" everything there is to hear, if you can bear it (= chapter 10). Most of all—and to pull this off, the play will *need* to level "actor, audience, troupe, producer impresarios, and booking agents" (2–3)—*The One about the Donkeys* will kill off claims to special status among specimens of humanity up and down the town: OYEZ, ass-ass-inate the lot of them, and us. All just as bad (jokes) as the rest (4):

face . . . omnem auritum poplum.

~

All ears, mind (= chapter 10).[7]

> Ears will be an asset in Plautus' word-famous circus.
> Expect a histrionic thrash of hybrid, mutant, rhetorics.

Asinaria

Text and Translation

Key to Text

→	in left margin: entrance of a character
→	in right margin: exit of a character

SERVVS	role
LIBANVS	name of character, with its **abbreviation in bold**
LIB	name of character abbreviated

{LIB}	character speaks aside to another character or to us
>	in left margin: addressed to another character
1–126 *senarii*	in right margin: name of metre

hoc̣ agite ṣ^{iu}ultis	i.e., sublinear dots = start of *invariably* long (‾) *or* resolved (˘˘) syllable of each metrical unit
-tis spect-	i.e., gap in text: = "main caesura" (i.e. word-break within the 3rd foot) in *senarii;* = midline break in longer verses
ăgĭtĕ	i.e., supralinear ˘ = the marked syllable is "short"
quaĕquidem	i.e., supralinear ˘ **in bold** = the metre counts the marked syllable as "short"
dicám	i.e., supralinear accent = the metre counts the marked syllable as "long"
Leōnida	i.e., supralinear makron = the marked vowel is a separate long syllable
pro͡inde	i.e., supralinear arc = synizesis and the like (i.e., the marked vowels are a diphthong or slur together metrically)
s^{i u}ultis, mihⁱ atque	elision or syncope (i.e., the words slur together so that the raised syllables do not count metrically)
dicam | huic	hiatus and the like (i.e., adjacent words do *not* slur together metrically)
ˀobsequellamˀ	the text is damaged beyond rescue

Key to Translation

→	in left margin: entrance of a character
→	in right margin: exit of a character
SLAVE	role
LIBANUS	name of character
LIB	name of character abbreviated
{ }	spoken aside to another character or us
>	addressed to another character
spoken verse	in right margin: type of verse

→

PROLOGVS

hoc ăgĭtĕ s^{iu}ultis, spectatores, nuncĭam,   1–126 *senarii*

quaĕquĭdem mĭhⁱ atquĕ uobis res uertat bĕne

grĕgĭqu^e huic et dŏmĭnis atquĕ conductorĭbus.

{fac^e nuncĭam tu, praec^o, omn^{em} auritum pŏplum.

ăgĕ nunc rĕsĭde, căuĕ mŏdo ne gratĭis.}   5

nunc quid processĕr^{im} huc et quid mĭhĭ uŏluĕrim,

dic^{am}: ut sciretis nomen huius fabŭlae.

nam quŏd ăd argument^{um} attĭnet, sane brĕue ^est.

nunc quod me dixi uellĕ uobis dicĕre,

dicám: | huic nomen Graec^e Ŏnago ^est fabŭlae.   10

Demŏphĭlus scripsit, Maccus uertit barbărĕ,

Ăsĭnarĭam uult essĕ, sĭ per uos lĭcet.

ĭnest lĕpos ludusqu^e in hac comoedĭa,

ridĭcŭlă res est. dătĕ bĕnign^e ŏpĕram mĭhi

ut uos, ŭt ălĭas, părĭter nunc Mars adiŭuet.   →

→→

SERVVS CALLIDVS = **LIBANVS**

+ SENEX = PATER = DEMAENETVS

LIB   sicut tŭum uis unĭcum natum tŭae   16

sŭpĕressĕ uitae sospĭt^{em} et sŭperstĭtem

ĭtă ted obtestor per sĕnectutem tŭam,

perqu^e illam, quam tu mĕtŭĭs, uxorem tŭam,

siquid med erga | hŏdĭe falsum dixĕris,   20

ut tĭbĭ sŭperstes uxor aetatem sĭet

atqu^e illa uiua uiuŭs ut pest^{em} oppĕtas.

DEM   per Dĭum Fĭdĭum quaeris: iurato mĭhi

uĭdĕo nĕcess^e essĕ elŏqui quidquid rŏges   24

proĭnd^e actut^{um} istuc quid sit quod scir^e expĕtis   27

elŏquĕr^e: ŭt ipsĕ scibo, te facĭ^{am} ut scĭas.

LIB   dic obsĕcr^o herclĕ serĭo quod te rŏgem,

căuĕ mĭhĭ mendaci quidquam.

DEM   quin t^u ergo rŏgas?   30

LIB   num m^e illuc ducĭs ŭbĭ lăpis lăpĭdem tĕrit?   31

ăpŭ^d fustĭtŭdĭnas, ferrĭcrĕpĭnas insŭlas,   34

ŭbĭ uiuos hŏmĭnes mortŭⁱ incursant bŏues?   35

→
THE PROLOGUE

Do it, spectators, if you will. Act right here and now.   1–126:
Hope this one'll turn out well, for me and for all of you.   spoken
For the troupe here, their lordship producers, the agents.   verse
{Now you, Mr. p. a. man, make the whole nation all ears.
SHHH! BRAY SILENCE!
And now act . . . sitting down. Only, mind it's not for free.}   5
Why did I step out here? What was it I was wanting?
I shall say. For you to know the *name* of this play.
As for the plot, see, it sure takes *no* time at all.
Now as for saying I wanna have my say to you,
I shall say. The play's name in Greek is *Conducteur des Ânes.*   10
Demophilus wrote it. Clown Plautus put it in pidgin;
wants it to be *The One About Asses,* if ok by you.
In it there is wit, and there is fun, in this comedy.
This one is a gas. Do give it up for me. Real fit.
Then, hope is, Mars'll back you. On a par with the past.   →

SLAVE: "THE BRAINS" = LIBANUS
+ SENIOR CITIZEN = FATHER = DEMAENETUS

LIB   So. As you will want for your one and only son   16
       to outlive your lifetime, out of harm, outlasting,
       so be my witness, by your status of elder,
       and by that woman, the one that you fear, the wife,
       if this day, as regards me, you tell me anything false,   20
       that said wife of yours shall outlast your span of time,
       and that in her life—your life shall fall to the plague.

DEM   In Gods' Truth, huh? I see that I am under oath
       and obliged to speak up, whatever your question.   24
       So right now. What is it you are seeking to know,   27
       speak up. So far as *I* know, I'll make it so *you* know.

LIB   I beg, lordy, don't mock, but answer my question.
       Watch it, no lying to me.

DEM   Why don't you ask your question?   30

LIB   You're not taking me off to the land where rock grinds rock,   31
       away in the Ironbongo-Clubbery Isles,   34
       the place where dead oxen assault live human beings?   35

DEM mŏdŏ pol perçepi, Lĭbănĕ, quĭd ĭstuc ṣit lŏçi:
     ŭbĭ fit pŏḷentă, te forṭassĕ ḍicĕr^e.

LIB   ah,
     nĕqu^e hercl^e ĕg^o istuc ḍico ṇec dictum uŏḷo,
     tequ^e obsĕçr^o hercl^e ut quae lŏçutu^{s e}s ḍespŭas.

DEM fiạt. gĕratur ṃos tĭbⁱ.

LIB   ăg^e, ăg^e, usqu^e excrĕạ.   40

DEM ĕtĭạmn^e?

LIB   ăgĕ quaes^o herçl^e usqu^e ex pĕnĭtis fauçĭbus,
     ĕtĭ^{am} amplĭus.

DEM   nam quoūsqu^e?

LIB   usqu^e ad morṭem uŏḷo—

DEM căuĕ si^{ui}s mălam r^{em}.

LIB   —uxoris ḍico, ṇon tŭam.

DEM dono t^e ŏb istuc ḍict^{um} ut expers ṣis mĕṭu.

LIB di tĭbĭ dent quaecumque optes.

DEM   ṛedd^e ŏpĕram mĭḥi.   45
     cụr hoc ĕg^o ex te quaer^{am}? aut çur mĭnĭṭer tĭbi
     proptĕrĕa quod me ṇon scĭẹntem feçĕris?
     aut çur posṭremo filĭọ susçensĕạm,
     pătres ut făçĭunt çetĕri?

LIB   quĭd ĭsṭuc nŏuị ^est?   50
     demịror quid siṭ et qu^o euadat ṣ^{um} in mĕṭu.

DEM ĕquĭdem scĭọ iam, filĭus quŏd ămet mĕus
     isṭanc mĕrĕtric^{em} e proxĭmọ Phĭḷaenĭum.
     estṇ^e hoc ut ḍico, Lĭbănĕ?

LIB   rect^{am} insṭas uĭam.
     ĕă ṛes est. ṣĕd ĕum ṃorbŭs inuaṣit grăuis.   55

DEM quid ṃorbi ^est?

LIB   quĭă non ṣuppĕṭunt dicṭis dăṭa.

DEM tun^e es adịutor ṇunc ămanti filĭọ?

LIB sum uer^o, ĕt alter ṇostĕr est Lĕọnĭda.

DEM bĕn^e herçlĕ făçĭtĭs ĕt ă m^e ịnitis gratĭam.
     uerum m^{eam} uxorem, Lĭbănĕ, ṇescis quali^s ṣit?   60

LIB tu primus ṣentis, ṇos tămĕn in prĕtĭọ sŭmus.

DEM fătĕor ĕam ẹss^e importun^{am} atqu^e inçommŏdam.

LIB posṭĕrĭuṣ istuc ḍicis quam creḍo tĭbi.

DEM   Sure, Libanus, I have just seen what that place is:
"where pasta's made" is maybe what you're saying.

LIB   Ow.

No I'm not saying that, lord, and I don't want it said,
and I beg, lordy, do gob out that talk of yours.

DEM   Done. Just to humour you.

LIB   Go, go, hawk up all the way.   40

DEM   More?

LIB   Go, please, lord, all the way from deep down the throat.
Still more.

DEM   All the way . . . where?

LIB   All the way to death, I'd like.

DEM   Watch out for trouble, ok . . .

LIB   —Oh no, not yours. Your wife's.

DEM   My prize for that is you'll have no cut in the . . . fear.

LIB   The gods grant your every wish.

DEM   Now do a job for me.   45

Why would I ask you this? And why would I menace you,
'cos of the fact that you didn't put me in the know?
And, last in line, why would I get cross with my son,
the way that all other fathers do?

LIB   What's this new one?   50

I'm fazed. What's this? Going where? Here I *am* "in the fear."

DEM   I already know it: that son of mine. Love. Sex.
With that whore from next door. With her—Philaenium.
Is it as I say, Libanus?

LIB   You're on the right track.

That's it. But a *pox* has gone for him, something chronic.   55

DEM   What pox is that?

LIB   Not having the fees to match the talk.

DEM   Are you my son's lieutenant, now running loverboy?

LIB   I am indeed. And our number two's Leonida.

DEM   Lord, that's kind of you. You're both winning points from me.
But, my *wife*, Libanus. You know the way she is?   60

LIB   You feel it first, but we star on her list, all the same.

DEM   I must admit, she's . . . discouraging, . . . disagreeable.

LIB   Your saying that comes second to my crediting it.

DEM   omnes părentes, Lĭbănĕ, lĭbĕris sŭis

qui m^i auscultabunt, făcĭent obsĕquentiam   65

quipp^e qui măg^e ămic^o utantur nat^o et bĕnĕuŏlo.

atqu^e ĕgŏ m^e id făcĕrĕ stŭdĕo, uŏl^o ămar^i a mĕis,

uŏlŏ me pătris mei sĭmĭlem, qui causa mĕa

naucleric^o ips^e ornatu per fallacĭam

qu^{am} ămab^{am} abduxit ab lenonĕ mŭlĭĕrem,   70

nĕquĕ pŭdŭit ĕ^{um} ĭd aetatis sycŏphantĭas

strŭĕr^e et bĕnĕfĭcĭis m^e ĕmĕrĕ natum sŭum sĭbi.

eos me decretum ^{e}st persĕqui mores pătris.

nam m^e hŏdĭ^e orauit Argӯrippus filĭus

ŭti sĭb^i ămanti făcĕr^{em} argenti copĭam,   75

ĕt ĭd ĕgŏ percŭpĭ^o obsĕqui nato mĕo:

uŏl^o ămar^i ?obsĕcutam? illius, uŏl^o ămet me pătrem.

quamqu^{am} illum mater arte contentequ^e hăbet,

pătres ut cons^{u}euerunt—ĕgŏ mitt^o omnĭ^a haec.

praesertim c^{um} is me dignum cui concredĕret   80

hăbŭit, m^e hăber^e hŏnor^{em} eius ingĕnĭo dĕcet.

cum m^e ădĭit, ut pŭdentem nat^{um} aequum ^{e}st pătrem,

cŭpĭ^o ess^e ămicae quod det argentum sŭae.

LIB   cŭpĭs id quod cŭpĕrĕ te nequiqu^{am} intellĕgo.

dotalem seruum Saurĕ^{am} uxor tŭă tĭbi   85

adduxit, cui plus in mănu sit quam tĭbi.

DEM   argent^{um} accepi, dot^e impĕrĭum uendĭdi.

nunc uerb^a in paucă confĕram quid te uĕlim.

uiginti ĭ^{am} usu^s ^{e}st filĭ^o argenti mĭnis:

făc^e ĭd ut păratum iam sit.

LIB   undĕ gentĭum?   90

DEM   me defraudato.

LIB   maxĭmas nugas ăgis:

nudo detrăhĕrĕ uestimentă me iŭbes.

defraudem tĕ | ĕg^o? ăgĕ si^{ui}s tu, sĭnĕ pennis uŏla.

ten^e ĕgŏ defraudem, c^{ui} ipsi nĭhĭl est in mănu

nĭsĭ quid tu porr^o uxorem defraudauĕris?   95

DEM   qua me, qu^a uxorem, qua tu seruum Saurĕam

pŏtes, circumduc^e, aufer. promitto tĭbi

DEM Parents the world over, Libanus, will take their kids,
   —if they'll hear me out—and do some favouritism: 65
to get more out of a positive friend of a son.
Yes I'm keen to do it: I wanna be loved by my kid.
I wanna be like my father, who on my behalf—
in a ship cap'n's rig, to enable a con—personally
stole the She I was going with, from a pimp. 70
He felt no shame, at that time of life, at skulduggery
mongering—and buying *his* son (me) with good turns.
I've decided to follow this, my, father's approach.

Today, see, my son pleaded with me—Argyrippus—
to make available cash funds for loverboy. 75
And here I feel passionate about favouring my child.
I wanna favourize his love—want he should love me.
All the same, mother keeps tight and taut rein on him,
the way *fathers* habitually do: *I* renounce all this.
Specially as he held me to deserve his credit, 80
decency says I should pay tribute to his spirit.
'Cos he came to me, it's fair, modest son to his father,
my passion's for cash, so he can pay for his playmate.

LIB Your passion—I know this passion of yours is in vain.
In her dowry was a slave—Saurea—and your wife 85
brought him over: to have more in his hand than you do.

DEM I took cash delivery, sold command for a dowry.

Now to get what I want from you in a few words:
my son needs twenty minae cash, immediate.
See it's there ready right away.

LIB   Where on earth from? 90

DEM You swindle *me*.

LIB   You are talking utter nonsense.
You're telling me to rip off someone naked's clothes.
"*Me* swindle *you*?" P-lease, you, go fly—without wings.
"*You* swindled? *Me*?" When you have nothing in your hand,
except anything you've gone and swindled from your wife? 95

DEM Any way you can: me. Or wife. Or slave Saurea.
Take 'em round the houses, unload 'em. I promise you

          noṇ offŭṭurum, ṣi | ĭd hŏdĭᵉ effecĕris.

LIB   iŭbĕas uṇᵃ ŏpĕra me pisçarⁱ ĭṇ aĕre,

          uenarⁱ auṭem reṭé iăçŭlᵒ in mĕdĭọ măṛi.   100

DEM   tĭḅⁱ optĭọnem ṣumĭṭo Lĕōnĭdam,

          făbrĭçarĕ quiduis, quiduis çommĭniscĕre,

          perfĭçĭtᵒ argentŭm | hŏdĭᵉ ŭṭ hăbĕat fĭlĭus

          ămĭcae quod det.

LIB   quĭd ăis ṭu, Demaenĕṭe?

DEM   quid ụis?

LIB   si fortᵉ ĭṇ insĭdĭas deụenĕro,   105

          tunᵉ rĕdĭmes me, si mᵉ hosteṣ interçepĕrint?

DEM   rĕdĭmam.

LIB   tum tᵘ ĭgĭtŭr ălĭud çura quidlĭbet.

          ĕᵒ ĕgᵒ ad fŏṛum, nĭsĭ quid ụis.

DEM   i, bĕṇᵉ ambŭḷa.

          atquᵉ audiˢṇᵉ ĕtĭăm? |

LIB   eccĕ.

DEM   ṣi quid ṭe uŏḷam,

          ŭḅⁱ ĕrĭs?

LIB   ŭbĭçumquĕ lĭbĭtᵘᵐ ĕrĭt ănĭmo mĕọ.   110

          prŏfecto ṇemo ᵉst quem iam ḍehinc mĕtụam mĭḥi

          ne quid nŏçerĕ poṣsit, çum tu mĭḥĭ tŭạ

          orạtĭọnᵉ omṇᵉᵐ ănĭmᵘᵐ ostendisṭi tŭụm.

{LIB}   {quin ṭe quŏquᵉ ipsum făçĭᵒ hauᵈ ṃagni, ṣⁱ hoc pătro.}

LIB   pergam quᵒ occeṗⁱ atquᵉ ĭbĭ consĭlĭᵃ exordĭar.   115

DEM   audịˢṇᵉ tᵘ? ăpŭd Archĭbulᵘᵐ ĕgᵒ ĕṛᵒ argentạrĭum.

LIB   nempᵉ in fŏṛᵒ?

DEM   ĭbĭ, si quĭd ŏpus fŭĕrit.

LIB   mĕmĭnĕṛo.   →

DEM   non essĕ ṣeruus peioṛ hoc quisquam pŏtest

          nec măgĭˢ uerṣutus ṇec quᵒ ab çăuĕạs aegrĭus.

          ei͡dᵉᵐ hŏmĭni, si quid recṭe çurạtum uĕḷis,

          manḍes: mŏriri ṣese mĭsĕre mauŏḷet   120

          quam ṇon perfectum reḍdat quod promĭsĕrit.

          nᵃᵐ ĕgᵒ ĭllŭc argentum ṭam părạtum filĭọ

          scĭᵒ esse quam mᵉ hunc ṣcipĭọnem çontŭī.

	it'll do you no harm at all if you get this job done today.
LIB	You could tell me in the same deal, "Go fish the . . . sky,"
	or, "Go hunt mid ocean, with nets for catching . . . game." 100
DEM	For sergeant, you must take along Leonida.
	Scheme up anything, anything you like, think it up.
	You are to see that my son gets the cash today
	to pay for playmate.
LIB	Whaddya say, Demaenetus?
DEM	What do you want?
LIB	If I happen to get in a trap, 105
	will you buy me out, if the enemy cut me off?
DEM	Yes, I'll buy you out.
LIB	Then boss something else. What you like.
	I'm off to the mall, if that'll be all?
DEM	Go, walk good.
	You still listening?
LIB	See?
DEM	Should I want you at all,
	where'll you be?
LIB	Wherever my mind sees fit to ad lib. 110
	For a fact, from now on, there's no one for me to fear,
	in case they could do me some harm. Not when you've
	shown me
	the whole of your mind, in the course of speaking your plea.
{LIB}	{Why, I won't rate you much, either, if I get this farther.}
LIB	I'll go on where I started for, 'n' there get weaving plans. 115
DEM	You listening? I'll be at Archie Plotter, the banker's.
LIB	You mean in the mall?
DEM	Yep, there, if need be.
LIB	I shan't forget. →

DEM	No slave, not a one, can be badder than this 'un,
	nor more wily, nor harder for you to watch out for.
	The same person, if you want something seen to right, 120
	you'll hand it him. He'll prefer to die a sorry death
	than to deliver what he's promised non-complete.
	See, that cash is good as there ready for my son,
	I ken it, as I behold this here walking kane.

sed quĭd ĕgŏ cessŏ irᵉ ad fŏrum, quᵒ incepĕram?   125

ibᵒ atquᵉ ĭbi mănebᵒ ăpŭd argentarĭum.   →

→   ADVLESCENS **AMATOR**

AMAT   sicĭnᵉ hoc fĭt? fŏras aedĭbus mᵉ ëĭci?   127–32:
                                            cretic

promĕrentⁱ optĭmᵉ hocĭnᵉ prĕti reddĭtur?   tetrameters

bĕnĕ mĕrenti măla ᵉs, mălĕ mĕrenti bŏna ᵉs.

at mălo cum tŭo. nam iăm | ex hoc lŏco   130

ibᵒ ĕgᵒ ad tresuĭros uestrăquᵉ ĭbĭ nomĭna

faxᵒ ĕrunt, căpĭtĭˢ te perdᵃᵐ ĕgᵒ et filĭam—

pellĕcĕbrae pernĭcĭeˢ ădŭlescentᵘᵐ   133: choriambic
     exĭtĭum—   dimeter
nam mărᵉ haud est mărĕ, uos mărᵉ   134–7: cretic
     acerrĭmum.   tetrameters
nᵃᵐ in mări reppĕri, | hic elaui bŏnis.   135

ingratᵃ atquᵉ irrĭtᵃ essᵉ omnĭᵃ intellĕgo
quae dĕdⁱ et quod bĕnĕ fecⁱ at posthac tĭbi—

—mălĕ quod pŏtĕro făcĕrĕ făcĭam, mĕrĭtoquᵉ id   138–380:
     făcĭam tŭo   trochaic
ĕgŏ pol te rĕdĭgᵃᵐ eodᵉᵐ undᵉ orta ᵉs, ăd ĕgestatis   *septenarii*
     termĭnos.
ĕgᵒ ĕdĕpol te făcĭᵃᵐ ut quae sis nunc et quae fŭĕris scĭas.   140

quae prĭŭˢ quᵃᵐ istᵃᵐ ădĭⁱ atquᵉ ămans ĕgᵒ ănĭmum mĕŭm |
     isti dĕdi,
sordĭdo uitᵃᵐ oblectabas panᵉ in pannis ĭnŏpĭa,

atquᵉ ĕă sⁱ ĕrănt, magnas hăbebas omnĭbus dis gratĭas;

But why dawdle, not go to the mall, where I was bound? 125
I'm off, and there I shall stay put at the banker's. →

→
BOY

LOVER-**BOY** ONE

Hey, can this really be
   happ'ning?

I . . . me? . . . chucked
   out of the house? sing-song

Way ahead in deserving
   well,

And *this* must be my
   reward?

Someone deserves well,
   you treat bad.

And bad, you go and
   treat well.

Well, bad is coming to
   you, too.

Right now, away from 130
   this place,

I'm off, to the courthouse

And it's there your names
   will lodge.

I'll fix it, and I'm gonna
   waste

You and your daughter for life—

E-ternyi-ty, . . . par-a-a-dise,

O boy, that home ay-cross ballad
the road line

'Cos . . . the sea . . . is
   never . . . the sea

When *you* are the sea more song
   of pain.

'Cos . . . wealth . . . I
   found . . . down in
   the sea

But here was my wipe-out, 135
   clean.

It's all inane, it's all in vain.

I know that all this is so.

All those payments I paid,
   the deeds

I have done. From now on, you—

—will find I'll do you the bad I can, and you'll 138–745:
   deserve that I do. recitative

I'll drag you down, sure, where you came from, to the verse
   pit of privation.

Surely, I'll see you know what you are now, and just what
   you were then. 140

You. Before I was into your girl, and gave her loverboy's heart,

you used to spice up your life, with filthy rags and crusts,
   on skid row.

And if you got that, you'd give the whole pantheon
   almighty thanks.

ĕădem nunc, cum ᵉst mĕlĭus, me cuĭuṣ ŏpĕra ᵉst ignoṛas
mălạ.

reddᵃᵐ ĕgŏ tᵉ ex fĕra fặme mansᵘetem, me specṭa mŏdọ.　　145

nᵃᵐ isti quid susẹensĕᵃᵐ ipsi?　ṇil est, ṇil quidquam mĕṛet:

tuo fặcit iussụ, tuᵒ impĕrĭo　ạaret: ṃater tᵘ, eadᵉᵐ ĕra ᵉs.

tĕ | ĕgᵒ ulc̣iscar, tĕ | ĕgᵒ ut ḍigna ᵉs　perdᵃᵐ atquᵉ ut de ṃe
mĕṛes.

ạt scĕlestă uĭdĕˢnᵉ ut nᵉ ĭd quĭdem,　me dignᵘᵐ essᵉ existĭmat

quĕm | ădĕạt, quem c̣ollŏquatur,　c̣uĭquᵉ irato ṣupplĭc̣et?　　150

atquᵉ ecc̣ᵃᵐ illĕcĕbrᵃ exit ṭandᵉᵐ. ŏpinọr hic antᵉ ostịụm

meo mŏdọ lŏqu̇ăr quae uŏḷam, quŏnĭᵃᵐ ịntus ṇon lĭc̣ĭtum
ᵉst mĭhị.

→　　　　　　　　　　**+ LENA**
LENA　　unum quodquᵉ istorum ụerbum　ṇummis Phĭlĭppis aurĕis

non pŏtest auferrᵉ hinc̣ a me　ṣi quĭṣ emptor ụenĕṛit.

ṇec rectẹ quae tᵘ in nos ḍicĭṣ,　aurᵘᵐ atquᵉ argenṭum
mĕṛum ᵉst.　　　　　　　　　　　　　　　155

fixŭs hic ăpŭd ṇos est ănĭmus　tŭŭˢ claụo Cŭpidĭnis.

remĭgĭọ ueḷoquĕ quantum　pŏtĕris fẹstinᵃ et fŭge:

quam măgĭˢ tĕ | ĭn alṭum c̣ăpessis,　tᵃᵐ aestus tᵉ in porṭum
rĕfert.

AMAT　　ĕgŏ pŏl istum porṭĭtorem　priuabọ porṭorịo.

ĕgŏ te ḍehinc ut mĕrĭta ᵉs ḍe mᵉ et　mea re tractarᵉ
exsĕquar,　　　　　　　　　　　　　　160

You, now it's better. It was my doing, but you don't know me.
    Bad'un.
I'll get you eating outa my hand from starving wild—just
    you watch me.   145

So. Why should I be cross with *her*? No reason. She deserves
    it—*not.*
Does what you tell her, obeys your command. You're mother,
    you're own-her.
I'll get you back, I'll waste you, as deserved, and merited
    from me.

The wicked witch. See how she don't even think this . . .—
    think me worthwhile
for her to get close to, to swap words with, or kneel to,
    in a stew?   150

Just look. Out comes the vamp. At last. I guess that here,
    at the porch,
I'll say, in my way, what I like. Since, inside, it was verboten.

→   **+ MADAME**

Mme

Never a one of these words of yours, not for dosh in gold
    sovereigns,
can a buyer unload from me here, should one appear on the
    scene.
The verbals you wrong us with are twenty-four carat gold,
    pure cash.   155
Your heart is nailed to my establishment by The Rivet Of Eros.
Row all your oars, spread those sails to the wide, go faster,
    go flee:
as you launch yourself at the deep, so the tide brings you back
    into port.

BOY   Sure, I'm gonna starve this harbour-master of the harbour dues.
Next up, I'm gonna treat you as you've deserved, for me
    and my stash.   160

cum tu me | ut mĕrĭtus sum non   tractas, cumquĕ eĭcis
dŏmo.

LENA   mằgĭs istuc percĭpĭmus lingua   dici quam factis fŏre.

AMAT   solus solĭtudĭnᵉ ĕgŏ ted   atquᵉ ăb ĕgestatᵉ abstŭli:
solus si ductem, rĕferrĕ   gratĭam numquam pŏtes.

LENA   solus ductato, si semper   solus quae poscam dăbis.   165

semper tĭbĭ promissᵘᵐ hằbetᵒ hac   legĕ, dum sŭpĕres dătis.

AMAT   qui mŏdus dandi? nam numquam   tu quĭdᵉᵐ expleri pŏtes.

mŏdŏ cᵘᵐ accepistĭ, hauᵈ multo post   ălĭquid quod poscas
pằras.

LENA   quid mŏdi ᵉst ductandᵒ, ằmando?   numquamnᵉ
expleri pŏtes?
mŏdŏ rĕmisisti, contĭnŭo   ĭᵃᵐ ut rĕmittᵃᵐ ad te rŏgas.   170

AMAT   dĕdĭ ĕquĭdem quod mecᵘᵐ egistĭ.
LENA   et   tĭbĭ ĕgŏ misi mŭlĭĕrem:

par pằri dătᵘᵐ hostimentum ᵉst,   ŏpĕră pro pĕcunĭa.

AMAT   mằlᵉ ằgis mecum.
LENA   quid mᵉ accusas, si fằcĭᵒ offĭcĭum mĕum?
nam nĕquĕ fictᵘᵐ usquam ᵉst nĕquĕ pictum   nĕquĕ
scriptᵘᵐ in pŏëmằtis
ŭbĭ lenằ bĕnᵉ ằgat cum quiquᵃᵐ ằmantĕ quae frugĭ
essĕ uult.   175
AMAT   mĭhĭ quĭdem te parcĕrᵉ aequum ᵉst   tandᵉᵐ, ut tĭbĭ
durem dĭu.

LENA   non tu scis? quᵃᵉ ằmanti parcĕt, ĕằdem sĭbĭ parcet pằrum.

quằsĭ pĭscĭs ĭtĭdem ᵉst ằmator   lenae: nequam ᵉst nĭsĭ
rĕcens—

One, you don't treat me as I deserve, and two, chuck me out of
    doors.

Mme   This strikes us as more how a tongue talks, not a realistic
    prospect.

BOY   I was solo, you desolate: I rescued you from privation.

If I took her home solo, you could never repay the favour.

Mme   "Take her home solo," if you'll forever *pay* "solo," on
    demand.   165

Your promise, this, forever. Just one condition: long's you
    pay top whack.

BOY   And with what ceiling for paying? You ne'er can be filled to the
    brim.

You just took delivery: not long since you set some other
    demand.

Mme   What ceiling for take-home-'n'-sex? *You* "ne'er can be filled to
    the brim."

You just return-delivered: post-haste, "return-delivery
    to you"?   170

BOY   I've paid up on your deal with me.

Mme   And *I've* delivered you
                                 the girl.

Par for par payment. This is equity rendered: service for fee.

BOY   You do me a bad deal.

Mme   Why accuse me if I'm doing my bit?

See, nowhere is there story told, picture painted, or scene
    penned in verse,

where madam cuts a good deal with some loverboy, and . . .
    means . . . to do . . . right.   175

BOY   You spare me, that's fair, after this long. Then I'll last you
    for ages.

Mme   Don't you *know*? Madam spares loverboy—she won't spare
    madam enough.

For madam, the lover's just . . . like . . . a . . . *fish:* rotten unless
    it's fresh—

ĭs hăbet suc^{um}, is s^uauĭtat^{em}, eum   quouis pacto condĭas

uel pătĭnarĭum uĕl assum,   uerses quo pacto lĭbet;   180
is dărĕ uult, is s^e ălĭquid posci.   n^{am} ĭbĭ de pleno promĭtur,

nĕqu^e ĭllĕ scit quid det, quid damni   făcĭat: illi rei stŭdet.

uult plăcerĕ ses^e ămicae,   uult mĭhi, uult pĕdĭsĕquae,

uult fămŭlis, uult ĕtĭ^{am} ancillis,   et quŏquĕ cătŭlo mĕo

subblanditur nŏuŭs ămator,   s^e ut cum uĭdĕat gaudĕat.   185

ueră dic^o: ad suum quemqu^e hŏmĭnem   quaest^{um} ess^e
      aequum ^est callĭdum.

AMAT   perdĭdĭcⁱ istaec essĕ ueră   damno cum magno mĕo.

LENA   sⁱ ecastor nunc hăbĕas, quod des,   ălĭă uerbă praehibĕas;

nunc quĭă nĭhĭl hăbes, mălĕdictis   t^e eam ductarĕ postŭlas.

AMAT   non mĕum ^est.
LENA   nec meum quĭd^{em} ĕdĕpŏl   ad t^e ut
                  mittam gratĭis   190
uer^{um} aetatĭs atqu^e hŏnoris   gratĭa hoc fiet tŭi,
quĭă nobis lŭcro fŭisti   pŏtĭus quam dĕcŏri tĭbi:
si mĭhĭ dantur dŭŏ tălent^a argenti nŭmĕrat^a in mănum,
hanc tĭbĭ noct^{em} hŏnoris causa   gratĭis dono dăbo.

AMAT   quid si non est?
LENA   tĭbĭ non essĕ   credam, ill^a ălĭ^o ibit tămen.   195

AMAT   ŭbⁱ illaec quae dĕdⁱ ant^e?
LENA   ăbusă. nam sⁱ ĕă durarent mĭhi,

mŭlĭer mittĕretur ad te,   numquam quidquam poscĕrem.

fresh has got juice, fresh got sugar, sweet you can season any
    which way,

as in pan-fry or bakeria, you turn 'em which way you like.   180

He *wants* to pay, *wants* his demand. See, here the order's
    from full stores,

he don't know the sum he pays, the hole he's making—loving
    the job:

wants to pleasure playmate, wants it for me, wants it for lady's
    page,

wants it for slaves of the house, wants it for maids, too; plus,
    my pup

gets sweet talk from the brand new lover, so *he's* overjoyed
    to see him.   185

It's the truth I tell: it's fair each person should be smart for
    their trade.

BOY   I've learned my lesson, this is the truth, with a vast loss come
    to me.

Mme   Our Lady, if you could pay now, you'd have different words
    up front.

Now 'cos you have nothing, you press for taking her home,
    with abuse.

BOY   *Not* my scene.

Mme   Not *my* scene, surely, to deliver her to you,
    free.   190

And yet, for the sake of your age and esteem, this shall be done,

'cos you have brought profit to us rather than kudos to yourself:

if one-twenty minae are paid me, cash, counted out in my hand,

then, out of esteem, I shall grant you . . . tonight . . . free . . . for a
    bonus.

BOY   What if there's zilch?

Mme   I'll credit your zilch—she'll go
    elsewhere, all the same.   195

BOY   Where's what I paid in the past?

Mme   Spent 'n' gone. If it was lasting
    me out,

the She would be delivered to you, I'd never demand a thing.

dĭᵉᵐ ăquam solem lunam noctem | —haec argento
   non ĕmo;
cetĕră quae nos ŭŏlŭmŭs ŭti Graeca mercamur fĭde.

cᵘᵐ a pistorĕ panem pĕtĭmus, ŭinᵘᵐ ex oenŏpolĭo,   200

sⁱ aes hăbent, dant mercem: ĕădem nos discipliṇᵃ utĭmur.

sempĕr ŏcŭlatae mănus sunt nostrae, credunt quod ŭĭdent.

ŭĕtŭs est: 'nĭhĭli c͡oactĭo est'—scis cuius. non dĭcᵒ amplĭus.

AMAT   ălĭam nunc mⁱ oratĭonem despŏlĭato praedĭcas,   204

              ălĭᵃᵐ atque olim cᵘᵐ illĭcĭebas mᵉ ad te blandᵉ
                 ac bĕnĕdĭce.   206
              tum mⁱ aedes quŏquᵉ arridebant cᵘᵐ ad te ŭĕnĭebam tŭae.

              mᵉ unĭcᵉ unᵘᵐ ex omnĭbus tᵉ atquᵉ illᵃᵐ ămarᵉ a͡ibas mĭhi.

              ŭbĭ quid dĕdĕram, quăsĭ cŏlumbae pullⁱ ịn orᵉ ambae mĕo

              usquᵉ ĕratis, m͡eo de stŭdĭo stŭdĭᵃ ĕrant uestrᵃ omnĭa,   210

              usquᵉ ădhaerebatis. quŏd ĕgŏ iussĕram, quod ŭŏlŭĕram,
              făcĭebatis, quod nolebᵃᵐ ac ŭĕtŭĕram, de industrĭa
              fŭgĭebatis, nĕquĕ conarⁱ id făcĕrᵉ audebatis prĭus.

              nunc nĕquĕ quid uĕlim nĕquĕ nolim făcĭtis magni, pessĭmae.

LENA   non tu scis? hic noster quaestŭs auⁱcŭpi sĭmillĭmuˢ ᵉst.   215

              auⁱceps quandŏ concinnauit arĕᵃᵐ, offundit cĭbum;

              assᵘescunt: nĕcessᵉ est făcĕrĕ sumptum qui quaerit lŭcrum.

Day 'n' water 'n' sun 'n' moon 'n' night . . . these things no cash
    buys me
—the rest of the things we want to use, we purchase on Greek
    credit.
When we go get bread from the baker, wine from the
    marchant de vin,   200
it's "If they got brass, they give goods": *we* apply the same
    regulation.
Always open-eyed hands, that's what we have: they credit what
    they see.
Oldasthehills: "Credit limit zero," you know who gets *that*—say
    no more.

BOY   Changed! You plead in a different style, now that I've been
    asset-stripped,   204
Changed from way back when you were vamping me to
    you, all sex 'n' smarm.   206
Then even walls had smiles, when I used to come to you,
    round at your place.
"Of them all, I was your one 'n' only love," you'd tell me, from
    you 'n' her.
When I had paid up, like dove chicks, the pair of you, that's
    what you were,
all the way; and all your soft spots were copied from soft
    spots of mine;   210
all the way, you would cling on to me. My orders and my wishes,
you *did*. My dislikes and my taboos, you took elaborate pains, and
you did *not*. You'd run, you'd not have the nerve to do it, not
    before.
Now, wish or veto, you don't rate me high, worst women in the
    world.

Mme   Don't you *know*? This trade of ours is most . . . like . . .
    the . . . Catcher of Birds.   215
When the fowler has prepared a piece of ground, he tips
    feed on it,
the birds get used to it: investment's a must if you want profit.

ṣaep^e ẹdunt: sĕṃel si ṣunt capṭae, rem ṣoluunṭ auⁱcŭpi.

ĭtĭd^{em} ăpud noṣ: aedes ṇobiṣ   arĕạ ^est, auⁱceps
    ṣ^{um} ĕgo,   219+220
ẹsca ^est mĕrĕtrix, ḷectŭṣ illex   est, ăṃatọres ăụes.

bĕnĕ sălutandọ cons^uescunt,   ḅompellandọ ḅlandĭter,
osḅŭlandọ, ọratĭọnĕ uinnŭḷa, uĕṇustŭḷa.
ṣi păpillam pertracṭauit,   haud ĭḍ est ab ṛ^e auⁱcŭpis,
ṣauĭum si ṣumpsit, ṣumĕr^e ẹum lĭḅet sĭnĕ ṛetĭḅus.   225

haecĭnĕ ṭ^e ess^e obḷit^{um} in ḷudo   qui fŭisti ṭam dĭụ?

AMAT   ṭŭ^a ĭstă ḅulpa ^est, quae discĭpŭlum   ṣemĭdoct^{um} abs ṭ^e
            amŏụes.

LENA   ṛĕmĕaṭ^o audacṭer, merḅedem   ṣĭ | ĕris ṇactus. ṇunc ăḅi.

AMAT   măṇĕ, măṇ^e, audi. ḍic, quid ṃ^e aequum   ḅenses pro illa ṭĭḅĭ
            dăṛe,
            ann^{um} hunc ṇe cum quiqu^{am} ălĭọ sit?

LENA   ṭunĕ? ụiginṭi mĭṇas,   230

atqu^e ẹa ḷegĕ: ṣⁱ ălĭŭṣ ad me   prĭŭs attŭlĕrit, ṭu uăḷe.

AMAT   ăṭ ĕgo ^esṭ ĕtĭam prĭŭs qu^{am} ăḅis quod   ụŏlŏ lŏqui.
LENA   dic quod
                                         lĭḅet.
AMAT   ṇon omṇino ịam pĕrĭị ^est rĕḷĭḅŭum quo pĕrĕam măᶃis.

hăbĕ^o und^e istuc ṭĭḅĭ quod poscis   ḍem, sĕḍ in leges mĕaṣ

dăḅ^o, ŭti ṣcirĕ possis, perpĕtŭ^{um}   aṇṇ^{um} hanc   mĭhⁱ ŭti
            ṣeruĭat   235
ṇec quemqu^{am} intĕrĕ^a ălĭ^{um} admịttat   prorsus quam m^e
            ad ṣe uĭṛum.
LENA   quịn, si ṭu uŏḷes, dŏmĭ ṣerui   qui sunt ḅastraḅo uĭṛos.

postrem^o ut uŏḷes noṣ essĕ,   syngrăphum făḅĭṭ^o affĕṛas;

They eat often: just the once—if they're caught—clears the
    catcher's account.
It's the same way round ours: the house is our ground,
    I play fowler,   219+220
bait is the hooker, divan is vamp, and the lovers, they're
    the birds.
They get 'em used to it, with nice hello's, and with sexy petnames,
with kissing, with pleas that go, "a lil' bit 'wo,' lil' bit 'wow.'"
If a nipple gets fondled, that's no skin off the bird-catcher's nose.
If a kiss gets snatched, he can just bag him, and no need
    for a net.   225
You have forgotten this stuff, after being so long in the school?

BOY   That's your fault. Expelling your pupil halfway through the
    syllabus.

Mme   Come back, don't be shy . . .—when, if, you get the finance.
    For now: so long.

BOY   No, wait. Listen. Say, what do you reckon fair to pay you, for her,

    for her to go with no one else this year?

Mme   For you?
                              Twenty minae.   230
Plus this condition: should someone else fetch 'em first,
    it's bye bye you.

BOY   Umm, I . . . there's . . . before you go . . . something
    I want to say.

Mme   Say what you like.

BOY   I'm not completely wasted. There's what's left—to help me waste
    some more.
I have funds to pay what you demand. And I'll pay, but on my
    terms.
So you're aware: (1) she's to be my slave the whole livelong
    year through,   235
(2) she'll, in the time stipulated, let no man near her but me.

Mme   Why, if you like, the slaves I have at home, I shall go and neuter,
    the men.
For clincher, see you fetch a contract, tell us the way you like us.

　　　ut uŏḷes, ut tĭbĭ lĭḅebit,　ṇobis lĕgᵉᵐ imponĭto:
　　　mŏdŏ teċᵘᵐ unᵃ argentᵘᵐ afferto,　fǎcĭlĕ pǎtĭar cẹtĕṛa.　　　240

　　　portĭtorum sĭmĭllĭṃae sunt　ianŭae lenonĭae:

　　　ṣⁱ affers, ṭum pǎṭent, si ṇon est　quod deṣ, aedes ṇon pǎṭent.　→

AMAT　　intĕṛĭi si ṇon inuĕnĭ° ĕg°　illas ụiginṭi mĭṇas,
　　　et prŏfecto, ṇĭsⁱ ĭllud perd° argentum, pĕṛĕunḍum ᵉst mĭḥi.

　　　ṇunc pergᵃᵐ ad fŏṛᵘᵐ atquᵉ expĕṛĭǎṛ　ŏpĭḅŭṣ, omni ċopĭa,　245

　　　ṣupplĭċab°, eẋobsĕċrab° ut　quemquᵉ ǎṃicum ụidĕṛo,

　　　dignos, indignos ǎḍirᵉ atquᵉ ?expĕṛiṛi?　cerṭum ᵉst mĭḥi.
　　　ṇam si mutŭas non pŏtĕṛo,　certum ᵉst ṣumam faenŏṛe.　　→

→　　　　SERVVS CALLIDVS = **LIBANVS**
LIB　　herclĕ uero, Lĭbǎnĕ, ṇunc te　mĕlĭuˢ ᵉst expergiscĭer
　　　atquᵉ argento ċompǎṛando　fingĕṛĕ fallacĭam.　　　　250
　　　iam dĭụ ᵉst facṭum cum ḍiscesṭⁱ　ǎb ĕṛ° atquᵉ ǎbĭisṭⁱ ad
　　　　fŏṛum.　　　　　　　　　　　　　　　　　　　251
　　　ĭbĭ tᵘ ǎḍ hoc dĭẹī ṭempus　ḍormĭtaᵘⁱsṭⁱ ĭn otĭọ.　　　253

　　　quin tᵘ abs ṭe sŏcordĭᵃᵐ ọmnem　reicᵉ ac ṣegnĭtĭᵉᵐ amŏụe

　　　atquᵉ ǎḍ ingĕnĭụm uĕtus uersutum ṭe rĕċĭpis tŭụm?　　　255

　　　ṣeruᵃ ĕṛum, cǎụĕ tŭ | ĭdem faxiṣ　ǎlĭi quod serụi ṣŏḷent,

　　　quĭ | ǎḍ ĕṛi fraudatĭọnem　ċallĭḍᵘᵐ ingĕnĭụm gĕṛunt.

　　　ụndĕ ṣumam? quᵉᵐ interụertam? quọ hanc cĕḷocem
　　　　ċonfĕṛam?

As you like it, what turns you on: load me up with conditions.
Only—just fetch the cash along with you: I'll stand the rest,
    easy.   240

Just like the door to a Customs House, same for the door to
    madame's.
Fetch stuff—open sesame. If you can pay zilch—the place is
    shut.   →

BOY   I really am done for if I don't come upon the twenty minae.
For a fact, if I don't waste the cash, it must be *me* gets wasted.

Now I'll head for the mall and give it a try, by hook or
    by hock,   245
get down on my knees 'n' intensify pleas, as each friend
    comes in sight.
High-ups, low-downs: go up to them and try it on, I've decided.
'Cos if I can't borrow 'em, I've decided, I'll take out *a loan*.   →

→
LIB   SLAVE ONE: THE BRAINS = **LIBANUS**
Well, lord, Libanus, you best get on and wake yourself up now,
and plot a cunning plan for organizing a bash at the cash.   250
It was yonks ago you split from master, and went off to the
    mall.   251
There you slept like you're on vacation, through to *this*
    hour of the day.   253
Why don'tcha throw off all your sluggishness and expel all
    your sloth?
Wont'cha make a recovery, find your formerly versatile self?   255

Serfguard master. Don't you do the same as other slaves
    normally do
—applying talented brains to set up a swindle on master.

Where'll I take it from? Who'll I send the wrong way?
    Where'll I point my yacht?

impĕtrit^{um}, ĭnaugŭratum ^est: quouis admittunt ăŭes,

picŭs et cornix ab ḷaeua, ̣coruus, parr^a ab ḍextĕra   260

cons^uaḍent. cert^{um} hercle ^est ŭestram ̣consĕqui sententĭam.
ṣed quĭḍ hoc quod picŭs ulmum ̣tundĭt? hau^d tĕmĕrarĭum ^est.
 ̣certe hercḷe ĕgŏ quant^{um} ex augŭrĭo hoc ̣auspĭcĭoqu^e intellĕgo,
ạut mĭḥi in munḍo sunt ŭirg^{ae} aut ̣atrĭensi Ṣaurĕae.

ṣed quĭd ĭḷḷuc quŏḍ exănĭmatus ̣currĭt huc Lĕōnĭḍa?   265

m̥ĕtŭo quŏd ĭḷḷĭc obscaeụauit m̂eae falṣae fall̠acĭae.

→   + SERVVS CURRENS = LEONIDA
LEO   ŭbⁱ ĕgŏ nunc Lĭbănum rĕquir^{am} aut fămĭlĭarem filĭum,
                ŭt ĕg^o iḷḷos lĭbentĭores făcĭam quam Lĭbentĭa ^est?
                maxĭmam praeḍ^{am} et trĭumph^{um} iṣ affĕr^o aduentu mĕo.

                quanḍŏ m̥ecum părĭter potant, părĭter ṣcortạri sŏḷent,   270
                ḥanc quĭdem quam n̥actus praedam părĭter c^{um} illis partĭam.
{LIB}   {iḷḷĭc hŏm̥o aedis compiḷauit, m̥orĕ ṣi fecĭt sŭo.
                ụ^{ae} illi qui t^{am} indĭlĭgentĕr obserụauit ianŭam.}
LEO   aetatem uĕḷim serụirĕ, Lĭbăn^{um} ut conuĕnĭam mŏḍo.
{LIB}   {m̂ea quĭd^{em} herclĕ lĭbĕr ŏpĕra n̥umquam fieṣ ocĭus.}   275

LEO   ĕtĭam de tergo dŭ ̣centas plagas praegnat̠is dăḅo.

{LIB}   {ḷargitur pĕcuḷĭ^{um}, ọmn^{em} in ̣tergo thesaurum gĕrit.}

LEO   n̥am sⁱ occasĭonⁱ huic tempus ṣese ṣubterḍuxĕrit,
                n̥umqu^{am} ĕdĕpol quăḍrigiṣ albiṣ indĭpiscet postĕa.
                ĕrŭm | ĭn obsĭdĭọnĕ linquet, ĭnĭmic^{um} ănĭmoṣ auxĕrit.   280
                ṣed si mec^{um} occasĭon^{em} opprĭmĕr^e hanc qu^{ae} obuenit stŭḍet,

                maxĭmas ŏpimĭtates, gaudĭo effertissĭmas,
                ṣuis ĕris iḷḷe una m̥ecum părĭet n̥atoqu^e et pătri,
                ặdĕo ŭt aetat^{em} amb^o ambobus n̥obis ṣint obn̥oxĭi,

Now I'm father forward, unbirdened: the birds bless any
    direction.
Woodpecker 'n' crow to the left of me, raven, barn-owl to
    the right.   260
Same advice from all: I've decided, lord, I shall follow your line.
But what's *this*? Pecker bashes elm? Now that's no way accidental.
Sure, lord, I . . .—far as I can tell from the birden of the birdlore,
birches either in store for me, or else they're for steward Saurea.

But what's this? Gasping for breath, and steaming this way:
    Leonida.   265
I'm afraid—that bird's put the mockers on my cheating cunning
    plan.

→	**+ SLAVE TWO IN A HURRY = LEONIDA**
LEO	Where o where shall I track down Libanus or our 'ouseold's son
	so I can make 'em even more libidinous than Libido
	The biggest prize 'n' triumph Thats what I'm fetchin' 'em My
	grand entry
	Seein' it's on a par they drink with me go whorin' on a par 270
	now I've got this prize I shall share it with 'em on a par In part . . .
{LIB}	{This person's burgled a house, on his usual behaviour pattern.
	Damn blast the guy that got so casual about watching the door.}
LEO	. . . I'd willin'ly slave all my time Just let me 'n' Libanus meet . . .
{LIB}	{Well, lord, nothing *I* do's gonna get you your liberty
	quicker.} 275
LEO	. . . I'll even pay off my own back two 'undred lashes worth of
	bump . . .
{LIB}	{That's him splashing out his stash. He carries his whole hoard
	on his back.}
LEO	. . . 'cos if time does a disappearin' trick on dis opportunity
	surely four white chargers won' ever catch 'im nor ever after
	'e'll be leavin' master under siege buildin' up enemy morale 280
	Where's if we two look lively 'n' we jump this break that's
	come up
	then there'll be the biggest bonanza stuffed to burstin' with joy
	that he 'n' me'll spawn as one for his masters father & son
	so much both of them'll be be'olden to both of us for life

nostro dĕuincti bĕnĕfĭcĭo.

{LIB}   {'uinctos' nescĭŏquos ăit: 285

non plăcet: mĕtŭ° ịn communĕ ne quam fraudem
  frausŭˢ sit.}
LEO   pĕrĭ ĕg° oppĭdo nĭsĭ Lịbănᵘᵐ inụĕnĭo ịᵃᵐ, ŭb ŭbi ᵉst
  gentĭum.
{LIB}   {ịllĭc hŏmo sŏcĭᵘᵐ ạd mălam rem quaerit quᵉᵐ
  adiungat sĭbi.
non plăcet: pro mọnstr° extemplo ᵉst quandŏ qui sụdat
  trĕmịt.}
LEO   ṣed quĭd ĕg° hic prŏpĕṛans concesso pĕdĭbus, ḷingua
  lạrgĭọr?   290
quin ĕg° hanc iŭbĕo tăcerĕ, quae lŏquens lăcĕṛat dĭem?
{LIB}   {ĕdĕpŏḷ hŏmĭnĕm | infelicem, qui pătronam comprịmat.
  nam si quid scĕḷeste fecit, linguă pr° illo peiiĕṛat.}

LEO   apprŏpĕṛabo, ne post tempus praedae praesĭdĭum părem.
{LIB}   {quᵃᵉ illaec praeda ᵉst? ib° aduersᵘᵐ atquᵉ electabo,
  quidquĭd est.}   295
LIB   iŭbĕo te salụerĕ ụocĕ ṣumma, quōad uiṛes uălent.

LEO   gymnăsĭum flăgri, salụeto.
LIB   quĭd ăgis, cụstos cạrcĕṛis?

LEO   ọ cătenạrum cŏḷonᵉ.
LIB   o ụirgạrum lasciuĭa.
LEO   quot pondo ted essĕ censes nudum?
LIB   ṇon ĕdĕpol scĭọ.
LEO   scibᵃᵐ ĕgŏ te nescirᵉ, at pŏl ĕgŏ, qui ted expendi, scĭo: 300

nudus uinctus centum pond° es, quandŏ pendes per pĕdes.
LIB   qu° argụment° istuc?
LEO   ĕgŏ dicam qu° argụment° et quo mŏdo.

ad pĕdes quandˌ° allĭgatum ᵉst aequum centumpondĭum,
ŭbĭ mănus mănĭcae complexae ṣunt atquᵉ adductᵃᵉ
  ad trăbem,

bound fast by our good turn . . .

{LIB}
        {"Bound," he's calling some

           people or other: 285

I disapprove. I'm afraid. He may've scammed some scam, for
    the team.}

LEO   . . . I've straight 'ad it if I don't find Libanus now where
    o where's 'e . . .

{LIB}   {This person's after a partner in crime, to yoke up with him.

    That's a no-no: it's a red alert, shivering in a sweat is.}

LEO   . . . But I'm in a dash 'ere why cop out on feet but full on
    with *tongue*   290
    Why don' I tell it 'ush Its mutterin's mutilatin' the day . . .

{LIB}   {Surely, a luckless person, having to go jump his *patroness:*
    See, anything he's done devilish, Ms. *Tongue* does perjury
    for him.}

LEO   . . . I'll speed up so I don" fix the prize an escort after time's up—

{LIB}   {What "prize" is that? I'll go right up and lure out whatever
    it is.}   295

LIB   IBIDYOUGOO'DAY, top of my voice, far's my powers can
    muster.

LEO   Goo'day workout centre for the whip

LIB   How you doin', prison

              screw?

LEO   Awmighty grower of manacles

LIB   Mighty orgasm of birches!

LEO   How many pounds ya think ya weigh in ya skin?

LIB   Surely, I dunno.

LEO   I knew ya don' know but sure *I* know 'cos I'm the one that
    weighed ya   300
    In ya skin and bound you are way up at 1 cwt weighed by feet

LIB   How d'you work that out?

LEO   I'll tell ya on what basis how it
         works out
    Once a fair level cwt has been strung up tight to the feet
    when the 'andcuffs hug ya 'ands in their clasp pulled up right to
    the beam

nec dependes nec propendes —quin mălus nequamquĕ sis. 305

LIB   uae tĭbⁱ.
LEO   istuc testamento Seruĭtus lĕgat tĭbi.
LIB   uerbiuelĭtatĭonem fĭĕri compendi uŏlo.

           quĭd ĭstuc est nĕgoti?
LEO   certum ᵉst credĕrᵉ.
LIB   audacter lĭcet.

LEO   siᵘⁱs ămanti subuĕnirĕ fămĭlĭari filĭo,

           tantᵘᵐ ădest bŏnⁱ improuiso, uerum commixtum mălo: 310

           omnes de nobis carnĭfĭcum   concĕlĕbrabuntur dĭes.
           Lĭbănĕ, nunc audacĭᵃ usuˢ ᵉst nobis inuentᵃ et dŏlis.
           tantum făcĭnus mŏdŏ | inuenⁱ ĕgᵒ, ut nos dicamur dŭo

           omnĭum dignissĭmⁱ essĕ quo crŭcĭatus conflŭant.
LIB   ergo mirabar quod dudum scăpŭlae gestibant mĭhi,   315

           hărĭŏlari quᵃᵉ occeperunt sĭbĭ | essᵉ in mundo mălum.

           quidquĭd est, elŏquĕrĕ.
LEO   magna ᵉst praedă cum magno mălo.
LIB   si quĭdᵉᵐ omnes coniurati crŭcĭamentă confĕrant,
           hăbĕᵒ ŏpinor fămĭlĭarem —tergum, ne quaeram fŏris.

LEO   sⁱ istam firmĭtudĭnᵉᵐ ănĭmi | obtĭnes, salui sŭmus.   320

LIB   quin si tergo res soluenda ᵉst, răpĕrĕ cŭpĭo publĭcum:

           pernĕgabᵒ atquᵉ obdurabo, peiĕrabo denĭque.
LEO   ᵉᵐ istă uirtus est, quandᵒ usuˢ ᵉst qui mălum fert fortĭter:

           fortĭter mălum qui pătĭtŭr, idem post pŏtĭtur bŏnum.

ya ain't way over, ya ain't way under—... bein' a no-good
    thug   305

LIB   Damn you.

LEO   That's what Mme Slavery is leavin' you in her will

LIB   This wordwarmongering! There's some economizing I want
    done.

What's that prob of yours?

LEO   Its decided: I'll credit you.

LIB   Feel free,
    be bold.

LEO   Please come show support for the son in our 'ouseold the
    loverboy

There's that much of a good thing just turned up But jumbled
    up with bad   310

Thanks to us each day executioners will 'old a jamboree

Libanus what we need now is to find us bravura and shtick

There's that much of a heist I've just found Pull it off 'n' we
    two'll be

called the 'ombrés most deservin'—... of torture by the bucketful

LIB   *That's* why I've been amazed my shoulder-blades've been itching
    for ages.   315

They've started soothsaying what there is in store for them.
    Something bad.

Whatever it is, air it.

LEO   The prize is big In with a *Big Bad.*

LIB   If one and all come join in and fetch the instruments of torture,

I believe I do own a household . . .—*back,* no need to look
    outside.

LEO   If ya keep possession of that strength of mind of yours then
    we're saved   320

LIB   Look, if a *back* must clear the bill, I'm game, rob the National
    Bank.

I'll deny it all the way, stay tough, and it's perjury for me.

LEO   Pow that's the cream of courage for ya When someone brave's
    bad bravely

"Bravely endure bad," the sayin' would run, "ensure good
    thereafter"

LIB   quin rᵉᵐ actŭtᵘᵐ ĕdissĕris? cŭpĭọ mălụm nancĭscĭẹr.   325

LEO   plăcĭdᵉ ergᵒ unum quidquid rŏgĭtᵃ, ŭṭ acquĭẹscam.
              ṇon uĭdes
              mᵉ ex cursụrᵃ ănḥelĭtᵘᵐ ĕtĭam ḍucĕrᵉ?
LIB   ăgᵉ ăgĕ, ṃansĕṛo . . .

              . . . tᵘᵒ arbĭtratu, ụĕl ădĕᵒ ụsquĕ ḍum pĕṛĭs.

LEO   ŭbĭṇam ᵉst ĕrụs?
LIB   ṃaiŏr ăpụd fŏṛum ᵉst, mĭnŏṛ hic esṭ intus.
LEO   ịam sătĭṣ est mĭḥi.
LIB   tᵘᵐ ĭgĭtur ṭu diụes es fạctus?
LEO   ṃittĕ ṛidĭcŭḷarĭa,   330

              Lịbănĕ.
LIB   ṃittᵒ. isṭuc quŏḍ affeṛṣ aureṣ expecṭant mĕạe.

LEO   ănĭmᵘᵐ adụertᵉ, ŭṭ aeque ṃecŭm | ḥaec scĭạs.

LIB   tăcĕọ.
LEO   bĕạs.

              ṃemĭnistiˢnᵉ ăsĭṇos Arcădĭcos ṃercaṭori Pellaĕọ
              nostrum ụendĕrᵉ atrĭẹnsem?
LIB   ṃemĭni. quid tum posṭĕa?   334+335

LEO   ẹᵐ ergᵒ ĭs argentᵘᵐ huc rĕṃisit, quod dăṛetur Ṣaurĕạe
              prŏ | ăsĭṇis. ădŭḷescens ụenit ṃŏdŏ, quᵘⁱ ĭḍ argentᵘᵐ attŭḷit.

LIB   ŭbⁱ ĭs hŏṃo ᵉst?
LEO   ịam ḍeuoṛandum censes, ṣi conspexĕṛis?

LIB   ĭtᵃ ĕnim ụero. ṣed tăṃen tu ṇempᵉ eos ăsĭnos praedĭcạs

              ụĕtŭlos, cḷaudos, quĭbŭˢ subtritᵃᵉ ad fĕmĭnă iăm | ĕranṭ
              ungŭḷae?   340

LIB   Why don't you tell the tale right away? I fancy bagging
     The Bad.   325

LEO   Gently then One question at a time to calm me down Can't
     ya see
     I'm still pantin' 'n' gaspin' from the 'urry

LIB   There, there, I can
     wait . . .
     . . . It's all up to you. All the way till you are . . .
     —dead.

LEO   Well where's master?

LIB   Big master's at the mall, little master's in here.

LEO   Enough for me.

LIB   Did you just get rich quick, then?

LEO   Do drop the stand-up
     comedy bit,   330
     Libanus.

LIB   Dropped it is. What's that you're fetching? Mine ears
     are a-g-o-g.

LEO   Focus your mind. You'll know it, I'll know it,
     fair do's.

LIB   I'm shtoom.

LEO   You saint.

     Recall an Assyrian dealer buying them Arcadian asses
     off our household steward?

LIB   I do recall. So what is it comes
     next?   334+335

LEO   There. So. He's only gone and sent the cash to be paid to Saurea
     for them asses. The young guy's just got here, and he's fetching
     the cash.

LIB   Where is this person?

LEO   Your immediate thought? "Swallow him
     whole. On sight."

LIB   Yes, just so, true. And yet, hang on, you must be meaning *those*
     donkeys—
     clapped-out, gone lame, the ones with their hooves worn
     down right up to the hocks?   340

LEO   ipsos, qui tĭbĭ subuectabant   rur^e huc uirgas ulmĕas.

LIB   tĕnĕ^o, atqu^e idem t^e hinc uexerunt   uinctum rus.

LEO   mĕmŏr es
                                               prŏbe.
uer^{um} in tonstrin^a ut sĕdebam,   m^e infit percontarĭer

ecquem filĭum Strătonis   nouĕrim Demaenĕtum.
dico me nouiss^e extempl^o et   m^e eius seruum praedĭco   345

ess^e, ĕt aedis demonstraui   nostras.
LIB   quid tum postĕa?

LEO   ait s^e ŏb ăsĭnos ferr^e argentŭm | atrĭensi Saurĕae.
uiginti mĭnăs, sĕd ĕum sese   non no^{ui}ss^e hŏmĭnem qui sĭet,

ipsum uero se nouissĕ   callĭde Demaenĕtum.

quŏnĭ^{am} ill^e elŏcutŭs haec sic—
LIB   —quid t^{um}?
LEO   auscult^a
                               ergo, scĭes.   350

extemplo făcĭo făcetum   m^e atquĕ magnĭfĭcum uĭrum,
dico med ess^e atrĭensem. sic hoc respondit mĭhi:
'ĕgŏ pol Saurĕam non noui   nĕquĕ qua făcĭe sit scĭo.

te non aequum ^est suscenserĕ. sĭ | ĕrum uis Demaenĕtum,
quĕm | ĕgŏ nouⁱ, adduc^e: argentum   non mŏrabor quin
     feras'.   355
ĕgŏ me dixⁱ ĕr^{um} adductur^{um} et   me dŏmi praesto fŏre.
ill^e in bălĭnĕas ĭturu^s ^est,   ind^e huc uĕnĭet postĕa.

quid nunc cŏnsĭli captandum   censes? dic.
LIB   ^{em} istuc ăgo

LEO   That's the ones. They once used to hump here the birches of
      elm for you.

LIB   Got it. Same ones carted *you* off to the farm, bound
      fast.

LEO   Good memory.

      Now. There I was sitting in the barber's, he starts
          questioning me.
      Do I know a son of Armée, by the name of Demaenetus?
      I say, "Yes, I know him," right away, and pipe up "I am his
          slave."   345
      And I gave the directions to our house.

LIB   So what is it comes next?

LEO   He says he's carrying cash for asses to steward Saurea.
      Twenty minae. "But," he says, "I don't know that person from
          Adam,"
      Though, true, brainbox *does* know the man himself, i.e.,
          Demaenetus.
      Now since he'd told me it all this way . . .

LIB   —What next?
LEO   —So listen,
                                              you'll
                                              know. 350

      Right then I fashion a facetious, epic-faceted, hero:
      me. I say that the steward is I. This was his answer to me:
      "Sure, I don't know Saurea. And nor do I know what he looks
          like.
      It's not fair if you get cross. Please get your master Demaenetus,
      him I do know, bring him to me. You'll get cash, no stalling
          from me."   355
      I said I would bring master, and that I'd be home, at his service.
      He's going off to the baths, and from there he'll come here after
          that.
      Whaddya rate now to cop for a plan? Do say.

LIB   Pow—here's where
                                              I'm at.

quomŏdŏ argentŏ interuertᵃᵐ ĕt̬ aduentorᵉᵐ et Ṣaurĕam.

i̬am hoc ŏpŭṣ est exascĭato.   n̬am sⁱ ill̬ᵉ argentum prĭuṣ   360

h̬ospeṣ huc affert, contĭn̬ŭo   n̬os amb̬ᵒ exclusi̬ sŭm̬us.

n̬am mᵉ hŏdĭe sĕn̬ex seduxit   ṣolum ṣorsᵘᵐ ăb̬ aedĭbus,
m̬ĭhĭ tĭbiqu̬ᵉ intermĭn̬atus   n̬os fŭturoṣ ulmĕ̬os,
n̬ĭ | hŏdĭ̬ᵉ Ạrgÿrippo | ẹssent   uigintⁱ argenṭi mĭn̬ae.
i̬ussit u̬el noṣ atrĭensem   u̬el noṣ uxorem sŭ̬am   365

d̬efraudarĕ, d̬ixit ṣese | ŏpĕram promisçam dăr̬e.

n̬unc tᵘ ăb̬ⁱ ad fŏr̬ᵘᵐ ăd ĕr̬ᵘᵐ et n̬arrᵃ haeç   ut noṣ acturi̬
     sŭm̬us:
t̬ᵉ ex Lĕ̬ōn̬ĭda fŭturᵘᵐ essᵉ   atrĭensem Ṣaurĕam,
d̬ᵘᵐ argentᵘᵐ affĕrat merçator   prŏ | ăsĭn̬is.

LEO   f̬ăcĭᵃᵐ ut iŭbes.
LIB   ĕg̬ᵒ ĭllᵘᵐ intĕr̬ĕᵃ hic oblectabo,   prĭŭˢ si fort̬ᵉ adu̬en̬ĕrit.   370

LEO   qu̬ĭd ăis?
LIB   quid uis?
LEO   pugno malam   si tĭb̬i perçussĕr̬o,

             m̬ox cum Ṣaurĕᵃᵐ ĭm̬ĭtabor, cău̬eto n̬e susçensĕ̬as.
LIB   h̬erclĕ u̬ero tu cău̬ebis   n̬e mᵉ attingas, s̬i săp̬is,

             n̬ĕ | hŏdĭe măl̬o cᵘᵐ auspĭçĭo   n̬omen çommutau̬ĕris.

LEO   quaesᵒ, aequᵒ ăn̬ĭmo păt̬ĭtor.
LIB   păt̬ĭtor   t̬ŭ | ĭtem ç̬ᵘᵐ ĕg̬ŏ
                                            te r̬ĕfĕrĭam.   375
LEO   d̬icᵒ ŭt ususˢ ᵉst fĭ̬ĕri.
LIB   d̬icᵒ herçl̬ᵉ   ĕg̬ŏ quŏqu̬ᵉ ut facturŭˢ sum.
LEO   n̬e n̬ĕga.

How to send cash one way, and the visitor 'n' Saurea another?

This needs chop-chop, pdq. 'Cos if he fetches the cash here
    first,   360
this stranger in town, the pair of us are forthwith good as
    shut out.

See, today the old boy took me off to one side, away from home.
He threatened me and you: we are both going to be over-elmed,
if there aren't twenty minae of cash for Argyrippus by today.
His order was, we can take his steward or we can take his
    wife,   365
and swindle 'em. He said he would back us up, the same
    either way.

Now. You. Off to the mall to master, tell how we're going to act.

You're going to stop being Leonida, you're steward Saurea,
till merchantman fetches us cash for asses.

LEO	I'll do what I'm told.
LIB	I. Meantime, shall entertain him, if he happens to get here
	first. 370
LEO	Answer me this.
LIB	Whassup?
LEO	If my fist lands a punch bang on
	your jaw,
	in a mo', when I'll be playing "Saurea," mind you won't get cross.
LIB	Lord, you'll mind you don't lay finger on me, not if you got any
	sense,
	case you find you changed your name on a day when the omens
	are bad.
LEO	Please take it. In fairness.
LIB	Same goes: you take it. When . . .—
	I hit you back. 375
LEO	I'm saying how it must go.
LIB	I'm saying too, lord, how *I* shall go.
LEO	Don't say no.

LIB   quin promitt°, inquᵃᵐ, hostĭrĕ contrᵃ ut mĕrŭĕris.
LEO   ĕg° ăbĕo, tu iam, scĭo, pătĭĕrĕ.

                                       sed quĭs hĭc est? ĭs est,
illᵉ est ipsus. iᵃᵐ ĕgŏ rĕcurro | huc. tᵘ hunc intĕrĕᵃ hic tĕne.

ŭŏlŏ sĕni narrarĕ.   →
LIB   quin t͡uᵘᵐ offĭcĭum făcĭs erg° ac fŭgis?   380

→ →   **+ MERCATOR CVM CRVMINA**
                         (+ PVER MVTVS)
MERC   ut dĕmonstratae sunt mĭhí, | hasᶜᵉ aedis essᵉ ŏportet   381–503:
           Dĕmaenĕtŭs ŭbĭ dicĭtur hăbĭtarᵉ. i, pŭĕrĕ, pulta   iambic
                                                  septenarii
           atquᵉ atrĭensem Saurĕam, sⁱ est intŭs, euŏcat° huc.
LIB   quis nostras sic frangit fŏris? ŏhᵉ, inquam, si quĭd audis.

MERC   nem° ĕtĭam tĕtĭgit. sanŭˢnᵉ es?
LIB   at censebᵃᵐ attĭgisse   385

           proptĕrĕᵃ huc quĭᵃ hăbebas ĭter. nol° ĕgŏ fŏres conseruas
           meas a te uerbĕrarĭer. sanᵉ ĕgŏ sᵘᵐ ămicus nostris.

MERC   pŏl hauᵈ pĕriclum ᵉst cardĭnes ne fŏrĭbŭs effringantur,

           si | istoc exemplº omnĭbus qui quaerunt respondebis.
LIB   ĭtᵃ haec morata ᵉst ianŭá: | extemplo ianĭtorem   390

           clamat, prŏcul si quem uĭdet irᵉ ad se calcĭtronem.

           sed quid uĕnis? quid quaerĭtas?
MERC   Dĕmaenĕtum uŏlebam.

LIB   si sit dŏmi, dicam tĭbi.
MERC   quĭd eiŭs atrĭensis?

LIB   nĭhĭlo măgᵉ intŭs est.

LIB   I hereby promise to make it quits as you'll deserve.

LEO   I, I am off. You will, I know, take it.

                                    But who's this 'ere? It's 'im,
            he's the one. I'll hurry. Back 'ere in no time. Meanwhile you hold
                'im 'ere.
            I wanna tell the old 'un.   →

LIB   Why not play your role, run like
                             the windy?   380

→ →   + **MERCHANT WITH POUCH**
                       (+ PAGE, NON-SPEAKING PART)

MERC   According to the directions given me, this must be the house,
               where I am told that Demaenetus has his home. Go on, boy,
                   knock,
               and steward Saurea, if he's inside, see that he gets called out here.

LIB   Who's smashing our door this way? *Basta,* I say, can you hear
                   at all?

MERC   No one even touched it. Are you well?

LIB   Well, I reckoned you'd
                                            touched it   385
               'cos you were travelling this way. I do *not* want one of us slaves,
               my mate the door, to get a beating. 'Course I am all our lot's
                   friend.

MERC   No danger, sure, the hinges aren't going to get smashed off the
                   doors,
               not if you reply on this model to everyone that calls by.

LIB   That's the character of Ms. Door. Right away yells to call
                   doorman,   390
               if she spots far off, coming her way, one with a kick like a mule.

               But why're you here? Whaddya want?

MERC   It was Demaenetus I
                                            wanted.

LIB   If he was at home, I would tell you.

MERC   Well, what about his
                                            steward?

LIB   He's no more in.

MERC   ŭbⁱ est?

LIB   ad tonsor^{em} irĕ dixit.

MERC   conueni. sed post non rĕdit?

LIB   non ĕdĕpol. quid uŏlebas?   395

MERC   argenti uiginti mĭnas,   sⁱ ădesset, accepisset.

LIB   qui pr^o istuc?

MERC   ăsĭnos uendĭdit   Pellaeo mercatori

mercatu.

LIB   scĭŏ. t^u id nunc rĕfers?   i^{am} hic crede^e ĕ^{um} affŭturum.

MERC   qua făcĭe uester Saurĕa ^est?   sⁱ ĭs est, iam scirĕ pŏtĕro.

LIB   măcĭlentis malis, rufŭlús,   ălĭquantum uentrĭosus   400

trŭcŭlentis ŏcŭlis, commŏda   stătura, tristi fronte.

MERC   non pŏtŭit pictor rectĭus   descrībĕr^e eius formam.

LIB   atqu^e hercl^e ips^{um} ădĕo contŭor: quassanti căpĭt^e incedit.

   quisqu^e obuĭ^{am} huic occessĕrĭt   irato, uapŭlabit.

MERC   sĭquĭd^{em} hercl^e Aeăcĭdĭnis mĭnis   ănĭmisqu^e expletus cedit,   405

   si med iratus tĕtĭgĕrĭt,   iratus uapŭlabit.

→   + ‘*ATR*IENSIS’ = SERVVS IRATVS

      (= SAVREA, A LEONIDA PERSONATVS)

ATR   quĭd hŏc sĭt nĕgoti nemĭnem   meum dictum magni făcĕre?

   Lībăn^{um} in tonstrin^{am} ut iussĕram   uĕnir^e, is nullus uenit.

   n^e ill^e ĕdĕpol terg^o et crurĭbus   consŭlŭit hau^d dĕcore.

{MERC>LIB}   {nĭmĭs impĕrĭosu^s ^est.}

{LIB>MERC}   {uae mĭhí. |}

ATR>LIB   hŏdĭe saluerĕ iussi   410

   Lībănum libertum? iam mănu | emissu^s ^es?

MERC	Where is he?
LIB	Told me he was off to the barber's.
MERC	I met him. But he's not come back since?
LIB	Surely, no. Why'd you want him? 395
MERC	Twenty minae. He would've taken delivery, if he'd been here.
LIB	That's for what?
MERC	Asses he sold to a merchant from Assyria. Trade.
LIB	I know. You're fetching it in now? I credit he'll be here soon.

MERC   What's your Saurea look like? Is he the one? I'll soon be able to
know.

LIB   Lean-jawed, rather tawnyish, with a pronounced surplus at the
belly;   400
mean-eyed, a pretty fair size, and wearing a frown on his
forehead.

MERC   No painter could have got down his shape and kept so close to
the line.

LIB   Yep, lord, it really is, I got him in view. Head shakes as he walks.
There'll be a beating for anyone who meets *him* in a stew.

MERC   If, lord, an Achilles' menace 'n' mettle fill him as he walks,   405
still, one finger on me in his stew, he'll get beat up in his stew.

→   + *STEWARD* = SLAVE IN A STEW
              (= SAUREA, TAKEN OFF BY LEONIDA)

STEW   What's this prob? Nobody rates what I tell them as worth all
that much?
Libanus. My orders were to come to the barber's. He did *not*.
Means that, surely, he's not looked out for back and legs, good
and proper.

{MERC>LIB}   {It's Commander O.T.T.}

{LIB>MERC}   {Ow, damn me.}

STEW>LIB   My order of the
day's   410
"Libanus liberated, goo'day"? Just done, your
manumission?

{LIB>MERC}   obsĕcro te.
ATR>LIB   ne t͏ͧ herclĕ cum magno mălo   mĭhĭ obuĭᵃᵐ occessisti.

                 cur non uenistⁱ, ut iussĕrᵃᵐ, in tonstrinᵃᵐ?
LIB>ATR   hic me mŏratuˢ ᵉst.

ATR>LIB   sĭquĭdᵉᵐ herclĕ nunc summum Iŏuem   te dicas detĭnŭisse

                 atquᵉ is prĕcator adsĭet,   mălam rᵉᵐ effŭgĭes numquam.   415

                 tu, uerbĕrᵒ, impĕrĭum mĕum   contempsisti?

{LIB>MERC}   {pĕrĭⁱ, hospes.}
MERC>ATR   quaesᵒ herclĕ noli, Saurĕă,   mͤa causᵃ hunc uerbĕrare.

ATR   ŭtĭnam nunc stĭmŭlŭs in mănu   mĭhĭ sit—
MERC>ATR   —quĭescĕ, quaeso.

ATR>LIB   —qui lătĕră contĕram tŭă,   quᵃᵉ occallŭĕrĕ plagis.

ATR>MERC   abscedᵉ ac sĭnĕ mᵉ hunc perdĕrĕ,   qui semper mᵉ irᵃ
                    incendit,   420
                 cuͥ numquᵃᵐ unam rem me lĭcet   sĕmel praecĭpĕrĕ furi,

                 quin centĭens ĕădᵉᵐ impĕrᵉᵐ atquᵉ   ogganniᵃᵐ, ĭtăque iᵃᵐ
                    hercle
                 clamorᵉ ac stŏmăcho non quĕo   lăbori suppĕdĭtare.

                 iussinᵉ, scĕlestᵉ, ab ianŭa | hoc stercŭs hinc auferri?

                 iussinᵉ cŏlumnis deĭci | ŏpĕras ărănĕorum?   425

                 iussinᵉ in splendorem dări   bullas has fŏrĭbus nostris?

                 nĭhĭl est. tamquam si claudŭˢ sim,   cum fusti ᵉst ambŭlandum.

                 quĭă trĭdŭᵘᵐ hoc unum mŏdo   fŏrᵒ ŏpĕrᵃᵐ assĭdŭam dedo,
                 dum rĕpĕrĭam qui quaerĭtet   argentᵘᵐ in faenŭs, hic uos

{LIB>MERC}	{Help!}
STEW>LIB	Means for sure, you done crossed my path. Lord, walked right in, with a Big Bad.

Why'd you not come, as per orders, to the barber's?

LIB>STEW

He held

me up.

STEW>LIB

If you said, lord, you were detained by Jove the Almighty himself,

were *He* here to pray mercy for *you* . . .—you'll never get off Bad News.   415

You whipping boy. Scoffed at my command,
       did you?

{LIB>MERC}   {I've had it, guest, friend.}

MERC>STEW

Please, Saurea, lord, don't give him a beating, not for my sake, no.

STEW

Right now, wish I'd got a whip here in my hand . . .

MERC>STEW

—P-lease, do

be calm.

STEW>LIB

. . . so I could give those hips of yours a good scour, so toughened to blows.

STEW>MERC

Back off. Let me waste 'im. He's always the fire-starter for my stew.   420

I never can give him orders the once, not one single thing, the thief.

No. A hundred times must I give—no, bark—the same commands—so now,

lord, with the decibels of spleen. I just can't keep up with the work.

Ordered or not: first, this shit here, for fetching away from the door?

Ordered second: the spiders' handiwork, knocking off the columns?   425

Ordered third: these here door studs, putting a shine on 'em for our doors?

Nought out of three. As if I'm lame, I have to walk round with a stick.

'Cos just these 1-2-3 days past, I've assigned full time to the mall,

while I'm hitting the "Desperately seeking cash loan," here you lot

dormĭtīs intĕrĕa dŏṃⁱ atquᵉ ĕrŭṣ ĭn hărᵃ, haud aedĭbŭṣ,
hăbĭtat.   430
ᵉᵐ ergᵒ hoc tĭbⁱ.

{LIB>MERC}   {ḥospes, ṭᵉ obsĕc̣ro, def̣endĕ.}
MERC>ATR   Ṣaurĕᵃ, oṛo
mĕạ cauṣᵃ ut miṭṭas.

ATR>LIB   ĕḥᵒ, ecquis pṛo uecṭụrᵃ ŏḷiui
rem ṣoluit?
LIB>ATR   ṣoluit.
ATR   c̣u͡i dăṭum ᵉst?
LIB   Stĭc̣ho uĭc̣arĭᵒ ịpsi

t͡uo.
ATR   ụáh, deḷeniṛᵉ appăṛas, scĭŏ ṃi uĭc̣arĭᵘᵐ ẹsse,

nĕquᵉ ĕᵒ ẹssĕ ṣeruᵘᵐ ĭṇ aedĭbụ́s | erⁱ qui sit pḷuris
quᵃᵐ ille ᵉst.   435
sed ụină quaĕ | hĕri ụendĭḍi uiṇarĭᵒ Ẹxaeṛambo,

iam pṛŏ | ĕis ṣăṭĭˢ feç̣it Stĭc̣ho?
LIB   fec̣issĕ ṣăṭĭs ŏpinor.
nam ụidⁱ huç̣ ipsᵘᵐ addụcĕṛe trăpeziṭᵃᵐ Ẹxaeṛambum.
ATR   sic dĕdĕro. prĭŭˢ quae c̣redĭḍi, uix anno post exegi:

nunc ṣăṭăgĭt, adduc̣it dŏṃúm | ĕtĭᵃᵐ ultṛᵒ et ṣcribit
ṇummos.   440
Drŏṃo merc̣edem ṛetṭŭḷit?
LIB   diṃĭdĭo ṃĭnŭs ŏpinor.
ATR   quid ṛĕlĭc̣ŭᵘᵐ?
LIB   a͡ibat ṛeddĕṛé c̣ᵘᵐ extemplo ṛeddĭṭᵘᵐ esset.

nam ṛĕṭĭneṛⁱ, ut quod ṣit sĭbí | ŏpĕris lŏc̣atᵘᵐ effĭc̣ĕret.

ATR   scȳphos quoṣ utendos dĕḍi Phĭlŏḍamo, ṛetṭŭḷitne?
LIB   noṇ ĕtĭăm.

back home sleep the while, and master's abode is a sty, not a
   house.   430
Pow, you got it coming.

{LIB>MERC}   {Help me, guest, friend, I beg you.}

MERC>STEW   Saurea, *please*.
For my sake, do let him be.

STEW>LIB   Hey. Olives, shipment of: somebody
cleared the bill?

LIB>STEW   Bill cleared.

STEW   Payment made to . . .?

LIB   Le Compte
                                       himself.
                                   Deputy
to you.

STEW   Pah. You're trying t' soft soap me. I know my own
                Deputy.
And no there ain't a slave in master's house that's worth more
        than he is,   435
Now, wine: sold yesterday, by me. To Extraordinaire, the
        wine-mart.
Le Compte satisfied now for that lot?

LIB   I guess he's been satisfied.
'Cos I saw him bring the banker in person. That Extraordinaire.

STEW   *The* way to pay. Last credit from me barely recouped one year
        down.
Now, he satisfies. Glad to bring him to our base. And, signs for
        dosh.   440
Le Coureur: fee fetched and paid in?

LIB   50% short is my guess.

STEW   The balance, then?

LIB   He said yes, it's in . . .—the moment it's in
                to him.
'Cos it's withheld, so he'll complete the worksheet
        sub-contracted to him.

STEW   Goblets handed to Philodamus, for the use of: returned, no?

LIB   Not yet.

ATR	| hem non? si uĕlis, da, commŏdᵃ
	hŏmĭnⁱ ămico. 445
{MERC>LIB}	{pĕrⁱ herclĕ, ⁱᵃᵐ hic mᵉ ăbĕgĕrit sŭᵒ ŏdĭᵒ.}
{LIB>ATR}	{heus iam sătis tu.

audⁱˢnᵉ quae lŏquĭtur}

{ATR>LIB}	{audĭᵒ et quĭesco.}
{MERC>LIB}	{tandᵉᵐ, ŏpinor,

contĭcŭit. nunc ădĕᵃᵐ optĭmum ᵉst, prĭŭˢ quᵃᵐ incĭpit
tinnire.}

MERC>ATR	quam mox mⁱ ŏpĕram das?
ATR>MERC	ehem, optĭme. quam dudum
	tᵘ aduenisti?
	non herclĕ te prouidĕram —quaeso, ne uĭtĭo uertas— 450

ĭtᵃ iracundĭᵃ obstĭtít ŏcŭlis.

MERC	non mirum factum ᵉst.

sed si dŏmi ᵉst, Demaenĕtum uŏlebam.

ATR	nĕgăt essᵉ intus.
	uerᵘᵐ istuc argentum tămen mĭhĭ si uis denŭmĕrare,
	rĕpromittᵃᵐ istoc nomĭnĕ sŏlutam rem fŭturam.

MERC	sic pŏtĭŭs ut Demaenĕto tĭbⁱ ĕro praesentĕ reddam. 455
LIB>MERC	ĕrŭs istunc nouit atquᵉ ĕrᵘᵐ híc.
MERC>LIB+ATR	ĕrᵒ huic praesentĕ reddam.
LIB>MERC	da mŏdŏ mĕo pĕrĭcŭlo, rem saluᵃᵐ ĕgᵒ exhĭbebo.

nam si scĭat noster sĕnex fĭdem non essᵉ huic hăbĭtam,
suscensĕăt, cui \| omnĭum rerᵘᵐ ipsus semper credit.

ATR	non magni pendo. ne dŭĭt, si non uult. sic sĭnᵉ astet. 460

{LIB>MERC}	{dᵃ, inquam. uah, formĭdo mĭser nᵉ hic me tĭbⁱ arbĭtretur

STEW   "No"? Ugh. If you like, *give* it away: be nice to a friend.   445

{MERC>LIB}   {Lord, *I've* had it. This mo', his puke'll chase me off.}
{LIB>STEW}   {Hey.
                                                        Enough
                                                          now,
                 you hear what he is saying?}
{STEW>LIB}   {I do. I'll simmer down.}
{MERC>LIB}   {At last.
                                                     I guess
                 he's hushed, now's best to approach him. Before the tinnitus
                    begins.}
MERC>STEW   How soon can you see to me?
STEW>MERC   Oops. Great. How long since you
                                                got here, sir?
                 No, lord, I never saw you coming—will you please take no
                    offence)—   450
                 Getting in a stew like that blocked my eyes.
MERC   No surprises there,
                                                     then.

                 Now. If he's home, I'm after Demaenetus.
STEW   *He* says he's not in.
                 But that cash of yours, nonetheless, if you will count it me out,
                 I'll promise back that the account down under your name will
                    be cleared.
MERC   *This* way, instead: I'll deliver it you, master in attendance.   455
LIB>MERC   Master knows him, he knows master.
MERC>LIB+STEW   I'll pay him, master
                                                attending.
LIB>MERC   Just hand it over, risk all my own. I'll have the account cleared
                    safe.
                 See, if our top elder knew this guy hadn't had trust shown to him,
                 he'd be cross, and himself always gives him universal credit.
STEW   No big deal to me. Won't pay, need not. Leave him on stand-by,
                    just so.   460
{LIB>MERC}   {Pay, I say. Yukkh, poor me, I dread it, he'll judge that I advised
                    you

sᵘasissĕ sĭbĭ ne credĕres. da, quaesᵒ, ac ne formida:

saluᵘᵐ herclᵉ ĕrit.}

{MERC>LIB}   {credam fŏrĕ —dum quĭdᵉᵐ ĭpsᵉ in
mănŭ | hăbebo.

pĕrĕgrinŭs ĕgŏ sum, Saurĕam non nouⁱ.}

{LIB>MERC}   {at noscĕ sane.}

{MERC>LIB}   {sit, non sit, non ĕdĕpol scĭo. sⁱ ĭs est, ĕᵘᵐ essᵉ ŏportet.   465

ĕgŏ certe mᵉ incerto scĭᵒ hoc dăturum nemĭnⁱ hŏmĭni.}

ATR>LIB   herclᵉ istum dⁱ omnes perdŭĭnt. uerbo căuĕ supplĭcassis.

ferox est uiginti mĭnas mĕas tractarĕ sese.

ATR>MERC   nemᵒ accĭpĭt, aufer te dŏmᵘᵐ. abscedᵉ hinc, mŏlestus ne sis.

MERC>ATR   nĭmĭs iracunde. non dĕcet sŭperbᵘᵐ essᵉ hŏmĭnem
seruum.   470

ATR>LIB   mălᵒ herclĕ iam magno tŭo, nⁱ isti nec recte dicis.
LIB>MERC   impurĕ, nĭhĭli.
{LIB>MERC}   {non uĭdes irasci?}
ATR>LIB   pergĕ porro.
LIB>MERC   flăgĭtĭŭm | hŏmĭnis.
{LIB>MERC}   {dᵃ, obsĕcrᵒ, argentᵘᵐ huic, ne
mălĕ lŏquatur.}

MERC>LIB+ATR mălᵘᵐ herclĕ uobis quaerĭtis.
ATR>LIB   crurᵃ herclĕ diffringentur,
nⁱ istᵘᵐ impŭdicum percĭes.

{LIB}   {pĕrĭⁱ herclᵉ.}
LIB>MERC   ăgᵉ, impŭdice,   475

scĕlestĕ, non audes mĭhĭ scĕlesto subuĕnire?

not to give him the least credit. Pay, please, and don't you dread
   a thing.
Lord, it will be safe.}

{MERC>LIB}   {I'll credit it will, long's it's . . .—here, in my
                         hand.
I come from abroad. I don't know Saurea.}

{LIB>MERC}   {*Get* to know him,
                                 then.}

{MERC>LIB} {Him? Not him? . . . Surely, I dunno. If it is, it just must
               be him.   465
I *am* certain I'll pay this to no person where I'm *un*certain.}

STEW>LIB   Lord, may the pantheon waste him. Mind you don't kneel to
               him out loud.
He's running wild from getting to handle *twenty minae of mine.*
STEW>MERC No one takes delivery. Fetch yourself home. Push off, don't be a
               pain.
MERC>STEW O.T.T. stewing. That's wrong: overblown pride from a slave
               person.   470

STEW>LIB   Lord, a Big Bad's all yours, unless you talk to him right out of line.
LIB>MERC   Unclean! S.F.A.!
{LIB>MERC}   {See him stewing?}
STEW>LIB   Keep going, you, right on.
LIB>MERC   Scandal person!
{LIB>MERC}   {Pay him the cash, I beg, or else he'll
                         badmouth you.}

MERC>LIB+STEW You two, lord, are asking for bad.
STEW>LIB   Your legs, lord, they will get
                                 shattered,
         if you don't stun sir shameless.
{LIB}   {Lord, I've had it.}
LIB>MERC   Come on, sir
                                 shameless, 475
     you're the accursed, won't you just dare . . .—come and rescue
         me, *the* accursed?

ATR>LIB	pergi^sn^e prĕcari pessĭmo?
MERC>ATR	quae res? tun^e lĭbĕr^o hŏmĭni

mălĕ seruus lŏquĕrĕ?

ATR>MERC	uapŭl^a.
MERC>ATR	id quĭdem tĭbⁱ herclĕ fiet

ut uapŭles, Demaenĕtum   sĭmŭl ac conspexĕr^o hŏdĭe.

in ius uŏco te.

ATR>MERC	non ĕo.	
MERC>ATR	non is? mĕmento.	
ATR>MERC	mĕmĭni.	480
MERC>ATR	dăbĭtur pol supplĭcĭum mĭhi de tergo uestro.	
ATR>MERC	uae te.	

tĭbĭ quĭdĕm supplĭcĭum, carnĭfex,   [?]de nobis detŭr?

MERC>ATR	ătqu^e ĕtĭam?

pro dictis uestris mălĕdĭcis   poenae pendentur mⁱ hŏdĭe.

ATR>MERC	quid, uerbĕr^o? ai͡^sn^e tu, furcĭfer? nosmet fŭgĭtarĕ

         censes?   484+485

i nunci^{am} ăd ĕrum, quo uŏcas, iamdudum quo uŏlebas.

MERC>ATR	nunc demum? tămĕn numqu^{am} hinc fĕres argenti nummum,

         nĭsĭ me

dărĕ iussĕrit Demaenĕtús.

ATR>MERC	ĭtă făcĭt^o, ăg^e ambŭl^a ergo.

tu contŭmelĭ^{am} altĕri   făcĭas, tĭbĭ non dĭcatur?

t^{am} ĕg^o hŏmŏ sum quam tu.

MERC>ATR	scilĭcét. ĭtă res est.
ATR>MERC	sĕquĕr^e

                       hac ergo.   490

praefiscĭnⁱ hoc nunc dixĕrim: nem^o ĕtĭam m^e accusauit

mĕrĭto mĕo, nĕquĕ m^e altĕr est Ăthenis hŏdĭe quisquam

cui͡ credi rect^e aeque pŭtent.

STEW>LIB   Keeping on praying to the pits?

MERC>STEW   What's this going on?

                                      A free person,

                and you a slave badmouth him?

STEW>MERC   Get beaten.

MERC>STEW   Lord, you got it

                                          coming,

                your beating. The minute I clap eyes on Demaenetus today.

                I'm taking you to court.

STEW>MERC   I won't go.

MERC>STEW   Won't go? Don't forget.

STEW>MERC   I won't.   480

MERC>STEW   Sure and it's retribution will be mine. On your back.

STEW>MERC   Goddam you.

                Retribution will be yours, executioner? On me?

MERC>STEW   Yes, plus

                the penalty for your verbal abuse will be paid me today.

STEW>MERC   You what, whipping boy? You don't say, ball-'n'-chain? Think

                    we'll bolt for it?   484+485

                Off, now, to master. Where you're "taking" us. Where you've

                    wanted long since.

MERC>STEW   Now? At last. Still, you'll never fetch one coin from this cash,

                    not unless

                Demaenetus orders me to pay.

STEW>MERC   That's the way. So . . .—get

                                  walking.

                You can use vitriol on a twin, and have none spoken at you?

                I'm a person as much as you.

MERC>STEW   Course. That's life.

STEW>MERC   So this way,

                                      follow.   490

                Now let me say this, no skin off your nose: no one's ever taken me

                to court and me deserve it. There's no one else in today's Athens

                they reckon gets so much credit, as me, right 'n' proper.

MERC>ATR   fortassis. sed tămen me

numquᵃᵐ hŏdĭᵉ induces ut tĭbi credᵃᵐ hoc argentᵘᵐ ignoto.
lŭpŭs est hŏmᵒ hŏmĭni, non hŏmŏ, cum qualis sit
    non nouit.   495

ATR>MERC   iam nunc sĕcundă mĭhĭ făcis. scibᵃᵐ huic te căpĭtŭlᵒ hŏdĭe

facturum sătĭˢ prᵒ iniurĭă. quamquᵃᵐ ĕgŏ sum sordĭdatus,
frugi tămen sum, nec pŏtest pĕcŭlĭᵘᵐ enŭmĕrari.

MERC>ATR   fortassĕ. |
ATR>MERC   ĕtĭam Pĕrĭphănes Rhŏdo mercator diues
absentᵉ ĕro solus mĭhĭ tălentᵘᵐ argenti soli   500
annŭmĕrauit et credĭdit mĭhĭ, nĕquĕ deceptuˢ ᵉst ĭn ĕŏ.

MERC>ATR   fortasseᵉ.
ATR>MERC   atquᵉ ĕtĭam tu quŏquᵉ ipsĕ, sⁱ esses percontatus

mᵉ ex ăliis, scĭŏ pol credĕres nunc quod fers.
MERC>ATR   haudᵈ nĕgassim.→ → → →

→ →   **LENA + MERETRIX = PHILAENIUM**
LENA   nĕquĕonᵉ ĕgŏ ted interdictis făcĕrĕ mansᵘetem   504-44:
                    mĕis?   trochaic
                ?ăn ĭtă tŭ ᵉs ănĭmatᵃ, ut qui matrĭs expers   *septenarii*
                    impĕrĭis sĭes??   505
PHIL   ŭbĭ pĭem Pĭĕtatem, sⁱ istoc morĕ moratam tĭbi
                postŭlem plăcĕrĕ, mater, mĭhĭ quo pacto praecĭpis?

LENA   an dĕcorum ᵉst aduersari mĕis te praeceptis?
PHIL   quĭd est?
LENA   hocĭne ᵉst pĭĕtatem cŏlĕrĕ, matrⁱ impĕrĭum mĭnŭĕrĕ?
PHIL   nĕquĕ quae recte făcĭunt culpo nĕquĕ quae
                    delinquunt ămo.   510

MERC>STEW

P'raps,

and yet

you'll never lure me to credit you with this cash today. Unknown.
A man's a wolf, not a man . . .—to a man who don't know
  what he's like.   495

STEW>MERC   The way you're behaving now suits me. I just knew you would
  give me
satisfaction for damage to this noddle. Although I am grubby,
still I am good as gold, and . . .—my stash it just cannot be
  counted.

MERC>STEW   P'raps.

STEW>MERC   Even His Éminence, loaded merchant from Rhodes, today
paid me sixty minae cash, solo—master *not* in attendance— 500
counted it up, giving me credit, and in that, *he* wasn't conned.

MERC>STEW   P'raps.

STEW>MERC   You yourself, too, if you'd checked me out proper with
  other folk,
I know sure you'd credit me with what you bring now.

MERC>STEW

I shan't

dissent.

→ → → →

→ →   **MADAME + WHORE = PHILAENIUM**
Mme   Have I really no way to tame you to obey when I say no?

You're not minded of parting from mother's command,
  are you, this way?   505

PHIL   How could I be Devotion's devotee, if I demanded, in
your way, that my ways win your approval, mama . . .—as you
  teach me?

Mme   So it's decent for you to stand up to my teachings, is it?

PHIL   What?

Mme   So, *this* is tending Devotion, then: shrinking mothers' command?

PHIL   I don't slate what they do right. I don't love what they do
  wrong, either.   510

LENA　　　　　　sătĭˢ dĭcacŭla ᵉs ămatrix.

PHIL　　　　　　　　　　　　mater, is quaestus mĭhi ᵉst:

　　　　　　　lĭnguă poscit, corpus quaerĭt,　ănĭmŭs orat, res mŏnet.

LENA　　　　　　ĕgŏ te uŏlŭi castigarĕ,　tu mĭhⁱ ăccusatrix ădes.

PHIL　　　　　　nĕquᵉ ĕdĕpol tᵉ accuso nĕquᵉ ĭd me　făcĕrĕ fas existĭmo.

　　　　　　　uerᵘᵐ ĕgŏ mēas quĕror fortunas,　cᵘᵐ illo quĕm | ămo

　　　　　　　　prŏhĭbĕor.　　　　　　　　　　　　　　　　　　　　515

LENA　　　　　　ecquă pars oratĭonis　de dĭe dăbĭtur mĭhi?

PHIL　　　　　　et mĕam partem lŏquendi |　et tŭam trado tĭbi.

　　　　　　　ad lŏquendᵘᵐ atquᵉ ad tăcendum　tutᵉ hăbĕas portiscŭlum.

　　　　　　　quin pol si rĕpŏsiui remum,　solă ĕgŏ in casterĭa

　　　　　　　ŭbĭ quĭescᵒ, omnis fămĭlĭae　causă consistit tĭbi.　　　　520

LENA　　　　　　quĭd ăis tu, quᵃᵐ ĕgŏ unam uidi　mŭlĭĕrᵉᵐ audacissĭmam?

　　　　　　　quŏtĭens te uĕtŭⁱ Argўrippum　filĭum Demaenĕti

　　　　　　　compellarᵉ aut contrectarĕ,　collŏquiuᵉ aut contŭi?

　　　　　　　quid dĕdit? quid iussit ad nos　deportarⁱ? an tu tĭbi

　　　　　　　uerbă blandă essᵉ aurum rerĕ,　dictă doctă pro dătis?　　525

　　　　　　　ultrᵒ ămas, ultrᵒ expĕtessĭs,　ultrᵒ ad tᵉ accersi iŭbes.

　　　　　　　illos qui dant ēos derides;　qui deludunt depĕris.

　　　　　　　an tᵉ ĭd expectarᵉ ŏportet,　si quis promittat tĭbi

　　　　　　　te facturum diuĭtem, si　mŏrĭatur mater sŭa?

　　　　　　　ecastor nobis pĕriclᵘᵐ et　fămĭlĭae portendĭtur,　　　530

　　　　　　　dᵘᵐ eiŭs expectamus mortem,　ne nos mŏrĭamur făme.

　　　　　　　nunc ădĕŏ nĭsĭ mⁱ huc argenti |　affert uiginti mĭnas,

Mme   Full of quips, for a lovebug, aren't you?

PHIL   Mama, that's my
profession:
my tongue demands, my body asks, my mind pleads, the circs
give coaching.

Mme   I meant to tick *you* off, and you turn up and put *me* in the dock.

PHIL   Surely, I put you in no dock: no, my doing *that* isn't right.
I do lament my luck, when I'm kept away from the man
I love.   515

Mme   Will any part of the pleading be earmarked mine while there's
daylight?

PHIL   I pass over to you *both* my part of the speechmaking *and* yours.
For speaking and for shushing, you take that rhythm stick for
rowing.
Why sure if *I* put back my oar, and in the rowers' bunks, solo,
I then take some rest, the *whole* household firm grinds to a
halt on you.   520

Mme   What you saying? The one woman I've seen who has the most
daring.
Loves-Talk, how many times have I said no? Argyrippus, son of
Demaenetus: no naming, touching, talking, eyeballing together.
What fees he paid? What's he ordered for ferrying to us? You
think
seductive words are gold for you? Posh talk will do for fees? 525
You go and love him, go and chase him, go get him summoned
to you.
Laugh at the ones that pay up. Waste away over the ones that
mock.
Ought you to wait for it, if one should come to you with the
promise:
"I shall make sure you are rich if . . ."—"if," that is, his "mummy
dies"?
Our Lady, high risk's predicted for us and the whole family, 530
and meanwhile we're waiting for her death, when we may
die of hunger.

So, now. If he doesn't fetch me twenty minae over here, cash,

 nᵉ illᵉ ecastor hinc trudetur largus lăcrĭmarum fŏras.

hic dĭēs summuˢ ᵉst quo ᵉst ăpud me | ĭnŏpĭᵃᵉ excusatĭo.

PHIL   pătĭar, si cĭbo cărerĕ me iŭbes, mater mĕa.   535
LENA   non uĕtŏ ted ămarĕ qui dant cŭiᵃ ămentur gratĭa.

PHIL   quid sⁱ hic ănĭmŭs occŭpatuˢ ᵉst, mater, quid făcĭam? mŏnᵉ.

LENA   em,
        mĕum căput contemples, si quĭdᵉᵐ ex re consultas tŭa.

PHIL   ĕtĭᵃᵐ oᵘⁱpílĭo qui pascit, mater, ălĭenas ŏuis,   539+540

        ălĭquᵃᵐ hăbet pĕculĭarem qui spem soletur sŭam.
        sĭnĕ mᵉ ămarᵉ unᵘᵐ Argȳrippum | ănĭmi causa, quem uŏlo.

LENA   intrᵒ ăbi, nam te quĭdᵉᵐ ĕdĕpol nĭhĭl est impŭdentĭus.

PHIL   audĭentem dicto, mater, produxisti filĭam.   → →

→ →   LIBANVS + LEONIDA CVM CRVMINA
LIB   Perfĭdĭae laudes gratĭasquᵉ hăbemus mĕrĭto magnas,   545–745:
                                                                    iambic
        cum nostris sycŏphantĭis, dŏlis astutĭisque,   septenarii
        scăpŭlarum confĭdentĭa, uirtutᵉ ulmorum freti,
        quⁱ aduersum ?stĭmŭlos? lammĭnas crŭcesquĕ
            compĕdesque
        neruos cătenas carcĕres nŭmellas pĕdĭcas boias   549+550

        inductoresquᵉ acerrĭmos gnarosquĕ nostri tergi,

        ?qui saepᵉ antᵉ in nostras scăpŭlas cĭcătrĭces indĭderunt,?

Our Lady, he'll be shoved outa here, showering us with . . .—
    tears. Out!
This is the last day the "funds short" cop-out will run. Not in *my*
    place.

PHIL I'll stand it, if you order me to go without food, mama mine. 535
Mme I don't say "no, don't love ones who pay up" . . .—that's why they
    get loved.

PHIL What if mind-'n'-heart's hung up here? Ma, what do I do? Please
    advise.
Mme   Pow.
Take a good look at my *head,* if you're taking stock of your
    account.

PHIL Even the shepherd, mama, who pastures the ewes of other
    people,   539+540
owns one private, for his stash, as the consoling hope for himself.
Let me love just Argyrippus for heart-'n'-mind's sake. The one I
    want.
Mme Inside, go on, off with you. 'Cos, surely, nowt's more shameless
    than you.
PHIL She heeds what you say, mama, the girl you brought up for your
    daughter.   → →

→ →   LIBANUS + LEONIDA
               (WITH MONEY-POUCH)
LIB In praise of Broken Trust. In thanks. We deserve the epic
    we've earned.   545
We and our forces: the chicaneries, the cons, and the brainwaves.
Shouldered on trust in our blades. On quality elm we reposed.
Us up against whips 'n' branding-irons 'n' crosses 'n' shackles

fetters 'n' chains 'n' cells 'n' hog-ties 'n' leg-irons 'n'
    collars.   549+550
Plus those passionate daubers, with our backs for intimate
    canvas,
?who have routinely inscribed for us scars on our shoulder
    blades.?

eae nunc lĕgĭones, cŏpĭae | exercĭtusquᵉ ĕorum
ui pugnando, peiiurĭis nostris fūgae pŏtiti.   555

ᵎid uirtutᵉ huius collegaī mᵉaquĕ cŏmĭtateᵎ
factumst. qui me ᵉst uir fortĭor ad sŭffĕrendas plagas?

LEO   ĕdĕpol uirtutes qui tŭas non possis collaudare
      sicŭt ĕgŏ possim, quae dŏmi duelliquĕ mălĕ fecisti.

nᵉ illᵃ ĕdĕpol pro mĕrĭto tŭo mĕmŏrari multă possunt: 560

ŭbĭ fidentem fraudauĕris, ŭbĭ ĕrᵒ infĭdelis fŭĕris,

ŭbĭ uerbis conceptis scĭens lĭbenter peiiĕraᵘᵉris,
ŭbĭ părĭĕtes perfodĕris, in furtᵒ ŭbĭ sis prĕhensus,

ŭbĭ saepĕ causam dixĕris pendens aduersŭs octo
artutos, audacis uĭros, uălentis uirgatores.   565

LIB   fătĕor prŏfectᵒ ut praedĭcas, Lĕŏnĭdᵃ, essĕ uera.
      uerᵘᵐ ĕdĕpol nᵉ ĕtĭam tŭă quŏquĕ mălĕfactᵃ ĭtĕrari multa

et uero possunt: ŭbĭ scĭens fĭdelⁱ infidus fŭĕris,

ŭbĭ prensŭs in furto sĭes mănĭfestᵒ et uerbĕratus,

ŭbĭ peiiĕraᵘᵉrĭs, ŭbĭ săcro mănus sis admŏlitus,   570

ŭbⁱ ĕris damno, mŏlestĭᵃᵉ et dedĕcŏri saepĕ fŭĕris,
ŭbĭ credĭtum quod sit tĭbĭ dătᵘᵐ essĕ pernĕgaᵘᵉris,
ŭbⁱ ămicae quăm | ămico tŭo fŭĕris măgis fĭdelis,

ŭbĭ saepᵉ ad languorem tŭă durĭtĭa dĕdĕrĭs octo

uălĭdos lictores, ulmĕis adfectos lentis uirgis.   575

num mălĕ rĕlata ᵉst gratĭᵃ, ut collegam collaudaui?

LEO   ut mequĕ tequĕ maximᵉ atquᵉ ingĕnĭo nostro dĕcŭit.

Now those legions, that capability to engage their armies,
by force, fight, our perjuring ourselves, achieved their
 objective: flight. 555
Through my colleague's qualities, of courage, and camaraderie,
this materialized. What hero braver than I, for suffering blows?

LEO Surely, the courageous qualities of your own you could not praise,
not as I could, your feats on home front and out in the field:
 all *B-a-d.*
Surely, feats are legion, re-told in the name of all you
 deserve: 560
when you fleeced one man who came to trust you; when you
 breached master's trust;
when you ad-libbed perjury, with relish quoting set formulae;
when you tunnelled through to the vaults; when you got nabbed
 on a robbery;
when you regularly faced charges strung up against eight
supple musclemen, the no-holds-barred type, strong-arm
 brigade of birchers. 565

LIB May I confirm for a fact, Leonida, what you say is all *true.*
But, surely, your feats, too, are legion, all *B-a-d,* and bear
 repeating,
and in truth just so: when you broke trust with someone worthy
 of trust;
when you were nicked on a robbery, red-handed, and dealt a
 beating;
when you did perjury; when you weighed into hands-on
 sacrilege; 570
when you've regularly been a write-off, a pain, and a disgrace;
when you maintained what was paid never was credited to you;
when you deserved the trust of your playmate more than you
 did your teammates';
when you regularly used your tough-guy hardness, turned
 zombie eight
strongman lictors, an armed guard equipped with flexi elm
 birches. 575
I hope I've returned thanks, and not so *B-a-d,* in praise of my
 colleague?

LEO You and me both, couldn't be better, so so right for our talent.

LIB   iᵃᵐ ŏṃittᵉ isṭaec: hoc quod rŏgo   responde.
LEO   rọgĭta quod uis.

LIB   argenti uiginti mĭṇas   hăbesnĕ?
LEO | ḥărĭŏḷare.

ĕdĕpol sĕṇem Deṃaenĕṭum   lĕpĭḍum fŭịssĕ ṇobis: 580
ŭṭ assĭmŭḷabat Ṣaurĕam   meḍ essĕ quam fạ̄cẹte.
nĭmĭṣ aegre ṛisum cọntĭṇᵘi, | ŭḅⁱ hospĭtᵉᵐ inclaṃauit,

quod sẹsᵉ abṣentĕ ṃĭhĭ fĭḍém | hăbẹrĕ ṇolŭịsset.
ut ṃĕmŏrĭṭer me Ṣaurĕam   uŏc̣abăṭ atrĭẹnsem.

LIB   măṇĕḍum.
LEO   quĭḍ est?
LIB   Pḥĭlaenⁱᵘᵐ ẹstnᵉ   haec quᵃᵉ intŭṣ
                               exiṭ atque   585
un̄ᵃ Argȳṛippŭṣ?
LEO   opprĭṃᵉ os,   ĭṣ est. sŭḅauscuḷṭemus.
LIB   lăcrĭmantem lăcĭnĭạ tĕṇet   lăcrĭṃans. quidṇᵃᵐ essĕ ḍicam?

tăcĭṭⁱ ausculṭemŭṣ.
LEO   attăṭae,   mŏḍᵒ herclᵉ in ṃentem ụenit,

nĭmĭˢ ụellᵉᵐ hăbẹrĕ pertĭcam.
LIB   cu͡i ṛe͡i?
LEO   qui ụerbĕrarem
ăsĭṇos, si fortᵉ occepĕrint claṃarᵉ hinc ex crŭṃina.   590

→ →   ADVLESCENS = AMATOR = **ARGYRIPPUS**
             + MERETRIX = **PHILAENIUM**
ARG   cur me rĕṭentas?
PHIL   quĭă tŭị | ăṃans ăbĕụntĭṣ ĕgĕo.

ARG   uăḷe uăḷᵉ.

LIB	Now drop all that. Answer this question from me.
LEO	Ask away, whatever.
LIB	Twenty minae in cash. Is that what you got?
LEO	Quite a soothsayer.

Surely, a funster our old boy turned out to be: Demaenetus.   580
The way he played along with my act of being Saurea, so witty.
Too much! I just about held the laugh in, when he yelled at his
   guest
from abroad, for refusing to trust me in his non-attendance.
The way he kept calling me "steward Saurea," never fluffed his
   lines.

LIB	Wait a mo'.
LEO	Whassup?
LIB	That Philaenium coming out from inside, 585
	Argyrippus alongside?
LEO	Zip your mouth, it's him. Let's listen in.
LIB	He's in tears, she's in tears, and she's got a hold of him by the hem.
	Let's hush up now and listen.
LEO	Ooh-la-la. Just popped in my head, lord,
	I really do wish I had a pole.
LIB	Oh yeah, and what for?
LEO	To beat
	the asses with, happen they start yelling from the money-pouch here. 590

→ →	LOVERBOY TWO:
	ARGYRIPPUS + PHILAENIUM
ARG	Why are you holding me back?
PHIL	'Cos I love you, miss you when you're gone.
ARG	Farewell, farewell.

PHIL   ălĭquant̮ᵒ amplĭus uălerem, s̮ⁱ hic măn}eres.

ARG   salu̮e.

PHIL   saluerĕ m̮e iŭbes, cu͡i t̮ᵘ ăbĭens̮ offers m̮orbum?

ARG   mat̮er sŭpremam m̮ĭhĭ tŭa̮ dixit, dŏm̮ᵘᵐ irĕ i̮ussit.

PHIL   ăc̮erbum f̮unus fĭlĭae făc̮ĭet, si t̮e cărendum ᵉst.   595

{LIB}   {hŏm̮ᵒ herclᵉ hin̮c exclus̮usˢ ᵉst f̮ŏras.}

{LEO}   {ĭtă r̮es est.}

ARG   m̮ittĕ quaeso.

PHIL   quo n̮unc ăbis? quin t̮ᵘ hic mănes?

ARG   nox, s̮i uŏl̮es, măn̮ebo.

{LIB}   {audi̮ˢnᵉ hun̮c ŏpĕrᵃ ut l̮argŭs est nocturna? n̮unc ĕn̮ⁱᵐ esse

n̮ĕgotĭo̮sᵘᵐ int̮erdĭus ui̮delĭc̮et Sŏlonem,

leg̮es ut c̮onscribat, quĭb̮us se pŏpŭlus tĕnĕat. gerrae.   600

qui s̮ese parer̮ᵉ appăr̮ent hu͡ius legĭb̮us, prŏf̮ecto

numquam bŏn̮ae frugi sĭ̮ent, dĭ̮es noctesquĕ p̮otent.}

{LEO}   {nᵉ ist̮ᵉ herclᵉ ăb̮ ista n̮on pĕd̮em disc̮edat, s̮i lĭc̮essit,

qui n̮unc fest̮inat atqu̮ᵉ ăb̮ hac mĭn̮atur s̮esᵉ ăbire.}

{LIB}   {serm̮oni i̮am fin̮em făc̮ĕ tŭ̮ᵒ, hu͡ius serm̮onᵉᵐ accĭpĭam.}   605

ARG   uăl̮e.

PHIL   quo prŏpĕras?

ARG   bĕnĕ uăl̮e. | ăpŭ̮d Orcum t̮e ui̮debo.

n̮ᵃᵐ ĕquĭdem me i̮am quant̮um pŏt̮est a uitᵃ abi̮udĭc̮abo.

PHIL   cur t̮ᵘ, obsĕc̮rᵒ, immĕrĭto mĕo̮ mĕ m̮orti d̮edĕr̮ᵉ optas?

ARG   ĕgonᵉ te? quam s̮ⁱ int̮ellĕgam defĭcĕrĕ u̮ita, i̮ᵃᵐ ipse

PHIL	I'd feel a whole lot weller if you'd stay put here.
ARG	Goo'day.
PHIL	You tell me "*Good* day" when your pushing off gives me the plague.
ARG	Your mother told me the day's over. Ordered me: time I went home.
PHIL	She'll bring her daughter an early death if she must do without you. 595
{LIB}	{Lord, this person's shut right out of doors.}
{LEO}	{That's how 'tis.}
ARG	Please, lemme go.
PHIL	Where are you going? Why don't you stay here?
ARG	I'll stay the night if you like.
{LIB}	{Get him! D'you hear how he's showering out the night shifts? So now he's a workaholic Moses, no less, working the daytime through, the way he drafts conditions for the nation to keep. Cojones! 600 Any persons gearing up to obey *his* conditions, for a fact, they *shan't* ever do right, and round the clock, day 'n' night . . .— *shall* get pissed.}
{LEO}	{Sure, lord, he wouldn't shift a foot from her, not if the choice was his, Yet now, he's in a rush, threatens that he's going away from her.}
{LIB}	{Now you must put a stop to your chit-chat, so I can take in his.} 605
ARG	Farewell.
PHIL	Where you racing?
ARG	Goodbye. Farewell. I shall see you in Hell. See, I'm banning myself from living, far as I possibly can.
PHIL	Why? I'll give myself to death undeserved, I beg you, *is* that your wish?
ARG	Me . . . ? And . . . you . . . ? If I see that you're fading from life, I shall right now

uĭtam mĕam tĭbĭ ḷargĭar   et ḍe mĕᵃ aḍ tŭᵃᵐ aḍdam.   610

PHIL   cuṛ ergo mĭnĭtaṛis mĭhĭ́   te uĭtᵃᵐ esṣᵉ amisṣ̣urum?

nam quid me facturam pŭṭas,   sⁱ istuc quod ḍicis faxis?

certum ᵉst efficĕrᵉ in mᵉ omnĭạ́ | e͡adem quae ṭᵘ in te faxis.

ARG   oh mḛllĕ ḍulci ḍulcĭor   tu ᵉs.

PHIL   ċertᵉ ĕnĭm ṭu uĭtᵃ es mi.

complectĕṛĕ.

ARG   fâcĭo lĭbens.

PHIL   ŭtĭṇam siċ effĕramur.   615

{LEO}   {o Lĭbănᵉ, ŭṭi mĭsĕr est hŏṃo   quⁱ̄ ăṃat.}

{LIB}   {imṃᵒ herclĕ ụero

qui pendet ṃulto ᵉst mĭsĕrĭor.}

{LEO}   {scĭŏ qui pĕṛiclum feci.

cirċumsisṭamŭṣ, altĕṛ hinc,   hinċ altĕṛ appeḷḷemus.}

LEO>ARG   ĕṛĕ, ṣalue. ṣed num fumŭṣ est   haec ṃŭlĭer quᵃᵐ amplexare?

ARG>LEO   quiḍum?

LEO>ARG   quĭ̄ᵃ ŏċŭli ṣunt tĭbi   lăcrĭṃanteṣ, e͡o rŏgaui.   620

ARG>LIB+LEO   pặtronus qui uobis fŭịt   fŭturus, perdĭḍistis.

LEO>ARG   ĕquĭ̆dᵉᵐ herclĕ ṇullum perdĭḍi, | idĕọ quĭă ṇumquᵃᵐ uḷḷᵘᵐ

hăḅŭi.

LIB>PH   Phĭlaenĭụm, saḷue.

PH>LIB+LEO   dăḅunt   di quae uĕḷitis ụobis.

LIB>PH   noctem tŭᵃᵐ ẹt uiṇi căḍum   uĕḷim, sⁱ opṭată fiant.

ARG>LIB   uerḅum căuĕ faxis, ụerbĕṛo.

LIB>ARG   tĭḅⁱ ĕquĭdem, ṇon mĭhⁱ opto.   625

shower my life over you, and count some from me over to
yours.   610

PHIL   So why? Why are you threatening me, with throwing your life
away?

See, what do you think I'm gonna do, if you . . . go . . . do . . .
what you say?

My mind's made up. I'll do to myself all that you do to yourself.

ARG   Oh honey's sweet, you are sweeter.

PHIL   Sweeter than life to me,

you are.

Let's have a hug.

ARG   Oh yes please let's.

PHIL   Wish we can get buried

this way.   615

{LEO}   {Dear Libanus, how sad is a person in love.}

{LIB}   {Lord, no, no way,
someone strung up is far, far the sadder.}

{LEO}   {I know, I've done a
trial.

One call 'em from here, let's surround 'em, the other one call 'em
from there.}

LEO>ARG   Goo'day, master. Hey there now, is she smoke, this woman in
your arms?

ARG>LEO   Pardon me?

LEO>ARG   Because your eyes they are watering. Hence my
question.   620

ARG>LIB+LEO   The patron you two were going to have for the future, you've lost.

LEO>ARG   Well, lord, I sure haven't lost one: why? 'Cos I never have had one.

LIB>PH   Philaenium, goo'day.

ARG>LIB+LEO   The gods will grant you everything you want.

LIB>PH   I'd like a night of yours, a jug of plonk, if my wishes came true.

ARG>LIB   Mind, not a *beep* from you, boy to beat up on.

LIB>ARG   I'm wishing for
you not me. 625

ARG>LIB   tum tᵘ ĭgĭtur lŏquĕrĕ quod lĭbet.
LIB>ARG   hunc herclĕ ụerbĕṛare.

LEO>LIB   quisnᵃᵐ istuc accredat tĭbí,   cĭnaedĕ cặlặmistrate?
                 tunᵉ ụerbĕres, qui pro cĭbo | hặbĕạs te ụerbĕṛari?

ARG>LIB   ut ụestrae fortunae mĕịs   praecedunt, Lĭbặnĕ, lọnge,

                 qui | họdĭe numquᵃᵐ ad ụespĕṛum   uiụam.
LIB>ARG   quapropter,
                                                     quaeso?   630
ARG>LIB   quĭᵃ ĕgᵒ hanc ặmo | ĕṭ haec mᵉ ặmat,   huic quod dem
                    ṇusquam quidquam ᵉst,
                 hinc med ặmantᵉᵐ ex aedĭbús   eieciṭ huius ṃater.

                 argenti ụiginṭi mĭṇae   meḍ ad morṭᵉᵐ appừlerunt
                 quaṣ họdĭᵉ ặdừlescens Ḍĭặbŏlús   ipsi dặṭurus ḍixit,
                 ửṭ hanc ne quoquam ṃittĕṛet   nĭṣⁱ ad sᵉ hunc annum
                    ṭotum.   635
                 uĭdetiˢnᵉ ụiginṭi mĭṇae   quid pollent quiduĕ possunt?

                 illᵉ quⁱ illas perdit ṣaluừṣ est,   ĕgŏ qui non perdo pĕṛĕo.

LIB>ARG   iam ḍĕdĭt argentum?
ARG>LIB   ṇon dĕḍit.
LIB>ARG   bŏṇᵒ ặnĭmᵒ es, ne formĭda.

LEO>LIB   secedᵉ huc, Lĭbặnĕ, ṭe uŏḷo.
LIB>ARG   si quid uiṣ.
ARG>LIB   obsĕcro uos,
                 eȃdᵉᵐ istac ŏpĕra sᵘauĭuˢ ᵉst   complexos fabừḷari.   640

LIB>ARG   noṇ omnĭᵃ ĕặdᵉᵐ aequᵉ omnĭbús,   ĕrĕ, sᵘauĭᵃ ẹssĕ ṣcito:

                 uobịs est sᵘauᵉ ặmantĭbus   complexos fabừḷari.
                 ĕgŏ complexᵘᵐ huius ṇil mŏṛor,   mĕᵘᵐ aụtᵉᵐ hĭc aspernạtur.

ARG>LIB	Then say on what you like, ad-lib.
LIB>ARG	To whop *him* here a beating, lord.
LEO>LIB	Who would ever credit it? That from *you,* you pansy with a perm.
	You? Dish out a beat-up, when taking a whopping fills your lunchbox?
ARG>LIB	How you guy's fortunes leave mine far behind in their wake, Libanus.
	For this day I shall never live till evening.
LIB>ARG	Why and wherefore, please? 630
ARG>LIB	'Cos I love her and she loves me . . .—and nothing nowhere to pay her.
	So that her mother has chucked loverboy out of the house here. Me.
	Twenty minae of cash have driven me all the way unto death.
	The twenty the boy Diabolus today told her he'd pay her,
	so she'd send her off nowhere but to him, for the whole of this year. 635
	You guys see what twenty minae got going? Their strength, their power.
	The one wasting them is safe; I'm not wasting them. No, *I'm* wasted.
LIB>ARG	Has he already paid the cash?
ARG>LIB	No he hasn't.
LIB>ARG	Cheer up, don't dread.
LEO>LIB	Step aside here, Libanus, I want you.
LIB>ARG	As you please.
ARG>LIB	I beg you,
	in one and the same go, you'll find it's sweeter to chat in a clinch. 640
LIB>ARG	Master. You should know not everything's just as sweet to everyone:
	for the pair of you lovers, yes, it *is* sweet to chat in a clinch.
	I've got no time for a hug from him, and *he* is repelled by mine.

           proĭnde istuc făcĭas ipsĕ quod făcĭamus ṇobis ṣᵘades.

ARG>LIB   ĕgŏ ṷerᵒ, et quĭdᵉᵐ ĕdĕpol lĭbens.

ARG>LIB+LEO   intĕrĕa, ṣi uĭḍetur,   645
           conceḍĭtᵉ istuc.

{LEO}   {uiˢnᵉ ĕṛum deḷudi?}

{LIB}   {dĭgnuˢ ᵉst ṣane.}

{LEO}   {uiˢnᵉ făcĭᵃᵐ ut ṭe Phĭḷaenĭum praeṣentᵉ hoc amplexetur?}

{LIB}   {cŭpĭᵒ herclĕ.}

{LEO}   {ṣĕquĕrᵉ hac.}

ARG>LIB+LEO   ecquĭḍ est ṣăḷutis? ṣătĭˢ lŏcuti.

LEO>ARG+PHIL   auṣcultatᵉ atquᵉ ŏpĕram dăṭᵉ et mĕă ḍictă ḍeuŏrate.
           primᵘᵐ omnĭum seruos tŭoṣ nos esṣĕ ṇon nĕgamus,   650
           sed ṭĭbĭ si ṷiginṭi mĭṇae | argenti profĕrentur,
           quo ṇos uŏcabis ṇomĭṇé?

ARG>LEO   liḅertos.

LEO>ARG   ṇon păṭronos?

ARG>LEO   id pŏtĭus.

LEO>ARG   ṷiginṭi mĭṇae | hic insunṭ in crŭṃina.

           haṣ ĕgŏ, si ṷis, tĭḅi dăḅo.

ARG>LEO   di ṭe seruassint ṣemper,
           cusṭos ĕrilis, ḍĕcŭˢ pŏpᵘli, theṣaurus copĭarum,   655

           ṣăḷus intĕrĭor corpŏrís ămorisquᵉ impĕrator.
           hic ponᵉ, hic istam coḷlŏca crŭminᵃᵐ in collo plane.

LEO>ARG   noḷᵒ ĕgŏ te, quĭ | ĕrus ṣis, mĭḥí | ŏnŭṣ istuc ṣustĭnere.

ARG>LEO   quin ṭu lăḅorĕ liḅĕras tᵉ atquᵉ istᵃᵐ imponĭs in me?

LEO>ARG   ĕgŏ ḅaiŭḷabo, tᵘ, ut dĕcet dŏmĭnᵘᵐ, antĕ mᵉ itᵒ inanis.   660

ARG>LEO   quid ṇunc?

LEO>ARG   quĭḍ est?

ARG>LEO   quin ṭradĭṣ huc crŭṃinam pressatᵘᵐ
                 ŭmĕrum?

	So you should take your own advice, and do what you tell us to do.
ARG>LIB	I will, surely. And I'll take a liberty.
ARG>LIB+LEO	Meanwhile, if you like, 645
	Both go huddle there.

{LEO}	{Like some fun with master?}
{LIB}	{Sure got it coming.}
{LEO}	{Want me to have Philaenium give you a hug, with him in attendance?}
{LIB}	{Lord, I fancy that.}
{LEO}	{Come this way.}
ARG>LIB+LEO	Saving us at all? Enough talk.

LEO>ARG+PH	Listen up, both of you; pay attention; and gobble down my words.
	First of all, we do not deny it, certainly we are your slaves. 650
	But if you get twenty minae of cash brought out in front of you,
	what name are you going to call us?
ARG>LEO	Liberated.
LEO>ARG	Not "patrons"?
ARG>LEO	Yes, that instead.
LEO>ARG	There's twenty minae here, inside this money-pouch.
	If you like, I'll pay them over.
ARG>LEO	The gods keep you safe forever.
	Your master's guard, your nation's pride, cornucopian treasure-house, 655
	saviour within our walls, commander on love's physical field,
	do put your deposit here. Check this pouch here. Plain flat on my neck.
LEO>ARG	You're my master, I will not have you shoulder this burden for me.
ARG>LEO	Why don't you liberate yourself from labour, and stick it on me?
LEO>ARG	I'll be porter. You, as fits an owner, go ahead, unladen. 660
ARG>LEO	Hey now.
LEO>ARG	Whassup?
ARG>LEO	Why don't you hand it here to flatten my shoulder?

LEO>ARG   hanc cui dăturuˢ eˢ hanc, iŭbe pĕtĕrᵉ atquᵉ orarĕ mecum.

     nᵃᵐ istuc procliue ᵉst quo iŭbes me plane collŏcare.

PHIL>LEO   da, mĕŭs ŏcellus, mĕă rŏsá, mĭ | ănĭmĕ, mĕă uŏluptas,

     Lĕōnĭdᵃ, argentum mĭhí, ne nos diiungᵉ ămantis.   665

LEO>PHIL   dic mᵉ ĭgĭtur tuum passercŭlum, gallinam, coturnicem,
     agnellᵘᵐ, haedillum me tŭum dic essĕ uel uĭtellum.

     prĕhendᵉ aurĭcŭlis, compăra lăbellă cum lăbellis.

ARG>LEO   tenᵉ oscŭletur, uerbĕro?
LEO>ARG   quam uerᵒ indignum uisum ᵉst?

     atqui pŏl hŏdĭe non fĕres, ni gĕnŭă confrĭcantur. 670

ARG>LEO   quiduis ĕgestas impĕrat: frĭcentur. daˢnᵉ quŏd oro?

PHIL>LEO   ăgĕ, mi Lĕōnĭdᵃ, obsĕcro, fĕr ămantⁱ ĕro sălutem.
     rĕdĭmᵉ istoc bĕnĕfĭcĭo tᵉ ab hoc, et tĭbⁱ ĕmᵉ hunc istᵒ argento.

LEO>PHIL   nĭmĭˢ bellᵃ es atquᵉ ămabĭlís, et sⁱ hoc mĕᵘᵐ essĕt, hŏdĭe

     numquam mᵉ orares quin dărém: | illum tᵉ orarĕ
      mĕlĭuˢ ᵉst,   675
     ĭllĭc hanc mĭhĭ seruandam dĕdit. i sane bellă belle.

LEO>LIB   căpᵉ hoc sⁱᵘⁱs, Lĭbănĕ.

ARG>LEO   furcĭfér, ĕtĭam me delusisti?

LEO>ARG   numquᵃᵐ herclĕ făcĕrem, gĕnŭă ni tam nequĭter frĭcares.

LEO>ARG	Her—the one you will hand this to—tell *her* to beg and plead with me.
	Where you told me to check it, slopes on the vertical plane. That's flat.
PHIL>LEO	Pay, my fine eyelet, my rosy rose, my dear heart, my sweet pleasure,
	Leonida . . .—the cash . . . *to me*. . . . *Don't* unyoke us, we are lovers. 665
LEO>PHIL	So then call me your tiny sparrowlet, broody hen, quackin' quail,
	your little lamblet, your cute kiddikin, say that's me, your juicy veal.
	You lug me by the lugholes. You match luscious lips to luscious lips.
ARG>LEO	Kiss *you* . . ., *her* . . . you whipping boy?
LEO>ARG	So just how insulting did that look?
	And yet sure you'll not carry it off, unless knees get a massage. 670
ARG>LEO	What it takes—"needs must"—command away, massage 'tis. Pay what I beg?
PHIL>LEO	Go on, my Leonida, I beg. Loverboy master needs saving.
	Buy yourself out from him with this good turn. Buy him for you with this cash.
LEO>PHIL	Too much, such beauty, so lovely. Yes, and if this was mine, this day
	you'd never plead with me, and me not give it. Better you plead 675
	with *him*—*he* gave it me, to keep safe. Go like beauty, you real beaut.
LEO>LIB	Cop this, p-lease, Libanus.
ARG>LEO	Ball-'n'-chain, have you dared make fun of me?
LEO>ARG	Lord, I'd never've done it if . . . you weren't so . . .—bad at massaging knees.

LEO>LIB   ăgĕ sĭ^{uĭ}s t^u in partem nuncĭ^{am} hunc delude atqu^e amplexar^e
               hanc.

LIB>LEO   tăcĕas, me spectes.
ARG>PHIL   quin ăd hunc, Phĭlaenĭ^{um}, aggrĕdimur,   680

               uĭrum quĭdem pŏl optĭm^{um} et non sĭmĭlem furĭs huius?

LIB   ĭnambŭlandum ^est: nunc mĭhĭ uĭcissim supplĭcabunt.

ARG>LIB   quaes^o herclĕ, Lĭbănĕ, sĭ^{uĭ}s ĕrum t͡uis factis sospĭtari,
               da mⁱ istas uiginti mĭnas. uĭdes m^e ămant^{em} ĕgere.

LIB>ARG   uĭdebĭtur: factum uŏlo. rĕdit^o huc contĭcinno.   685

               nunc istanc tantisper iŭbe pĕtĕr^e atqu^e orarĕ mecum.

PHIL>LIB   ămandon^e exorarĭer uis ted ăn oscŭlando?

LIB>PHIL   ĕnĭm uer^o ŭtrumqu^e.
PHIL>LIB   erg^o, obsĕcr^o, et t^u ŭtrumquĕ nostrum
                   serua.

ARG>LIB   o Lĭbănĕ, mi pătronĕ, mi trad^e istuc. măgĭ^s dĕcorum ^est
               libertum pŏtĭus quam pătron^{um} ŏnŭs in uĭa portare.   690

PHIL>LIB   mi Lĭbăn^e, ŏcellŭs aurĕus, donum dĕcusqu^e ămoris,
               ămabo, făcĭam quod uŏles, d^a istuc argentum nobis.
LIB>PHIL   dĭc ĭgitur med ănĕtĭcŭlam, cŏlumbam uel cătellum,
               hĭrundĭnem, mŏnedŭlam, passercŭlum pŭtillum,
               fac proserpentem bestĭam me, dŭplĭc^{em} ut hăbĕam
               linguam,   695
               cĭrcumda torquem bracchĭis, m͡eum collum circumplecte.

ARG>LIB   ten^e complectatur, carnĭfex?
LIB>ARG   quam uer^o indignus uĭdĕor?

LEO>LIB	Come on, p-lease, now for your part. Make fun of him, give her a hug.
LIB>LEO	Hush and watch.
ARG>PHIL	Why don't we step over *his* way, Philaenium? 680
	Sure, there's none better than him, and no, he's not a bit like *this* thief.
LIB	Time I took a stroll. Now they'll be on their knees to me. It's my turn.
ARG>LIB	Lord I beg you, Libanus, please save your master, all down to you.
	Hand me the twenty minae. You can see my love-affair needs them.
LIB>ARG	It'll be looked into. I'd *like* to see it done. Come back here at dusk. 685
	For that amount of time, order her now to seek and plead with me.
PHIL>LIB	You want your pleading done with sexing, or you want it with kissing?
LIB>PHIL	*Both*, actually.
PHIL>LIB	So then, I beg, you as well, save *both* of us two.
ARG>LIB	Dear Libanus, my patron, hand it over to me. It's more fit someone liberated hump a load on the street than a patron. 690
PHIL>LIB	My Libanus, eyelet of gold, gift and glory of love,
	please lover, I will do anything you want, just give us the cash.
LIB>PHIL	So call me ugly duckling, lovey dovey, or floppy puppy,
	soaring swallow, jolly jackdaw-a-dum, sparrowlet chick-a-dee,
	You must make me a crawling snake . . .—give us a double two-forked tongue. 695
	Make me a collar of your arms, hug me tight all around the neck.
ARG>LIB	Hug you, executioner?
LIB>ARG	So just how insulting do I look?

n^e istuc nequiquam dĭxĕrĭs   in me t^{am} indignum dictum,
uĕhĕs pŏl hŏdĭẹ me, sị quĭd^{em} hoc   argentum ferrĕ speres.

ARG>LIB   tẹn^e ĕgŏ uĕham?

LIB   tuṇ^e hoc fĕras   hinc argent^{um} ălītĕr a me?   700

ARG   pĕrĭ^i herclĕ. sị uẹrum quĭd^{em} et   dĕcor^{um} ĕrŭm uẹhĕrĕ
           sẹruum,
           inṣcendĕ.

LIB   sịc istị sŏḷent   sŭperbi ṣubdŏmari.

ast^a ĭgĭtŭr, ut cons^{u}etŭs es   pŭẹr olim. scị^{s}n^e ut dịcam?
em sịc. ăbĭ, ḷaudo, nec t^e ẹquo   măgĭs est ĕquŭs ụllus săpĭens.

ARG   inṣcende^e actut^{um}.

LIB   ĕgŏ fecĕr^o. hem   quĭd ĭstuc est? ut t^u
                  inṣedis?   705
dem^{am} herclĕ ịam dĕ | hordĕọ,   tŏḷutim ṇi băḍissas.

ARG   ămabo, Lịbănĕ, ịam săt est.

LIB   numqu^{am} hercl^e hŏdĭ^e ẹxorabis.

nam ịam calcari quădrŭpĕdo | ăgĭṭab^o aḍuersum ḍiuum,

postĭdĕ^a ad pistọres dăbọ, | ŭt ĭbi crŭcĭẹrĕ ḍurrens.
ast^a ut deṣcendam ṇunci^{am} ịn   prŏḍliui, quamquam
           ṇequa^m ^{e}s.   710

ARG   quid ṇunc, ămabo? quŏṇĭ^{am}, ŭṭ est   lĭbĭṭum, nos ḍelusistis,

dăṭisn^e argentum?

LIB   sị quĭdem   mĭhĭ ṣtătŭ^{am} ĕt ạram ṣtătŭis
atqu^e ut dẹọ m^i hịc immŏḷas   bŏụem. n^{am} ĕgŏ ṭĭbĭ Săḷus sum.

LEO   ĕtĭam t^u, ĕr^e, istunc amŏụes $^?$abs t^e atqu^e ipṣé m^e aggrĕdĕre$^?$

atqu^e illă, sĭbị qu^{ae} hĭc ịussĕṛat,   mĭhĭ ṣtătŭis suppḷĭḍasque?   715

ARG>LEO   quem ṭ^e autem ḍiuum ṇomĭnem?

LEO>ARG   Fortụn^{am}, atqu^e
                                Obṣĕquentem.

No, you won't speak such an insult against me and not pay for it,
so you'll give me a ride, lord, today if you'll hope to fetch this cash.

ARG>LIB   *Me give *you* a *ride*?*

LIB   Gonna fetch this cash off me some
                                other way?   700

ARG   Lord, I've had it. If it is fit for owner to give slave a ride . . .

—climb on.

LIB   It happens. Here's how the overblown undergo
                                subdual.

So stand ready, the way you once did as a kid. Know how I mean?
Pow, that's the way. Get going. Well done, no horse smart as
    you, horsey.

ARG   Climb on right away.

LIB   I'll do it. Hey up, what's this? How you
                                going?   705

Lord, I'll take some feed away if you don't highstep à grand galop.

ARG   Please, Libanus, whoa, enough. ·

LIB   Lord, you'll never plead a yes
                                today.

'Cos now I'll use the spur, and drive you straight up the slope,
    at a trot.

Later I'll give you to the millers, for torture there at the races.
Steady, so I c'n climb down now on the slope, though you're
    one bad 'un.   710

ARG   What now, please? Now that you two've had your fun at us
              ad lib*itum* . . .

—give us the cash?

LIB   Yes, if you stand me statue and altar status,
sacrifice an ox to me here like a god: for you, I'm Salvation.

LEO   You just shoo him away from you, master, step my way on
              your own.

The orders he gave for himself, stand me them too, down
    on your knees?   715

ARG>LEO   Which god am I to name you?

LEO>ARG   Fortune, yep, Fortune In Your
                                Favour.

ARG>LEO	i^{am} istoc es mĕlĭor.
LIB>ARG	an quĭd est hŏmĭni Sălŭtĕ mĕlĭus?

ARG>LIB	lĭcĕt laudem Fortuṇam, tămén ut ne Sălutem culpem.
PHIL	ecastor ambae sunt bŏnae.
ARG	scĭ^{am} ŭbĭ bŏni quid dĕdĕrint.

LEO>ARG	opt^a id quŏd ŭt contingat tĭbí uis.
ARG>LEO	quid sⁱ opta^{ue}r^o?
LEO>ARG	euĕnĭet. 720

ARG>LEO	opt^o ann^{um} hunc perpĕtŭum mĭhí | huius ŏpĕras.
LEO>ARG	impĕtra^{ui}sti.

ARG>LEO	ais^sn^e uero?
LEO>ARG	certe^e inqu^{am}.
LIB>ARG	ad m^e ădi uĭciss^{im} atqu^e expĕrire.
	exopt^a id quod uis maxĭme tĭbⁱ euĕnirĕ. fiet.

ARG	quĭd ĕg^o ălĭŭd exopt^{em} amplĭus nĭsⁱ illud cuius ĭnŏpĭa ^est,
	uigintⁱ argenti commŏdas mĭnas, huius quas dem matri. 725
LIB>ARG	dăḅuntur, ănĭmo sis bŏno făc^e, exoptat^a obtingent.

ARG	ut cons^ueuer^e, hŏmĭnes Sălus frustratŭr et Fortuna.

LEO	ĕgŏ căpŭt huic argento fŭi tĭbⁱ hŏdĭe rĕpĕrĭendo.
LIB>ARG	ĕgŏ pes fŭi.
ARG	quin nec căput nec pes sermonⁱ apparet.
	nec quid dicatis scirĕ nec me cur ludatis possum. 730

{LIB>LEO}	{sătĭ^s iam delusum censĕo. nunc rĕm | ŭt est elŏquamur.}

LIB>ARG	ănĭm^{um}, Argўripp^e, aduertĕ si^{ui}s. păter nos ferr^e hoc iussit
	argent^{um} ad ted.

ARG>LEO	Now *that* makes *you* better.
LIB>ARG	Surely *nothing*'s better than Salvation?
ARG>LIB	It's legit to praise Fortune, and *not* so I *must* slate Salvation.
PHIL	Both, Our Lady, good goddesses.
ARG	I'll know *when* they hand me some good.

LEO>ARG	Wish to get what you want.
ARG>LEO	What if I do wish?
LEO>ARG	Yes, it will come true. 720
ARG>LEO	I wish for *her* services through this whole year round.
LEO>ARG	Look no farther.
ARG>LEO	You don't say?
LEO>ARG	I certainly do.
LIB>ARG	It's my turn. Step up and try me. You wish hard that what you want most of all will come true. So be it.
ARG	What else should I wish hard for? Has to be where the dearth is complete: the handy twenty minae cash, so I can pay them her mother. 725
LIB>ARG	Yes, they *shall* be paid, be of good cheer, your hard wishes *shall* come true.
ARG	That's ever their way, Salvation tantalizing people. And Fortune.

LEO	I was head of today's Operation Unearth The Cash for you.
LIB>ARG	I was foot.
ARG	How come both head and foot of this chat are lost to sight? I can't understand what you're saying, I can't know why you're playing. 730
{LIB>LEO}	{That's enough fun out of him, I propose. Now let's spell out the deal.}

LIB>ARG	Argyrippus, attention please. Father ordered us to fetch *this* cash here to you.

ARG>LIB   ut tempŏrⁱ opportunequᵉ attŭlistis.

LIB>ARG   hǐc ĭnĕrunt ṵiginṭi mĭṇae   bŏṇae, mălᵃ ŏpĕra partae.
has ṭĭbĭ nos pactis ḷegĭbus   dărĕ ịussit.

ARG   quĭd ĭd est, quaeso?   735
LIB>ARG   nocṭᵉᵐ hu͡ius et ҫenam ṣĭbⁱ ŭt dăṛes.

ARG   iŭbᵉ aduĕṇirĕ, quaeso:

mĕrĭtissĭmᵒ eius quae uŏḷet   făcĭẹmus, quⁱ hoscᵉ ăṃores

nosṭros dispulsos ҫompŭḷit.
LEO   pătĭẹrĭˢṇᵉ, Argÿṛippe,

pătᵣᵉᵐ hanc amplexaṛi tŭṵ́m? |
ARG   haec făcĭet făcĭlᵉ ut pătĭar.

Lĕōṇĭda, currᵉ, obsĕҫro,   pătᵣᵉᵐ huc oṛatᵒ ut ṵeṇiat.   740

LEO>ARG   iamḍudum ᵉsṭ intŭṣ.
ARG>LEO   hac quĭḍem   non ṵenịṭ.
LEO>ARG   angĭporto

illạc pĕṛ hortum ҫircŭṃit   clam, ṇe quis ṣe uĭḍeret

huҫ irĕ fămĭlĭaṛĭụm: nᵉ uxor reṣciscat ṃĕtŭit.

dᵉ argento ṣi maṭer tŭą́   scĭat ut ṣit factᵘᵐ —

ARG>LIB+LEO   — heia,
bĕṇĕ ḍicĭṭᵉ.
LIB>ARG+PHIL   itᵉ inṭro cĭṭo.
ARG   uăḷetᵉ.
LEO>ARG+PHIIL   et ṵos ăṃate.   → → → →

ARG>LIB   Great timing, spot on. You've fetched it right
                                                 on the dot.

LIB>ARG   In here there'll be twenty minae, good 'uns, we did bad to get 'em.
                 He told us pay you them on fixed terms and
                      conditions.

ARG>LIB   What's that, please?   735

LIB>ARG   You pay him his fee: the night with her, plus party.

ARG>LIB   Please, order
                                                                  him: come.
                 We'll do what he wants, he deservemosts it, 'cos he found our
                      romance
                 uncorralled, and he corralled it.

LEO   Will you endure it,
                                                        Argyrippus . . .
                 —your father hugging *her* tight?

ARG   *This*'ll ease me into enduring it.
                                                        Easy.
                 Leonida, do scurry off, I beg, plead with dad: come here.   740

LEO>ARG   He's long been inside.

ARG>LEO   Well he didn't come this way.

LEO>ARG   Through the
                                                                  alley,
                 that way he came, round through the garden, private, so no
                      one'd see him
                 come here, none of the household. Afraid his wife gets to know
                      about it.
                 The cash . . .—if your mother knew what happened about the
                      cash . . .

ARG>LIB+LEO   —Whoa! Shh . . .
                 —no bad talkin' . . .

LIB>ARG+PHIL   —In you go, quick.

ARG   Farewell, you two.

LEO>ARG+PHIIL   Make love,
                                                          you two.

                                                          → → → →

→ →　　　　　　　ADVLESCENS = A MATOR
　　　　　　　　= **DIABOLVS** + **PARASITVS**

DIAB　ăgĕd^{um} ist^{um} ostendĕ　quem conscripsti syngrăphum　　746–829:

　　　　　　　　　　　　　　　　　　　　　　　　iambic

　　inter m^e ĕt ămic^{am} et　lenam. leges perlĕge.　　*senarii*

　　nam tu pŏĕta ^{e}s　prorsŭs ăd ĕam r^{em} unĭcus.

PAR　horrescet faxo　lenă, leges c^{um} audĭet.

DIAB　ăgĕ quaeso m^i herclĕ　translĕg^e.

PAR　　　　　　　　　　audi^{s}n^e?

DIAB　　　　　　　　　　　audĭo.　　750

PAR　'Dĭăbŏlus Glauci filĭus Clĕărĕtae

　　lenae dĕdĭt don^o argenti uiginti mĭnas

　　Phĭlaenĭ^{um} ut sec^{um}　esset noctes et dĭes

　　hunc annum totum'—

DIAB　　　　　　—nĕquĕ cum quiqu^{am} ălĭo quĭdem.

PAR　addonĕ? |

DIAB　　　　add^e, et　scribas uĭdĕ plan^e et prŏbe.　　755

PAR　'ălĭenŭm | hŏmĭnĕm | intro mittat nemĭnem.

　　quŏd ill^a aut ămicŭm | aut pătronum nomĭnet,

　　aut quŏd ill^a ămicae sŭ^{ae} ămatorem praedĭcet,

　　fŏres occlusae | omnĭbus sint nĭsĭ tĭbi.

　　in fŏrĭbus scribat　occŭpatăm | essĕ se.　　760

　　aut quŏd illă dicat　pĕrĕgr^e allat^{am} ĕpistŭlam,

　　n^e ĕpistŭlă quĭdĕm | ullă sit ĭn aedĭbus

　　nec cerat^a ădĕo　tăbŭl^a, et si qu^a ĭnutĭlis

　　pictură sit, ĕăm　uendat: n^i in quădridŭo

　　ăbălĭena^{ue}rit　quo abs t^e argent^{um} accepĕrit,　　765

　　tŭŭs arbĭtratus sit, comburas, si uĕlis,

　　n^e illi sit cer^a ŭbĭ　făcĕrĕ possit littĕras.

　　uŏcet conuiuam　nemĭn^{em} illă, tu uŏces.

　　ăd ĕorum ne quĕm | ŏcŭlos ădĭcĭat sŭos.

　　si qu^{em} ălĭ^{um} aspexit, caecă contĭnŭo sĭet.　　770

　　tec^{um} una postĕ^a　aeque poclă potĭtet:

→ →   LOVERBOY **DIABOLUS** + **PALOOKA**

DIAB   *All right.* Show us. The contract you've scripted,   746–829:
            between: spoken
        me; playmate; madam. Rendition of conditions.   verse
        See, you're the one and only poet, straight up, for the deal.

PAL   I'll see madam shudder, when she hears the conditions.

DIAB   Go, please. Lord, a transmition for me.

PAL   Listening?

DIAB   Listening.   750

PAL   𝔇iabolus, son of 𝔏e 𝔊ris, to ℭle-areta,
        𝔐ᵐᵉ, pays the fee of twenty minae, cash, no strings,
        for 𝔓hilaenium to be with him both night and day
        this year's duration . . .

DIAB   —And with no one else, either.

PAL   Insert?

DIAB   Yes, insert. See your script is plain and proper.   755

PAL   𝔓erson or persons from outside: she shall let inside: none.
        𝔍tem, she does name said person "friend" or "patron";
        or, item, does proclaim him her playmate's lover:
        doors be shut for all & sundry, yourself excluded;
        on said door, she shall give written notice "𝔍'm engaged."   760

        𝔒r, item, a letter, quoth she, is fetched from abroad:
        no letter whatsoever even be in the house,
        nor so much as a wax tablet; in case there be dud
        daub, she shall sell; unless within a three day period,
        from receipt of cash from you, transfer is effected,   765
        it shall be in your writ, re: disposal by fire,
        so as to forbid her wax, viz: whereon she might write.

        𝔓arty-guest, invitations: she shall make: none; you shall.
        𝔒f which parties, she shall fix her eyes upon: none.

        𝔍n case she has eyed another, she shall go blind, forthwith.   770
        𝔗hereafter, in harness with you, she shall down glasses:

                   abs țed accĭpĭat,   tĭbĭ prŏpinet, țu bĭḅas,

                   nᵉ ilḷă mĭnŭṣ aut plus   quam tu șăpĭat.'

DIAB   șătĭˢ plăc̣et.

PAR   'șuṣpicĭọneṣ omniṣ ab se șegrĕget.

               nĕquᵉ illaec̣ ulli   pĕdĕ pĕdĕm | hŏmĭṇi prĕmat,   775

               cum șurgat. nĕquĕ cᵘᵐ in ḷectᵘᵐ inșcendat proxĭṃum

               nĕquĕ c̣um deșcendaț indĕ, ḍet cu͡iquam măṇum.

               spectạndum ṇe cui | aṇŭḷum det ṇĕquĕ rŏget.

               talọs ne c̣uiquăṃ | hŏmĭnⁱ admŏuĕat ṇĭsĭ tĭḅi.

               cum ĭăc̣iat, 'te' ne   ḍicat: ṇomen ṇomĭṇet.   780

               dĕᵃᵐ ịnuŏc̣et sĭbĭ   quam lĭḅebit prŏpĭtĭam,

               de͡um ṇullum. și măgĭˢ ṛĕlĭgĭọsă f̣úĕṛit,

               tĭḅĭ ḍicat: țu prᵒ ilḷᵃ   oreṣ ut sit prŏpĭtĭụs.

               nĕquᵉ ilḷᵃ ulḷⁱ hŏmĭni   ṇutet, ṇictĕṭ, annŭaṭ.

               post, și lŭc̣ernᵃ extinctă șit, ne quid sụ̆ị   785

               membri commŏuĕat   quidquᵃᵐ in țĕnĕbriṣ.'

DIAB   optĭṃe ᵉst.

               ĭtă șcilĭcet facturam. ụerᵘᵐ in c̣ŭbĭc̣ŭḷo,

               deṃᵉ istuc̣, ĕquĭdᵉᵐ illam mŏụeri gestĭọ.

               noḷᵒ illᵃᵐ hăḅerĕ c̣ausᵃᵐ et ụĕtĭtam ḍicĕṛe.

PAR   scĭŏ, c̣aptĭọnes   mĕtŭis.

DIAB   ụerᵘᵐ.

PAR   ergᵒ ut iŭḅes,   790

               tollạm?

DIAB   quidṇⁱ?

PAR   audi   ṛĕlĭc̣ụ̆ă.

DIAB   lŏquĕṛᵉ, audĭọ.

PAR   'nĕquᵉ ullum ụerbum   f̣ăc̣iat perplexabĭle

               nĕquᵉ ulla ḷingua   șcĭăt lŏqui nĭṣⁱ Attĭc̣a.

plied by you, she'll toast you, & hand back for you to drink,
so taste she'll have, no less no more, than: you.

DIAB
>Enough.
>Approved.

PAL   Behaviour giving rise to suspicion: stay aloof: all.
Neither shall she inch toe to toe with any person,   775
when she gets to her feet; nor when she mounts the next couch
or dismounts from it, shall she hold out her hand: to none.

Ring, inspection of: she shall offer, or request: none.

Ankle-bones, dicing with: she shall press them on: no one,
you excluded; when she throws, shan't say "For you":
>name names.   780

Prayers, to goddess: of her choice, "Show kindness": any;
prayers, to god: none; save that, should she be jinxed worse,
she shall tell you, and you plead in her stead, "Do be kind."

Nodding, to a person: she shall nudge, wink, nod "yes": to none.

After that, "afterwards": if the lamp snuffs, she shall not   785
move one limb of hers in the dark: not at all.

DIAB
>Perfect.
For sure, that's how she'll act. But . . .—but in the bedroom,
delete that bit, I do get off on the movements she makes.
I don't want her having a point, and saying she's barred.

PAL   I know: frightened of quibbles.

DIAB
>True.

PAL
>So, as *per* your orders,   790
I'll remove it?

DIAB
>Why not?

PAL
>Hear the rest.

DIAB
>Speak, I hear you.

PAL   Language: she shall utter no word of aporia: none.
and she shall know to speak in no tongue bar Attic: none.

fortᵉ si tussirᵉ occepsit, ne sic tussĭat
ut cui͡quam linguᵃᵐ in tussĭendo prosĕrat.   795

quŏd ĭllᵃ autem sĭmŭlet quăsĭ grăuedo proflŭat,
hoc ne sic făcĭat: tu lăbellᵘᵐ abstergĕas
pŏtĭus quam cui͡quam sauĭum făcĭat pălam.

nec mater lenᵃ ad uinᵘᵐ accedat intĕrim
nĕc ulli uerbo mălĕ dicat. si dixĕrit,   800
haec multᵃ eⁱ esto, uino uiginti dĭes
ut cărĕat.'
DIAB   pulcre scripsti. scitum syngrăphum.

PAR   'tum si cŏronas, sertᵃ, unguentă iussĕrit
ancillam ferrĕ Vĕnĕri | aut Cŭpidĭni,
tŭŭˢ seruus seruet Vĕnĕrinᵉ ea͡s det an uĭro.   805

si fortĕ pure uellᵉ hăberĕ dixĕrit,
tot noctes reddat spurcas quot purᵉ hăbŭĕrit.'

haec sunt non nugae, non ĕnĭm mortŭalĭa.
DIAB   plăcent prŏfecto leges. sĕquĕrᵉ intro.
PAR   sĕquor.   → →

→ →   ADVLESCENS = AMATOR
          = DIABOLVS + PARASITVS
DIAB   sĕquĕrᵉ hac.   810
                ĕgonᵉ haec pătĭar aut tăcĕᵃᵐ? emŏri
me malim quᵃᵐ haec non eĭŭs uxorⁱ indĭcem.

ai͡ˢnᵉ tᵘ? ăpŭd ămicam munŭs ădŭlescentŭli
fungarᵉ, uxorⁱ excuses tᵉ et dicas sĕnem?
praerĭpĭas scortᵘᵐ ămantⁱ atquᵉ argentᵘᵐ ŏbĭcĭas
lenae? suppiles clam dŏmⁱ uxorem tŭam?   815
suspendam pŏtĭus me quam tăcĭtᵃ haec tᵘ aufĕras.

iam quĭdᵉᵐ hĕrclᵉ ăd illᵃᵐ hinc ibo, quam tu prŏpĕdĭem,

Coughing: if she happens to start, she shall not cough, such
that in coughing so, she snakes out her tongue: at no one. 795

Item: suppose she does ham up a snot-runny cold,
she shall not make like this. You shall wipe her lip clean
rather than she openly fakes a kiss: for no one.

Mother: meanwhile, Mme shall not join in the wine: none;
nor badmouth: no one; not one word. In case she so does, 800
her fine shall be this: twenty days complete lay-off from
the wine: none.

DIAB   Lovely script from you. Real pro of a contract.

PAL   Next, votives: in case she gives orders to her maid, to fetch
crowns, or garlands, or oils, to Venus or to Cupid:
your slave shall watch, "Does she endow Venus?."
        "Or a man?" 805

Staying clean: in case she happens to say she wants that,
she shall make as many nights filthy as she stayed clean.

DIAB   Load of nonsense this is not. This is no wake, just asleep.
          Conditions approved. That's a fact. Follow me in.
PAL   I do.   → →

→ →
DIAB   LOVERBOY **DIABOLUS** + **PALOOKA**
          Follow this way.
                   Me? Suffer this? Keep mum? Sheer death 810
          I'd rather die than not inform on him to his wife.

You . . .—you reckon? You'd play the part of a boyo
at the playmate's, make excuses to the wife "I'm old"?
You'd snatch a tart from loverboy, and chuck cash at
madame? You'd pillage your wife back home and stay mum? 815
I'd sooner swing than let you take it away, and freeze.

Now, though, lord, I'm off to her. The woman you'll shortly

nĭsĭ quĭd^{em} ĭll^a ant^e occŭpassit t^e, efflĭges scĭo,
luxŭrĭae sumptus suppĕdĭtar^e ut possĭes.

PAR   ĕgŏ sic făcĭ_endum   censĕo: m^e hŏnestĭu^s ^est   820
quam te păl^{am} hanc rem făcĕrĕ, n^e ĭll^a existĭmet
ămoris causa   percit^{um} id fecissĕ te
măgĭ^s quam sŭa͡ caus^a.

DIAB   at   pol qui dixti rectĭus.

t^u ergo făc ŭt illi   turbas, litis concĭas,
cum su͡o sĭbí nat^o un^{am} ăd ămicam de dĭe   825
potar^e, ill^{am} expĭlarĕ narra.

PAR   ne mŏne,
ĕg^o ĭstuc curabo. |

DIAB   ăt ĕgŏ t^e oppĕrĭar dŏmi.   → →

→ → → →   ADVLESCENS **ARG**YRIPPVS
                  + SENEX DEMAENETVS
             (+ MERETRIX PHILAENIVM; PVERI MVTI)

ARG   ăgĕ decumbamus si^{ui}s, păter.

DEM   ŭt iussĕris,
mi nat^e, ĭtă fiet.

ARG   pŭĕri, mens^{am} apponĭte.

DEM   numquidnam tĭbĭ mŏlestum ^est, natĕ mi, sⁱ haec nunc
mec^{um} accŭbat?   830–50:

ARG   pĭĕtas, păter, ŏcŭlis dŏlorem prŏhĭbet. quamqu^{am} ĕg^o   iambic
ĭstanc ămo,   *octonarii*
poss^{um} ĕquĭd^{em} inducĕr^e ănĭmum n^e aegre pătĭar quĭă
tec^{um} accŭbat.

DEM   dĕcet uĕrecund^{um} ess^e ădŭlescent^{em}, Argў̆rĭpp^e.

ARG   ĕdĕpol, păter,
mĕrĭto tŭo făcĕrĕ poss^{um}.

DEM   ăg^e erg^o, hoc ăgĭtemus conuiuĭum

uin^o ut sermonĕ s^uaui. nol^o ĕgŏ mĕtŭⁱ, ămari mauŏlo,   835

mi natĕ, m^e abs te.

ARG   pŏl ĕg^o ŭtrumquĕ făcĭ^o, ŭt aequum
^est filĭum.

	rub out, if she hasn't nipped in front of you, as I know,	
	to feed the habit of high-maintenance luxury.	
PAL	I vote it be done this way: it's more respectable	820
	for me to do this deed than you. Or else she may think	
	you've done it for love, because you've been shattered,	
	more than for her sake.	
DIAB	Yes, sure, your way talks straighter.	

	Make sure you stir up lots of trouble and strife for him:	
	"His son alongside, with the one playmate, at the drink:	825
	partying by day; and pillaging her"—tell her all.	
PAR	No briefing,	
	I'll fix it good.	
DIAB	Well I'll be home waiting for you.	→ →

→ →

BOY **ARG**YRIPPUS

\+ SENIOR CITIZEN **DEM**AENETUS

(+ WHORE PHILAENIUM; PAGES, NON-SPEAKING PARTS)

ARG	Come, places please, father, let's loll.	
DEM	Thy will and command,	
	son of mine, will be done.	
ARG	Garçons, bring on the table.	
DEM	Not a bit of a nuisance, is it, son of mine, if she's installed	
	by my side?	830–947:
ARG	Devotion, father, keeps the pain out of my eyes.	recitative
	Even though I love her,	verse
	I *can* coax my mind, into not taking it hard she's installed by	
	your side.	
DEM	It's fitting a boy be respectful, Argyrippus.	
ARG	Surely, father,	
	you deserve it, so I can do it.	
DEM	So come on, let's make this	
	a *party* . . .	
	—sweet wine, sweet talk go together. I don't want your fear, I	
	prefer love,	835
	son of mine. From you to me.	
ARG	Sure I do—do both—it's fair a	
	son should.	

DEM   cred^{am} istuc, s^{i} essĕ t^{e} hĭlărum uidĕr^{o}.

ARG   an tu me tristem pŭtas?

DEM   pŭt^{em} ĕgŏ, quem uĭdĕ^{am} aequ^{e} essĕ maest^{um} ut quăsĭ dĭes si dictă sit?

ARG   ne dixĭs istuc.

DEM   ne sic fŭĕrĭs. ilĭc^{o} ĕgŏ non dixĕro.   839+840

ARG ^{em} aspecta: ridĕ^{o}.

DEM   ŭtĭnam mălĕ qui mĭhĭ uŏlunt sic ridĕant.

ARG   scĭ^{o} ĕquĭdem qu^{am} ob rem me, pătĕr,   tu tristem credas nunc tĭbi:

quĭ^{a} istaec est tec^{um}. atqu^{e} ĕgŏ quĭd^{em} hercl^{e} ut uerum tĭbĭ dicam, pătĕr,

ĕă res me mălĕ hăbet. at non eo quĭă tĭbĭ non cŭpĭam quae uĕlis,

uer^{um} ist^{am} ăm^{o}. ălĭam tec^{um} ess^{e} ĕquĭdem făcĭlĕ possum perpĕti.   845

DEM   ăt ĕg^{o} hanc uŏl^{o}.

ARG   ergo sunt qu^{ae} exoptas: mĭhĭ qu^{ae} ĕg^{o} exoptem uŏlo.

DEM   un^{um} hunc dĭem perpĕtĕrĕ, quŏnĭam tĭbĭ pŏtestatem dĕdi,

c^{um} hac ann^{um} ŭt esses, atqu^{e} ămant^{i} argenti feci cŏpĭam.

ARG ^{em} istoc me facto tĭbĭ deuinxti.

DEM   quin t^{e} erg^{o} hĭlărum das mĭhi?   849+850

→→   **MATRONA = ARTEMONA**
           (CVM ANCILLIS MVTIS) + **PARASITVS**

MAT   ai^{s}n^{e} tu meum uĭr^{um} hic potărĕ, | obsĕcro, cum filĭo   851–947:

ĕt ăd ămicam detŭliss^{e} argenti uiginti mĭnas   trochaic

septenarii

meŏquĕ filĭo scĭent^{e} id   făcĕrĕ flagĭtĭum pătrem?

DEM   I'll believe that if and when I see you're happy.

ARG   You think this is
                                               me blue?

DEM   I'm going to, aren't I, when I see you fair sad as if facing trial?

ARG   Don't talk that way.

DEM   Don't be like that. Right away I'll stop
                                  talking that way.   839+840

ARG   Ow, just watch me smile.

DEM   How I wish folk who mean me bad
                                would smile *that* smile.

ARG   Certainly *I* know why it is, Father, you credit me blue over you:

             'cos *she* is with you. And yes, too, lord, tell you the godhonest
                 truth, father,
             this scene hurts me bad. No, not that I'm not passionate for you,
                 all you want,
             but I love her. Certainly, I can endure some girl and you.
                 Easy.   845

DEM   Well, I want *her,* I do.

ARG   So you got your wish: I want my wish for me.

DEM   You'll endure this one single day through. *Because* I've handed
                 you power
             to be with her for a year, I've come up with the cash to fund
                 loverboy.

ARG   Ow! Doing that bound me to you, fast.

DEM   So won't you hand me
                                      a happy you?   849+850

→ →   MISTRESS = ARTEMONA
             (+ MAIDS, NON-SPEAKING PARTS) + PALOOKA

MRS   So you say my husband's at the drink, partying here with the son,
             that he's fetched the sum of twenty minae cash down to his
                 playmate,
             and with my son's full knowledge his father's perpetrating this
                 shame?

PAR   nĕquĕ diuini nĕquĕ mⁱ humani posthac quidquᵃᵐ
          accredŭas,
      Artĕmonă, sⁱ huius r͡eⁱ essĕ me mendacᵉᵐ inuenĕris.   855
MAT   at scĕlestᵃ ĕgŏ praetĕr ălⁱos mͤum uĭrum frugi răta,

      siccum, frugi, contĭnentᵉᵐ, ămantᵉᵐ uxoris maxĭme.

PAR   at nunc d͡ehinc scitᵒ illᵘᵐ antᵉ omnis mĭnĭmi mortalem prĕti,

      mădĭdum, nĭhĭlⁱ, incontĭnentᵉᵐ atquᵉ osorᵉᵐ uxoris sŭae.
MAT   pol nⁱ istaec uerᵃ essent, numquam făcĕret ĕă quae nunc
          făcit.   860
PAR   ĕgŏ quŏquᵉ herclᵉ illᵘᵐ ant͡ehăc hŏmĭnem semper sum
          frugi rătus,
      uerᵘᵐ hoc facto sesᵉ ostendit, qui quĭdem cum filĭo
      potĕt unᵃ atquᵉ unᵃ ămicam ductet, decrĕpĭtus sĕnex.

MAT   hoc ecastor est quŏd illᵉ it ad cenam cottĭdĭe.
      a͡it sesᵉ irᵉ ăd Archĭdemum, Chaerĕam, Chaerestrătum,   865

      Clinĭam, Chrĕmem, Crătinum, Dinĭam, Demosthĕnem:

      ĭs ăpud scortum corruptelae ᵉst libĕris, lustris stŭdet.
PAR   quin tᵘ illum iŭbes ancillas răpĕrĕ sublimem dŏmum?

MAT   tăcĕ mŏdo. ne illum mecastor mĭsĕrᵘᵐ hăbebᵒ.
PAR   ĕgᵒ ĭstuc scĭo.

      ĭtă fŏrᵉ illi dum quĭdĕm cᵘᵐ illo nuptᵃ ĕrĭs.
MAT   ĕgŏ censĕo.   870

      ĕᵘᵐ ĕtⁱᵃᵐ hŏmĭnᵉᵐ aut in sĕnatu dărᵉ ŏpĕrᵃᵐ aut
          clĭentĭbus,
      ĭbĭ lăbŏrĕ delassatum noctem totam stertĕre.

      illᵉ ŏpĕri fŏris făcĭendo lassus noctᵘ ad mᵉ aduĕnit:

PAL   In the realm of the gods, or mankind, credit me no more at all,

                 Artemona, if you find I'm lying about *any* of this.   855

MRS   Yes, accursed I am: I thought my husband was good past
                 other men . . .
                 —a stay-dry good guy, under control: loved his wife most of
                 them all.

PAL   Yet, now and henceforth, know he is, beyond all, the creature
                 worth least . . .
                 —a stay-wet nothingness, out of control: and his wife's loather.

MRS   Sure, if all that weren't true, he'd never do what he's doing
                 right now.   860

PAL   I too, lord, before now always thought him to be a good person,

                 but by this act he's shown who he is, having his son alongside
                 at the drink, to party and co-date playmate: one clapped-out
                 old boy.

MRS   Our Lady that's what was going on, "I'm out to dinner" each day.
                 Said "I'm off out, from A through Archie Premier's, Bonjour's,
                 Bonjourarmée's,   865
                 Couchette's, Hennir's, Kratinus', L'Estrange's, Orateur
                 Démosthène's.
                 Now he's chez tart. A freeborn child's perversion, lover of morass.

PAL   Why not order your maid servants: "Lift him high, kidnap him,
                 back home"?

MRS   Now, shh. By our lady, I'll make him pitiful.

PAL   That's for sure.
                                      I know
                 that's how it shall be for him, long as you're married.

MRS   I'll vote for
                                     that.   870
                 That hombré! It's "I must attend the senate" or "tend to clients."

                 It's "I'm worn out with the work there," and it's snoring all
                   through the night.
                   He's "been working away," so he's "tired" when he comes back to
                   me nights.

fund^{um} ălĭen^{um} arat, incultum fămĭlĭarem desĕrit.

ĭs ĕtĭam corruptus porro sŭum corrumpit fĭlĭum.   875

PAR   sĕquĕr^e hac me mŏdo, iam fax^o ips^{um} hŏmĭnem mănĭfest^o
           opprĭmas.
MAT   nĭhĭl ecastor est quod făcĕrĕ mauĕlim.

PAR   mănĕdum.
MAT   quĭd est?
PAR   possis, si fort^e accŭbantem tŭum uĭrum conspexĕris

           cum cŏron^a amplex^{um} ămĭcam, si uĭdĕas, cognoscĕre?

MAT   poss^{um} ecastor.
{PAR}   {em tĭbⁱ hŏmĭnem.}
{MAT}   {pĕrĭi.}
{PAR}   {paulisper mănĕ. 880
           auⁱcŭpemŭs ex insĭdĭis clancŭlum quam rem gĕrant.}

ARG   quid mŏdi, pătĕr, amplexando făcĭes?
DEM   fătĕor, natĕ mi—

ARG   —quid fătĕrĕ?
DEM   —m^e ex ămorĕ | huius corrupt^{um} oppĭdo.

{PAR}   {audi^sn^e quĭd ăit?}
{MAT}   {audĭ^o.}
DEM>PHIL   ĕgŏn^e ut non dŏm^o uxori mĕae
           surrĭpĭ^{am} in delĭcĭis pallam qu^{am} hăbĕt atqu^e ad te
           defĕram?   885
           non ĕdĕpol conduci possum uit^a uxorĭs annŭa.

{PAR}   {cense^sn^e t^u ill^{um} hŏdĭe prim^{um} ĭrĕ | ass^uet^{um} ess^e in
           ganĕum?}
{MAT}   {ill^e ecastor suppĭlabat me, quŏd ancillas mĕas
           suspĭcabar atqu^e insontis mĭsĕras crŭcĭabam.}

He's ploughing someone else's farmstead, leaves his own home
    abandoned.

And now he's full perverted, he's perverting his very
    own son.   875

PAL   Just follow this way. I'll soon see you drop the hombré, in
        the act.

MRS   There's nothing, Our Lady, I'd rather do.

PAL   Hang on a mo'.

MRS   Whassup?

PAL   You could, I suppose, happen you catch sight of your husband
        installed

    with crown, hugging playmate, if you saw him . . .—could you
        tell it is him?

MRS   Lady, I could.

{PAL}   {Pow. There he is, yours.}

{MRS}   {I'm done for.}

{PAL}   {Hang on a bit.   880

    Let's catch birds from our *am*bush, from the hide let's net
        'em . . .—their fowl play.}

ARG   What cap, father, will you put on hugging?

DEM   I admit, son of
                                        mine . . .

ARG   —"Admit" what? . . .

DEM   —that for love of her I'm now an . . .
                        instant . . . undone . . .—wreck.

{PAL}   {Hear what he says?}

{MRS}   {I hear.}

DEM>PHIL   Aren't I going to steal from the Mrs.,

    back home, a stole she rates one of her darlings, then fetch it
        to you?   885

    Surely, I can't be hired *not* to. Not for . . . a year of . . . the
        wife's . . .—life.

{PAL}   {You vote today's trip to an eatery's him starting up a habit?}

{MRS}   {Our Lady, he's been stealing from me. I suspected my servants,
    and I set about torturing those pitiful, innocent maids.}

ARG>DEM   păter,
iŭbĕ dăṛi uiṇum: iamḍudum   factum ᵉst ҫum priṃum bĭbi. 890

DEM>PUER   ḍa, pŭĕṛᵉ, ab summ°.

DEM>PHIL   ăgĕ tᵘ inṭĕrĭbⁱ ăḅ infiṃo da ṣauĭum.

{MAT}   {pĕrĭi ṃĭsĕrᵃ, ŭṭ oscŭḷatur ҫarnĭfex, căpŭḷi dĕҫus.}
DEM   ĕdĕpŏḷ ănĭmam sᵘauĭorᵉᵐ ăḷĭquanto quᵃᵐ uxoṛis mĕae.

PHIL   ḍic ăṃab°, an foetet ănĭmă | uxoṛis tūae?
DEM   ṇautĕam

bĭbĕrĕ ṃalim, si nĕҫessum ṣit, quᵃᵐ illᵃᵐ oscŭlarĭer.   895

{MAT}   {aiˢnᵉ tandᵉᵐ? ĕdĕpol ṇe tu |ịstuc ҫum mălo magno tŭọ

dixistⁱ in me. ṣĭnĕ, rĕụĕnĭas ṃŏdŏ dŏṃum, fax° ut scĭas

quid pĕricli ṣit doṭatᵃᵉ uxori ụĭtĭum ḍicĕre.}
PHIL>DEM   ṃĭsĕr eҫastor es.
{MAT}   {eҫastor dignŭṣ est.}

ARG>DEM   quĭd ăịs, păṭer?
ecquid ṃatrᵉᵐ ăṃas?
DEM   ĕgŏṇᵉ illam?   ṇunc ăṃo—quĭă ṇon
ăḍest.   900
ARG   quid cᵘᵐ ăḍest?
DEM   pĕrĭissĕ ҫŭpĭo. |
{PAR}   ăṃăt hŏṃ° hic tᵉ ut praedĭҫat.

{MAT}   {nᵉ illᵃ eҫastor faenĕrato fundĭtat: nam ṣi dŏṃum

rĕdĭĕrit hŏdĭᵉ, oscŭḷand° ĕg° ulciscar pŏtissĭmum.}

ARG>DEM   Father,
order wine be served. It's now donkey's years since my first
drink.   890

DEM>BOY   Garçon, serve from my right.

DEM>PHIL   Meanwhile, come, *you* serve, from
left field, a . . .—kiss.

{MRS}   {I've had it, poor thing. Those kisses! Executioner. Coffin's pride.}

DEM   Surely, this breath is con-sider-ab-ly sweeter than my wife's
breath.

PHIL   Tell me, please, lover, do. Does your wife's breath stink?

DEM   You know
bilge
water?
Well, I'd sooner drink that, if I had to, than have a kiss
with her.   895

{MRS}   {Finally come out with that? Surely, a Big *B-a-d*'s all yours, for
what
you've said against me. Lemme at you, just come home. I'll see
you know
what a risk goes along with abusing The Wife With A Dowry.}

PHIL>DEM   By Our Lady, you're pitiful.

{MRS}   {Lord he deserves it.}

ARG>DEM   Tell me, father,
d'you love mother?

DEM   Her? Me? I love her right now. For . . .—
not being here.   900

ARG   How 'bout when she's here?

DEM   I long for her . . .—dead.

{PAL}   {He *loves*
you . . .—
so he says.}

{MRS}   {Sure, Lady, he's pouring the stuff out—he'll pay . . .—*interest*:
once he's home,
returning today, then kissing shall be my ultimate . . .—revenge.}

ARG   i̯ăcĕ, pă̯ter, ta̯los, ut porro n̯os i̯ăci̯amus.

DEM   m̯axı̆m̯e.
                    t̯e, Phı̆l̯aenı̆um, mı̆h̯i atqu^e uχoris m̯ort^em. hoc
                        Vĕnĕrı̆um ^est.   905
                    pŭĕri, plaudı̆t^e, et m̯i ob i̯actum c̯anthă̯ro mul̯sum dă̯te.

{MAT}   {n̯on quĕo̯ dura̯rĕ.}
{PAR}   {s̯i non dı̆dı̆cis̯ti ful̯l̯onı̆am,
                    n̯on mira̯ndum ^es̯t, Artĕmon^a, ı̆n ŏ̯c̯ŭlo̯s inuad̯i optı̆mum ^est.}

MAT>DEM   ÈGŎ POL V̯IV^am et t̯^u istaec̯ hŏdı̆e c̯um tŭo̯ magn̯o mă̯lo
                    inuŏ̯casti. |
{PAR}   ecquis c̯urrit pollinctor^em acc̯ersĕre?   910
ARG>MAT   m̯ater, s̯alue.
MAT>ARG   s̯at să̯lutis.
{PAR}   {m̯ortŭu̯^s ^est De̯maenĕt̯us.

                    t̯empŭ̯s est subd̯ucĕr^e hinc me. pulchr^e hoc gliscit proelı̆um.

                    i̯b^o ad Dı̆ăbŏl̯um, mand̯ată d̯icam fact^a ut u̯ŏlŭĕrit,
                    atqu^e intĕrĕ^a ut d̯ecumbamus s̯^uadeb^o, hi dum l̯itı̆gant.

                    postĕ d̯em^um huc c̯ras add̯uc^am ad l̯en^am, ut u̯iginti mı̆n̯as   915

                    ei det, in part^em hac ă̯mant̯i ut lı̆cĕă̯t e͡i pŏt̯irı̯er.
                    A̯rgy̆rippŭ̯s exora̯ri spero pŏtĕrı̆t ut sı̆n̯at
                    ses^e alternas c̯^um illo n̯octes hac frŭi. nam n̯i impĕt̯ro,
                    r̯egem perdı̆d̯i: ex ă̯morĕ t̯antum ^es̯t hŏmı̆n̯i inc̯endı̆um.}   →

MAT>PHIL   quid tı̆b̯i hunc rĕc̯eptı̆^o ad te ^est m͡eum uı̆r̯um?

ARG   Throw the ankle-bones, father, then I can throw dice
                         next.

DEM   Certainly:
                 Philaenium for me, death for the wife. Bullseye, it's a Venus. 905

                 Garçons, clap your hands, and for my throw serve mead into
                         my tankard.

{MRS}   {I just cannot endure it.}

{PAL}   {If you didn't learn the fulling trade,
                 no wonder, Artemona. "Get into his sight" will be perfect.}

MRS>DEM   Sure, I *shall* live. A Big Bad is yours, for that cursing, that praying,
                 you went in for.

{PAL}   {Will someone run to get the undertaker, quick?}   910

ARG>MRS   Mother, goo'day.

MRS>ARG   Enough "goo'day"-ing.

{PAL}   {Demaenetus,
                                  Dead-meat-us.

                 My cue to subtract me from the scene. This battle's boiling up
                         beaut.

                 I'm off to Diabolus, to tell him his plans went as he wished.
                 Meantime we'll loll on a couch, I'll persuade him, while this lot
                         do strife.

                 Later, lastly, I'll bring him here to madam, with twenty
                         minae   915
                 to pay, so monopolizing *her* will be on for him, in part.
                 Argyrippus, I hope, will let pleading work on him, agree to
                 share with him, enjoy her alternate nights. See, if I'm no farther,
                 I've wasted a king. For love, this hombré turns to such a
                         fireball.}   →

MRS>PHIL   What's this, you taking my husband in to you at your
                         place?

PHIL   pol me
                                              quĭdem   920

mĭsĕrăm | ŏdĭo | enĭcauit.

MAT>DEM   ṢVRG^E, ĂMATOR, I DŎMVM.

DEM   nullus s^{um}.

MAT   imm^o es, ne nĕg^a, omnĭ^{um} hŏmĭnum
                    pol nequissĭmus.
ăt ĕtĭam cŭbat cŭculus. ṢVRG^E, ĂMATOR, I DŎMVM.

DEM   uae mĭhí.

MAT   uer^a hărĭŏlarĕ. ṢVRG^E, ĂMATOR, I DŎMVM.

DEM   abscede^e ergo paulŭl^{um} istuc.

MAT   ṢVRG^E, ĂMATOR,
                                I DŎMVM.   925

DEM   i^{am} obsĕcr^o, uxor—

MAT   —nunc uxorem me^e essĕ mĕmĭnisti tŭam?

mŏdŏ, cum dict^a in me gĕrebas, ŏdĭum, non uxor, ĕram.

{DEM}   {totus pĕrĭi.}

MAT   quid tand^{em}? ănĭmă foetetn^e uxoris tŭae?

DEM   murr^{am} ŏlet.

MAT   iam surrĭpŭisti pallam quam scorto dăres?

PHIL>MAT   ecastor qui surrupturum pallam promisit tĭbi.   930

DEM>PHIL   non tăces?

ARG>MAT   ĕgŏ diss^{u}adebam, mater.

MAT>ARG   bellum filĭum.

MAT>DEM   istoscin^e pătr^{em} aequum ^{e}st mores lĭbĕris largirĭer?
nilnĕ te pŭdet?

PHIL   Sure I'm   920

a poor thing, he's murdered me—his puke.

MRS>DEM   UP, LOVERMAN,
                    HOME YOU GO.

DEM   I don't exist.

MRS   You do, don't deny it: surely, you are the *pits*.

Yet, this cuckoo's still there in the nest. UP, LOVERMAN,
    HOME YOU GO.

DEM   Damn me.

MRS   Soothsayer, you divine right. UP, LOVERMAN,
          HOME YOU GO.

DEM   Give us space, just a bit, over there.

MRS   UP, LOVERMAN,
                 HOME YOU GO.   925

DEM   It's time. I beg you, wife . . .

MRS   —So now you've remembered, I am
            your wife?

Just now, you were piling insults onto me, I was "puke," *not* "wife."

{DEM}   {I've had it. A write-off.}

MRS   Finally, this: "stinks," does it, your
            "wife's breath"?

DEM   Myrrh's the scent.

MRS   You've already "stolen the stole, to give" to
            the tart?

PHIL>MRS   Lady, there's the one who promised he'd rob a robe off you.   930

DEM>PHIL   Will you shut up?

ARG>MRS   Tried talking him out of it, mother.

MRS>ARG   Lovely
                    son . . .

MRS>DEM   Is it right a father should shower *those* ways on a freeborn child?
Have you *no* shame?

DEM>MAT   pol, s̩ⁱ ălĭud n̩il sit, t͡uī mᵉ, uxo̩r, pŭd̩et.

MAT>DEM   c̩ano c̆ăpῐtĕ t̩e c̆ŭc̩ŭlŭm̩ | uxo̩r ex lus̩tris răpit.

DEM   n̩on lῐc̩et mănerĕ—c̩enă c̆ŏqŭĭtur—d̩um cen̩em mŏd̩o?   935

MAT   e̩cas̩tor cen̩abῐs̩ hŏdῐe, | ut dignuˢ ᵉs—magnum mălum.

DEM   m̩ălĕ c̆ŭb̩andum ᵉst: i̩udῐc̩atum m̩ᵉ uxo̩r abduc̩it dŏm̩um.

ARG>DEM   d̩iceb̩am, păt̩er, tῐb̩í ne matri c̩onsŭlĕr̩es măl̩e.

PHIL>DEM   de pall̩a mĕm̩entᵒ, ăm̩abo.
DEM>MAT   i̩ŭbĕˢnᵉ hanc̩ hinc absc̩edĕr̩e?

MAT>DEM   I̩ DŎM̩UM.

PHIL>DEM   da s̩auῐᵘᵐ ĕtῐam prῐŭˢ quᵃᵐ ăb̩itῐs.
DEM>PHIL   ⁱ in crŭc̩em.   → →

PHIL>ARG   i̩mmᵒ intus pŏtῐu̩s. sĕquĕr̩ᵉ hac me, m̩ⁱ ănῐmĕ. |
ARG>PHIL   ĕgŏ uero̩
                                    sĕqu̩or.   → →

→ → → → →   EPILOGVS = GREX
          h̩ic sĕn̩ex si quid clᵃᵐ uxorem s̩ŭᵒ ănῐmo fec̩it uŏl̩up,
          nĕquĕ nŏu̩um nĕquĕ m̩irum fec̩it n̩ec sĕc̩us quᵃᵐ ălῐi sŏl̩ent.
          n̩ec quisquᵃᵐ ᵉst tᵃᵐ ingĕnῐo d̩uro n̩ec tam f̩irmo pectŏr̩e
          quin ŭb̩í quidquᵉ occas̩ῐonis s̩it sῐb̩í făcῐa̩t bĕn̩e.   945
          n̩unc si u̩ultis d̩eprĕc̩ari | h̩uic sĕn̩i ne u̩apŭl̩at,
          r̩emu̩r impĕt̩rari possĕ, p̩lausum s̩i clar̩um dătῐs.

DEM>MRS	Sure, were there none else, wife, I'd be ashamed of . . .—you.
MRS>DEM	You're the grey-headed cuckoo; your wife's ripping you from the morass.
DEM	Can I not stay—dinner's being cooked—just long enough for dinner? 935
MRS	Lady, you'll have dinner today, the one you deserve . . .—a great Big . . . B-A-D.
DEM	Bad nesting, then: the wife has sentenced me, landed me to take home.
ARG>DEM	I did tell you so, father. Told you not to go against mother.
PHIL>DEM	Don't forget the stole, lover, please.
DEM>MRS	Order her to give us space here.
MRS>DEM	YOU, HOME, NOW.
PHIL>DEM	Give us a kiss before you all go.
DEM>PHIL	Up on your cross. → →
PHIL>ARG	Inside, instead. Follow me this way, heart of mine.
ARG>PHIL	Follow, yes please. →

→ → → → →   THE EPILOGUE = THE TROUPE
This senior citizen kept from his wife what he did for his kicks:
did nothing new, weird, or off the way other characters behave.
There's no one so hard-hearted, no one so intransigent minded,
he wouldn't, with the opportunity, do *himself* a good turn.   945
Now if you want to beg this senior off his beating, we believe,
it can be got farther forward, *if all your clapping pays out CL-EAR.*

Language, Metre, and Text

Plautin Language
and Latin Vocabulary

The glosses include several items of U.K. and of U.S. colloquialism used in the translation. *See also* Index, *Asinaria, s.v.* wordplay and puns.

Key

1–15, 1	line numbers
219+220	see note ad loc.

grex³, minitor¹	third declension, first conjugation, etc.
grex(g-)	in third declension, nominative (plus stem for other cases)

+	a second (or third) word in the same line
[ ]	additional comment

1–15 The Prologue tells all | there's nothing to tell, so listen

Plautus prologues come in all sizes. This one keeps itself to itself, plays as "para-text," preliminary to the play "proper." Here to tell us it won't tell us—much. In short, it does "short" (8). Defers to its audience: as ever, theatre needs your help (15). The fun will buzz to and fro between asses on stage and bums on seats. That's the deal.

1 *sultis = s^i ^{u}ultis,* if you will, plural of s^i ^{u}is, please [all over Plautus. Showing the slurred and elided vowels and semivowels makes the text look strange but read easy] **3** *grex(g-)³* theatre-company [but this word for a herd will set the pace for As.] + *dominus²*: slave-owner, manager + *con-ductor³*: hiring magistrate **4** *face = fac* [imperative] + *praeco(n-)³*: crier [p(ublic) a(ddress) man] + *auritus:* [long-]eared + *poplus*[2] = *populus* [more such original forms down the line] **15** *alias:* at other times, [e.g.] previously.

16–126 Somewhere in theatre Greece . . . Father enlists Slave One to swindle Mother and fund Loverboy Son

Dialogue sets the scene deferred from the prologue. Unusually, the focal comedy queen, pater, is already in the know; matrona will instead be the blocking power-figure, aka parent, holding the purse strings but in the dark. In colluding to buy his son time at the heterosex-for-hire agency (= "next door"), father plots along with and through the slave agents. From the off, they share (split and double) this single function. Hence their mateyness. Nice try, but it will never work: pater will still end up as fall guy. Our hero, without whom. . . . Our alibi for slipping the leash, for a play day away. . . . Now we're ready to roll.

18 *ted:* you [more original pronoun ablatives in -*d* ahead] **20** *med erga* = *erga me:* toward me **21** *siet* [not yet contracted] = *sit* **27** *actutum:* immediately **29** *hercle:* lordy, by Hercules [ubiquitous expletive, men only] **34** *fustitudinus, ferri-crepinus:* "nonce" (one-off) non-words [the slave skirts painful words for his world] **36** *pol:* sure, by Pollux [everybody's expletive] **37** *polenta*[1]: barley flour **39** *de-spuo*[3]: spit out **40** *morem gero*[3] [+ dative]: humour + *ex-screo*[1]: hawk up and spit out **41** *penitus:* innermost **43** *s*[i] *[u]is:* see on 1. **45** *ex-pers(t-)*[3]: with no part in [+ ablative] **47** *minitor*[1]: threaten [vigorously] **49** *sub-censeo*[2]: get cross **56** *sub-peto*[3]: be available to [**61** colloquial *tamen in pretio sumus,* "we are at a high value, are prized" here soundly trumps and displaces its unmarked prompt *primus sentis,* with *tu* + long syllables ↔ *nos* + shorts] **65** *ob-sequentia*[1]: obedience, favour (cf. **76**, *obsequi*) **66** *utantur* arguably/provocatively introduces "utilitarian" self-interest into this paternal policy of befriending a son (why else . . . ?) **69** *nau-clericus:* of a ship-captain [naturalized Greek] **70** *leno(n-)*[3]: pimp, brothel-keeper; *lena*[1] will be the female counterpart, cf. **175**. **77** *ob-secutam:* cf. 65 [same idea wanted, but the exact locution is lost to us] **78** *arte* + *con-tente:* tightly + restrictively **85** *dotalis,* of a dowry [= **87** *dos(t-)*[3]] **89** *usus*[4] *est* there is a need of [+ ablative] for [+ dative] **91** *nugae*[1]: trifles **95** *porro:* straight on, forward **97** *circum-duco*[3]: lead round the houses, con **98** *ob-sum:* get in the way **99** *una opera:* with the same trouble, it's one and the same **100** *rete*[3], *iaculum*[2]: net, net for casting **101** *optio(n-)*[3]: junior officer, assistant **102** *com-miniscor*[3]: think up **114** *patro*[1]: "father," bring to fruition, cf. *in-petro*[1]: obtain by pleading, *in-petrio*[4]: seek a good omen **117** *nemp*[e]: of course **119** *uersutus:* full of turns, wily + *quo ab* = *a quo* + *aegrius:* with more difficulty **121** *ma-uolo*[3] = *magis-uolo* = *malo,* prefer **124** *scipio(n-)*[3]: walking-stick (*dreadful* clang with *scio*[4], I know) + *con-tuor*[3] = *con-tueor*[2], cf. 403. **125** *cesso*[1]: dally, stop.

127–152 Loverboy's lament

Let action commence, with a shrill snatch of overpitched song. From some-one's poor son, bounced by Madame from next door. Impoverished, strung-out, reproachful: adolescent. She's on next.

127 *sicine* i.e. *sic* + *ne* [the original weak *-ce* is retained here, as often with *hici-ne,* e.g. **128** *hocci-ne*] + *me eici* from *e-icio*[3] that I am thrown out [exclamatory indirect statement] **132** *faxo:* I'll make sure [colloquial future of *facio,* used parenthetically] + *capitis:* [at the price] of your head **133** *per-lecebrae*[1]: enticement, vamp [nonce-word, see on 34: marking a "nonsense text," mocking the limitations of regular, so conformist, diction] + *per-nicies*[5]: destruction [also spelled, or fused with, *per-mities*. This verse makes an instant high point of o.t.t. parody, possibly (false-)echoing a tragic outburst] **135** *elauo*[1]: wash out, get cleaned out [Plautin slang] **139** *egestas(t-)*[3]: need, lack **140** *ede-pol* = *pol,* strengthened, surely, see on 36. **142** *pannus*[2]: rag **145** *man-sues(t-)*[3]: hand-used, tame **147** *era*[1]: mistress, female owner [of slave]; *erus*[2] will be the male equivalent, from 251. [**150** in a stew: see on 267] **151** *eccam* = *ec-ce-hanc-ce,* here she is + *in-lecebra*[1]: enticement, vamp [three times in Plautin], cf. 133, 206 + *ostium*[2]: doorway.

153–248 Loverboy spars with Madame: a deal is cut

The pair argue the toss for our benefit. She hears the complaints, silences them, steals the scene. Altercation ("like for like," 172) makes way for her cameo lecture on marketplace economics in the sexwork industry. The dame's "hard school of realism" tour de force features overblown metaphor, analogy, simile—the rhetorical kitchen sink. Not forgetting a personal demonstration showing how it's done (222–6, in best panto-style). Cowed, the boy comes up with an indecent proposal: he'll lease The Girl for a year, under contract. An exclusive deal, finance pending. Now we're sussed—and we (unlike pater and his team) have met The Competition.

153 *uerbum* = *uerborum* [the original form] + "dosh" is britslang for "dough" [the best things in life are free: comic spiel specializes in abuse/idolatry of lolly/loot] **156** *clauus*[2]: nail **158** *capesso*[3]: grasp **159** *portitor*[3]: customs-officer **162** *fore:* will be [future infinitive of *sum*] **164** *ducto*[1]: hire [a call-girl] **172** *hostimentum*[2]: requital, cf. *hostio*[4]: requite, 377. **175** *lena*[1]: see 69 + *qui* = *quo* [obsolescent ablative form] **178** *nequam* = bad [doesn't decline] **179** *sucus*[2]: juice + *condio*[4]: season **180** *patinarius:* in a pan + *assus:* baked **183** *pedi-sequa*[1]: woman attendant **184** *catulus*[2]: puppy **186** *quaestus*[4]: paying job **188** *e-castor:* By Castor, "(By) Our Lady" [expletive used by women] **200** *oeno-polium*[2]: wine shop [naturalized Greek, but extant only here—the Greek is found just once] **202** *oculatus:* fitted with eyes **203** *co-actio(n-)*[3]: collecting **209** *columba*[1]: dove + *pullus*[2]: chick **215** *auceps(cip-)*[3] = *auis-capio*, bird-catcher **216** *con-cinno*[1]: fix up [**219+220** "The line numbers were established by the major post-Ritschl Teubner editions of Götz, Löwe and Schöll. Before Ritschl himself the practice was to give numbers by Acts and Scenes. But G., L. and S. were very free with textual changes and supplements, so that editors who followed them often found it necessary to coalesce into one line what had been two" (Malcolm Willcock, *per litteras*, cf. id. [1997])]. **221** *esca*[1]: bait, tit-bit + *illex*[3]: enticing, decoy **222** *com-pello*[1]: address **223** *uinnulus:* coaxing [nonce-word] **224** *papilla*[1]: nipple **225** *sauium*[2]: kiss **228** *re-meo*[1]: come back **236** *prorsus* = *pro-uersus*, straight ahead, right though **238** *syn-graphus*[2]: contract [Greek] **240** *una:* at one and the same time, together [**242** *quod des, aedes* redoubles the point it makes by the noise it makes] **246** *ex-ob-secro*[1], beseech, is only found here. **247** [?]*ex-periri*[?]: try [sense clear but the words won't scan] **248** *mutuus:* on loan + *faenus(or-)*[3]: interest.

249–266 Slave One's wake-up call

The comic slave thinks he's here to dream up another cunning plan—how to redeploy capital, as usual, only this time it belongs to matrona. He thinks he's the play's Brains, but he has another think coming.

    249 ex-*pergiscier* = -*i*[3], wake up [the archaic passive infinitive in -*ier* makes a handy verse-end for trochaic septenarii (doubling as sense-unit end), cf. 325, 343, 895, 916, 932]. **251** *dis-cesti* = *dis-cedisti* [such "consonantal" forms, from -*sti*, not -*isti*, are frequent] + *erus*[2]: see 147. [**251** "yonks," "long ago," is britslang, "origin unknown" of coarse] **254** *abs* = *a(b)* **256** *faxim:* the old optative of *facio*, "would do" [a colloquialism] **258** *inter-uerto*[3]: cut out, swindle + *celox(c-)*[3]: yacht **259** in-*petritum:* see on 114 + *quouis:* in any direction **260** *picus*[2] + *cornix(c-)*[3] + *coruus*[2] + *parra*[1]: woodpecker + crow + raven + barn-owl **262** *ulmus*[2]: elm-tree [slaves hear only the wood to "birch" them] **264** *in* *mundo:* in store + *uirga*[1]: rod [for beating slave] **266** *ob-scaeuo*[1]: be a [bad] omen for [+ dative]: only found here and *Stichus* 460.

267–380 Slave Two's . . . brainwave

This time around, Brains must share (split and double) his role—with his underling: such luck! The Slave in a 'Urry, whose breath-and-mindlessness should mark him a mere messenger, has already arranged for the loot to be delivered to their door. Casts himself to star as The Impostor, playing the part of "Slave in a Stew." All on automatic pilot, too—running on instinct.

[**267** "in a stew" will be my daft version of "in a temper," all the rage (see 404–6). His breakneck 'Astiness will *talk* in nonstop spate not a mo' to waste aspiratin' no time for punctuatin'] **268** *Libentia*[1]: [pretend goddess] Pleasure **270** *scortor*[1]: go whoring, cf. *scortum*[2]: tart, 814. **271** *partio*[4]: share out **272** *con-pilo*[1]: steal, rob **273** *uae:* alas [for], woe [to = + dative] **275** *ocior:* quicker **276** *plaga*[1]: blow **277** *thesaurus*[2]: treasure [naturalized Greek] **279** *quadrigae*[1]: four-horsed chariot + *ind-apisco/or*[3]: gain, overtake **280** *inimi-cum:* genitive plural, cf. 153. **282** *opimitas(t-)*[3]: prosperity [Plautin; slang] + *ex-fertissimus (ex-farcio*[3/4]) stuffed fullest **284** *ob-noxius:* beholden to **287** *oppido:* utterly **289** *ex-templo:* at once + *sudo*[1]: sweat **290** *con-cesso*[1]: stop, rest [Plautin; cf. 125] **292** *con-primo*[3]: squeeze, "jump" [for sex] **295** *e-lecto*[1]: lure out **297** *flagrum*[2]: whip + *carcer*[3]: prison **300** *ex-pendo*[3]: weigh up [**301**, **303** "cwt" is short for uncool, unpoetic, non-metric, "hundred-weight"] **304** *trabs(b-)*[3]: beam **306** *lego*[1]: leave in a will **307** *uerbi-uelitatio(n)*[3]: word-skirmishing [nonce joke-word] **311** *carni-fex(fic-)*[3]: executioner [**312** shtick: Yiddish woid for U.S. "gimmick" **313** heist: U.S. for UK "job"] **315** *scapula*[1]: shoulder-blade + *gestio*[4]: itch **316** *hariolor*[1]: soothsay + *in mundo:* see on 264. [**317** "Big Bad" will be rend(er)ing "corporal violence on the body" whenever a slave is concerned; a key euphemism which *functions* as a key dysphemism] **319** *tergum*[2] (neuter): back, hide [the slave's bodily self]: the manuscripts read *familiare,* but the ancient lexicographer Nonius Marcel-lus noted *familiarem,* which we can see as a grammar-busting twist that substitutes the slave's own hide for anything or anyone else that might be available in the household (= *familiaris* + noun or *familiaris* as noun) **324** *potior*[4]: get possession of **325** *e-dis-sero*[3]: expound in full **327** *an-helitus*[4]: panting **332** ["shtoom" is more yiddish, "mum's the word," a noise that marks no noise, and (so) mocks mere orthography] *beo*[1]: bless, make happy **334+335:** see on 219+220. **340** *claudus:* lame [lame puns on "clapped out," worn-out britslang for "worn-out" (British *machinery,* Britons and Britain, etc.) will be over-done in this translation, to obvious good effect: cf. 670, 863] + *sub-tero*³: wear down (from) underneath + *femen(in-)*³ = *femur,* thigh, haunch + *ungula*¹: hoof **341** *sub-uecto*¹: carry, haul, up country **343** *tonstrina*¹: barber's shop, cf. *tonsor*³: barber + *per-contor*¹: prod thoroughly [**344** Armée, for *Strato* = Greek "army-man"] **347** *ob* = on account of [+ accusative] **355** *non . . . quin* = not . . . so not, not without . . . -ing [+ subjunctive] **356** *prae-sto*: ready on the spot, available **357** *bal(i)neae*¹: baths [naturalized Greek] **359** *inter-uerto*: see on 259. **360** *ex-ascio*¹: hack out, bash out [chop-chop is mock-Chinese pidgin English = p. d. q., or pretty/purty damn/darn quick] **362** *sorsum* = *se-uersum,* separately, apart **363** *inter-minor*¹: threaten, block with threats **366** *pro-miscam*: indiscriminately **370** *ob-lecto*¹: entertain, beguil **371** *mala*¹: jaw, cheek **375** *patitor(-ior*³): suffer [deponent-passive imperative singular] + *re-ferio*⁴: strike back **377** *hostio*⁴: see on 172. [**380** "windy" i.e. "cowardly" (on the run, as desperate slave from owner)]

381–406 The Courier arrives

The play's other messenger is here with the money, for matrona. Will he trust it to father's slaves?

382 *pulto*¹: bang, knock **384** *ohe:* whoa **386** *con-seruus*²: fellow-slave **388** *cardo(in-)*³: hinge **390** *moror*¹: have as my way, am trained **391** *calcitro(n-)*³: kicker **394** *mage* = *magis,* more + *tonsor:* see on 343. **397** *qui pro* = *pro qui,* for which **398** *mercatu* = at market **400** *macilentus:* lean + *rufulus:* reddish + *uentriosus:* pot-bellied **401** *con-modus:* full-size **403** *con-tuor:* see on 124 + *quasso*¹: shake vigorously **404** *uapulo*¹: be beaten [the ultimate slave-owner's *verbal* cruelty] **405** *Aeacidinus* = of Aeacus' grandson [Achilles] + *minae*¹: threat.

407–503 The con's too convincing: Saurea's world

Impersonating matrona's hateful steward to prise the cash from the courier, the slaves over-egg their play-within-a-play travesty. He will, however, trust only pater—and off they go.

409 *ne:* yes, indeed + *crus(r-)*³: shin, leg + *decore:* fittingly [only here in Plautin] [**410** "O.T.T." is over the top slang for "too much"] **412** [see on 317]

oc-cessisti from *ob-cedo*³, confront **416** *uerbero(n-)*³: whipping-boy **418** *stimu-lus*²: whip **420** *qui = quo*, with which + *ob-callesco*³: become hardened, callous **421** *fur*³: thief **422** *og-gannio*⁴: bark at **423** *stomachus*²: bad temper + *queo*⁴: be able + *sub-pedito*¹: supply, provide for [= dative] **424** *stercus(or-)*³: dung **425** *de-icio*³: throw down **426** *bulla*¹: knob, stud **427** *fustis(t-)*³: cudgel, big stick **428** *dedo*³: devote **429** *faenus*: see on 248. **430** *hara*¹: sty **433** *uicarius*²: deputy **438** *trapezita*¹: banker [Greek naturalized] **439** *sic do*¹: colloquial = "that's the way for me" **440** *sat ago*³: satisfy, bustle **441** *di-midium*²: half **443** *loco*¹: contract for **444** *scyphus*²: goblet [naturalized Greek] **445** *com-modo*¹: be obliging, give the use of something **448** *tinnio*⁴: make a high-pitched clang **449** *quam dudum*: how long ago **450** *uitio uerto*³: reckon as a fault ["turn to/for a flaw"] **459** *credo*³: trust + dative [of person] + genitive [parti-tive, of thing: "some of..."] **460** *duim*: let me give [optative of *do*, frequent in Plautin] + *a(d)-sto*¹: stand beside/aside, or stand ready, stand steady [slaves knew about this] **461** *formido*¹: dread **464** *peregrinus*²: foreigner + *sane*: for sure **467** *per-duim*: see on 460. **467** *sub-plic-assim*: I'll have knelt and begged [an optative form with the force of a future perfect; cf. 503] [**471** see on 317] **472** "s.f.a." is a charmer of a euphemistic acronym, = (*say*) "sweet Fanny Adams," aka "nothing at all" (*think* "sweet fuck all")] **475** *per-cieo*²/⁴: shake thoroughly **476** *scelestus*: wicked/wretched **481** *sub-plicium*²: begging for mercy, punishment, death-penalty **484+485**: see on 219+220 *furci-fer*²: bearing the "fork" [torture worse than wearing portable stocks] **491** *prae-fiscini*: averting the evil eye (*fascinum*), not putting the mockers on any-thing **493** *fortassis = fortasse*, perhaps **496** *secunda facio*: act favourably ["do favourable things"] + *capitulum*²: dear wee head, or person **498** *frugi* (= *bonae frugi*, e.g. 602) cropping well, worthy, good + *peculium*²: slave's nest-egg of savings.

504–544 The Sex Slave holds out on Momma

Time to meet The Girl Next Door. What's it like being Love for Sale? She has a mind of her own, but that's about all we can be sure of.

  504 *ne-queo*⁴: am unable (cf. 423) + *inter-dico*³: forbid **505** *ex-pers*: see on 45. **506** *moratam*: see on 390. [**510** "slate" is C19–21 Brit. for "dump on"] **511** *dicaculus*: talkative, glib [**512** i.e. "circ[umstance]s"] **516** *de die*: in the course of the day **518** *portisculum*²: hammer for beating stroke for rowers **519** *re-posiui = re-posui* from *re-pono*³: rest + *casteria*¹: deck for rowers' kip?

[found only here] **520** *con-sisto*[3]: come to a stop **523** *con-tui:* see on 124. **525** *rere* from *reor*[2]: you think **526** *ex-petesso*[3]: seek vigorously **533** *largus lacrimarum:* generous *with* tears **536** *cuius:* belonging to whom, whose [adjectival form] **538** *e(x) re:* in your interests **539+540:** see on 219+220 *o*[ui]*-pilio(n-)*[3]: shepherd **541** *peculiaris*[3]: belonging to your stash, your own [cf. on 498] + *solor*[1]: console.

545–590 We're in the money . . . *and* We're so pretty, o so pretty . . .

One song of praise deserves another (567, 576). The slaves congratulate each other in pulling off the crime de la crime in their long and distinguished careers of villainy. We missed it, but father went along with the imposture, and . . . signed for the cash.

546 *syco-phantia*[1]: trickery [Greek naturalized in Plautin] **547** *scapula:* see on 315 + *ulmus:* see on 262. **548** *lam(m)ina*[1] + *com-pes(d-)*[3] plate of metal [red-hot for torturing slaves] + shackles for the feet **549+550:** see on 219+220 *neruus*[2] + *numella*[1] + *pedica*[1] + *boia*[1]: string, rope + another kind of portable stocks worn around a slave's neck + more (foot-)shackles + yet another kind of portable stocks, or collar [This *is* the worst torturer's catalogue in Latin as well as in Plautin.] **551** *in-ductor*[3]: painter **553** *cicatrix(c-)*[3]: scar **555** *potiti:* see on 324 [+ genitive] **556** *con-lega*[1]: fellow magistrate [in Plautin only here and the matching **576**]; *-aï:* original ending of the genitive singular [here, *if* authentic, parody of high style?] **563** *per-fodio*[3]: dig through **565** *artutus:* [well-]limbed [this would be a nonce-word: it is a correction, by Fleckeisen, of *astutos*] + *uirgator*[3]: see on 264. **570** *ad-molior*[4]: put energy into, shove onto **574** *duritia*[1]: hardness [**576** the words *collegam collaudaui* collude in collapsing all "praise" into the 2-way street of old "pals" ("obl(ig)ation")] **577** *ut . . . decuit:* i.e. *decet* + [it seems] accusatives of person *and* ablative of thing [i.e. "How it became both you and me, in the highest degree, and was worthy of our character"?] **579** *hariolor:* see on 326. **580** *lepidus:* charming, witty **582** *contini = continui* from *con-teneo*[2], hold in **584** *memoriter:* in a non-forgetting way **585** *mane-dum:* "wait, do" + *intus:* inside, *from* inside [in Plautin] **587** *lacinia*[1]: hem **588** *attatae:* oh wow [naturalized Greek] **589** *pertica*[1]: pole **590** *crumina*[1]: pouch [worn round neck; not a big deal].

591–745 Lovers' last gasp lament *and* Slaves riding high:
Loverboy pays his dues

We and the slaves watch Romeo and Juliet bid a cruel world and each other goodbye for ever (and farewell for ever). It's curtains for both. But dry your eyes, the slaves will now make them sit up and beg for the money. In fact, he must crawl and scrape and watch her fake playing hot and horny. First Slave's turn, second Second's. This is where the comedy delivers—never mind the plot. It's a show-stopper of "improvisational" transgression, leapfrogging itself from blackmail over degradation to blasphemy. Yet the slaves' redoubled toying with The Kids for kicks acts out, ahead of pater's cameo, the dynamics of their master's strike for (self-) gratification. The price for a year's bliss (= hire) is one helluva night on the tiles for pa . . .

591 *egeo*[2]: lack, need [+ genitive] **594** *suprema* [i.e. *hora*]: last hour of the day [at an assembly, etc.] **595** *acerbus*: unripe, premature **597** *nox*: by night [archaic, perhaps a legal tinge? Only here in Plautin, and a correction, by Lipsius, at that] **599** *interdius*: by day [rarer form than *interdiu*] **600** *gerrae*: "pah, rubbish!" [mostly Plautin] **601** *ad-paro*[1]: prepare **606** *Orcus*[2]: [Lord of] Hell **614** *mel(ll-)*[3]: honey **615** *ec-fero*[3]: carry out [for burial] **619** *fumus*[2]: smoke **620** *quidum*: how so? **624** *cadus*[2]: flagon **627** *cinaedus*[2] + *calamistratus*[2]: pathic with permed hair [naturalized + bastardized Greek slang] **628** *cibus*[2]: food **634** *daturus dixit*: "he said he was going to give" [(Graecizing?) nominative and infinitive construction] **635** *quoquam*: in any direction **636** *polleo*[2]: have power **643** *a-spernor*[1]: scorn, reject **647** *am^{bi}-plexor*[1]: embrace vigorously **655** *erilis*[3]: of a master **656** may be neither Latin nor Plautin: *I* take *interior* [Bothe's conjecture, for *interioris*] with *salus*, and *both* genitives with *imperator* **662** *presso*[1]: weigh down [rare] **663** *pro-cliuis*[3]: sloping down **666** *passerculus*[2] + *gallina*[1] + *coturnix(c-)*[3]: sparrow-let + hen + quail **667** *agnellus*[2] + *haedillus*[2] + *uitellus*[2]: lambkin + kidlet + calfling [all found only here] **668** *labellum*[2]: lip **670** *atqui*: and yet + *genu*[4]: knee + *frico*[1]: rub **682** *uicissim*: in turn **685** *con-ticinnum*[2]: quietening of night, nightfall, pre-dawn [rare] **686** *tantis-per*: for the meantime **693** *aneticula*[1] + *columba*[1] + *catellus*[2]: duckling + see 209 + little 184. **694** *hirundo(in-)*[3] + *monedula*[1]: swallow + jackdaw + *putillus*: tiny wee, teeny weeny **696** *torquis*[3]: twisted chain-necklace **698** *nequiquam*: no way, in vain **699** *ueho*[3]: carry, allow to be ridden **702** *sub-domo*[1]: "tame underneath" [nonce-word] **706** *hordeum*[2]: barley + *tolutim*: at a gallop + *badizo*[1]: walk [Greek word: only here in Latin] **708** *calcar*[3]: spur + *quadri-pedum*[2]: trot + *cliuus*[2]: slope **709** *postid-ea*

= *postea,* afterwards + *pistor*[3]: miller **716** *diuum* = *diuorum* + *Ob-sequens*[3]: see on 65, 77. [**718** "slate": see on 519] **733** *tempori* (or *temperi*): locative of *tempus,* used adverbially, "in *good* time" **737** *meritissimum:* comic Plautin out-doing of *meritum*[2], "one good deed that deserves another" [so, nonce more, a nonce-word] **742** *angi-portum*[2]: blind alley **742** *clam:* secretly **743** *re-scisco*[3]: get to find out (and know).

746–809 Pal writes a contract for rival Loverboy

Back with credit card and contract, the rival shows up just too late. He and his stooge have written a script to beat all. Here's how to programme a customized-executive reserved-exclusive living doll. Here's how to stop a play in its tracks. Groan loud. Do.

748 *prorsus:* see on 236. **750** *trans-lege*[3]: read through [read through all Latin, and find the word only here] **752** *do*[1] *dono:* give as a gift (*the* "dative") **761** *peregre:* from abroad **763** *ceratus:* waxed **763–4** *inutilis* | *pictura* "no-good picture," i.e. pornographic tableau that doesn't pull it off ("dud daub") **764** *quadri-duum*[3]: a four-day period **765** *ab-alieno*[3]: transfer to another's ownership **766** *com-buro*[3]: burn up **770** *caecus:* blind **771** *poclum*[2] = *poculum,* goblet + *potito*[1]: booze vigorously **772** *pro-pino*[3]: toast with a drink **778** *anulus*[2]: ring **779** *talus*[2]: ankle-bone, used for dice **784** *nuto*[1] + *nicto*[1] + *ad-nuo*[3]: nod vigorously + blink, wink + nod yes **787** *cubiculum*[2]: bedroom **790** *captio(n-)*[3]: trick **791** *quid ni?:* why not? **792** *per-plexabilis*[3]: enigmatic [Plautin: nonce-word] **794** *tussio*[4]: cough **795** *pro-sero*[3]: stick forward **796** *grauedo(in-)*[3]: head-cold, snot **797** *abs-tergeo*[2]: wipe off **798** *palam:* openly **800** *uerbo* = with a word (ablative) **801** *multa*[1]: fine **802** *scitus:* clever **803** *sertum*[2]: garland **807** *spurcus:* filthy **808** *nugae:* see on 91 + *mortualia*[3]: death-rites, keening [rare].

810–827 Loverboy's Pal will snitch to Mother on his new rival: Father

Plot and sub-plot collide. Will everyone finally get even? First things first.

811 *in-dico*[3]: inform against **814** *scortum:* see on 270. **815** *sub-pilo*[1]: steal secretly **817** *prope-diem:* soon **818** *ec-fligo*[3]: destroy + *sub-pedito:* see 423. **822** *per-cieo*[3/4]: see 475. **823** *at pol qui* or *at . . . qui* or *pol qui:* yes-indeed-sure [strong asseveration] **824** *lis* (= *lit-*)[3]: dispute + *con-cieo*[3/4]: stir up **826** *poto*[1]: booze [cf. 771].

828–850 Dad's party swings

Pater has his moment. Gropes the Girl, makes the Boy grin and bear it. Digs himself a deep, deep hole. We know.

827 *de-cumbo*[3]: recline [to dine] **830** *ac-cubo*[1]: lie next to **833** *uerecundus*: respectful **839+840**: see on 219+220 *dixis*: another optative form, cf. 256. **847** *per-petere*: suffer [deponent-passive imperative] **849+850**: see on 219+220.

851–941 Mum fetches him home

All hell breaks loose. Caught bang to rights, pa is ceremonially hounded from the love-nest. The play's holiday party debouches in carnival exorcism of Geriatric Lechery. Ugh. Yukkh. Join in—sing the song—all the way home. Boo! Hiss!

854 *accreduas = ad-credas*, from *accredo*[3]: believe [cf. on 460] **856** *ratus*: from *reor*[2], having thought [past participle] **859** *madidus*: soaked + *osor*[3]: hater [Plautin] **861** *ratus*: see 856. **863** *de-crepitus*: having lost voice, clapped-out **864** *coti-die*: every day **867** *corruptela*[1]: corruption + *lustrum*[2]: bog, morass, hole, dive **869** *me-castor*: "By Our Lady" [strengthened *ecastor*: see on 188] **873** *sterto*[3]: snore **874** *fundus*[2]: farm **881** *clam-culum*: a bit secretly, see on 742. **885** *de-licium*[2]: pet + *palla*[1]: robe **886** *annuus*: i.e. lasting through the [whole] year **887** *ganeum*[2]: eating-place, dive **888** *sub-pilo*: see on 815. **889** *in-sons(t-)*[3]: not-guilty **891** *a(b) summo . . . ab infimo*: from the highest [couch, place, at table] . . . from the lowest **892** *capulus*[2]: receptacle, esp. coffin **893** *anima*[1]: breath **894** *foeteo*[2]: stink + *nautea*[1]: bilge-water [naturalized Greek] **902** *faenerato*: at interest [cf. 248] + *fundito*[1]: pour vigorously **903** *ulciscor*[3]: take revenge on + *potissimum*: most of all **906** *iactus*[4]: throw + *cantharus*[2]: tankard [Greek] + *mulsum*[2]: honeyed wine, mead **907** [*ars*] *fullonia*: art of fulling, cleaning clothes [**909** see on 317.] **910** *pollinctor*[3]: undertaker + *ad-cerso*[3]: summon **912** *glisco*[3]: grow **915** *poste = post* [**919** "wasted" in the [gunlaw] slang sense "destroyed," cf. 232, 244 for play with *perdo/pereo*] **920** *re-ceptio(n-)*[3]: act of receiving [Plautin: only here in this use] **921** *e-nico*[1]: kill dead **922** *immo*: no, not at all + *nequissimus*: worst [superlative of *nequam*, see 178] **923** *cuculus*[2]: cuckoo **925** *paululum*: a little bit/way **929** *murra*[1] + *oleo*[2]: myrrh + smell of [+ accusative] **934** *canus*: grey-haired **935** *coquo*[3]: cook.

942–947 Some curtain call: your applautus is appreciated

Sympathy for the devil? Root for your anti-hero. Before it's too late. You know you want to.

942 *uolup:* pleasurably [*uolup facio:* enjoy] **943** *secus:* in an other way, differently.

Outline of the Metres of *Asinaria*

Gratwick (1993) 40–63, 251–60, and MacCary and Willcock (1976) 211–32, are most help for understanding, scanning, and reading Plautine verse: both are model presentations, attempting to teach from first principles to expertise in a few short pages. Not many readers will read enough plays to make doing the verse justice a high priority, but through the notation added to the text any newcomer can join in right away, and the following short profile will give you a fair idea of how the rhythm of the play swings and thumps along.

The short solo "song" in *Asinaria* is quite clearly marked out as a run of word-phrases composed to repeat and vary rhythmic patterns (= 2 below; on Plautine music and dramatic structure: Moore [1998], pp. 183, 185). The rest of the script, however, is "sing-song/talk," written in Plautus' favourite (most common) regular metres (= 1A and 1B below). The lines feel extremely "free" (like some talking blues). They play off the drive of spoken intonation against the recurrence of chanted half-line and whole-line units; each line is "called home" by a regular verse-end cadence. In *iambic septenarii* the words' own ordinary accentuation reinforces the verse cadence; in the other metres, there is often a clash between the two patterns. Across the length of the line, the sub-unit, or *metron*, of each verse has no underlying metronomic pulse. Thus a *senarius* can last anywhere between a light run of *alternating* "short" and "long" syllables (= 18 time-units, where a long lasts twice as long as a short) and a heavy run of *continuous* long syllables (= 23 time-units; see Gratwick and Lightley [1982] on heavily and lightly dramatic syllables). Most senarii are of 22 units, with one short syllable at either the first or the second "c" (a notation to be explained next): but enough lines have 21 or 23 units to downplay this norm, and, while 19 (and esp. 18) unit lines are far between, the few 20-unit verses are a significant minority. The final metron of *every* verse ends with a "short" syllable before a final "long" (so no senarius can ever last for 24 time units). The longer lines work correspondingly further away from internal or overall isochrony.

[NB In the text, the usual mid-verse word-break found in most lines is marked by a g a p.]

1. Iambic-trochaic Verse

NB In each metron, "B" and "D" are always long; "a" and "c" are those tending to be long or short ("a" mostly long; "c" rather more longs than shorts). Any element may be *either* a long syllable *or* two short syllables except at line-end: here the final two syllables are always short followed by long, except in *iambic septenarii,* where the final two syllables are always long followed by long. Within these parameters, the verse abides by a complex of norms for relating syllable patterns to spoken accentuation; these norms all have their exceptions, and never explain *all* the lines, or all the words. Editing Plautus is forever a test of nerve in tolerating or eliminating transmitted anomalies and violations, in metre as in all other aspects. As with any formal poetry, *reading* Plautus is always an ongoing negotiation between the pull of verse and the impetus of word accentuation.

1A. Short Spoken Verse: Iambic Senarius

1–126, 746–829: senarius (usually with a word-break between *linked* "half-lines"). The final "c" is always a "short" syllable.

aBcDa BcDaBcD
or
aBcDaBc DaBcD

1B. Longer Recitative Verse

Here, any element may be resolved into two short syllables except *at mid-verse and* verse-end: cadences with "cD" have the penultimate syllable short; cadences in "BC" and "Da" have the penultimate syllable long; the final syllable of every verse counts as long.

Just three varieties. All three long enough to feel close to a double line—"two-for-the-price-of-one." This is why Plautin theatre is all gabble and patter.

830–50: iambic octonarius (varying between separate or linked half-lines)

aBcDaBcD aBcDaBcD
or
aBcDaBcDa BcDaBcD

381–503, 545–745: iambic septenarius (as if an octonarius minus its last syllable)

aBcDaBcD aBcDaBC

138–380, 504–44, 851–947: trochaic septenarius (as if a "cretic," or "long-short-long" pattern, is followed by an iambic senarius)

BcDaBcDa BcDaBcD

2. Sung and Scored Lyric Verse

127–32, 134–7: cretic tetrameter, i.e., a fourfold series of "long-short-long" patterns. The following are the main patterns, in any combination:

– ⏑ –	– ⏑ –		– ⏑ –	– ⏑ –
– ⏑ ⏑ ⏑	– ⏑ – ⏑ ⏑		– ⏑ ⏑ ⏑	– ⏑ – ⏑ ⏑
⏑ ⏑ ⏑ –	⏑ ⏑ ⏑ –		⏑ ⏑ ⏑ –	⏑ ⏑ ⏑ –
– – –	– – –		– – –	– – –

Thus, for *Asinaria:*

127, 128, 130, 134	– ⏑ –	– ⏑ –	– ⏑ –	– ⏑ –
129	⏑ ⏑ ⏑ –	– ⏑ –	⏑ ⏑ ⏑ –	– ⏑ –
131	– ⏑ –	– ⏑ –	– ⏑ ⏑ ⏑	– ⏑ –

132   – ◡ –   ◡◡ ◡ –   – ◡ –   – ◡ –

135, 137   – ◡ –   – ◡ –   – – –   – ◡ –

136   – – –   – ◡ –   – ◡ –   – ◡ –

133: choriambic tetrameter (‾ ◡◡ ‾ with an "ionic" as the third element: ◡◡ – –)

– ◡◡ –   – ◡◡ –   ◡◡ – –   – ◡◡ –

Differences That
Make a Difference

Differences from the Oxford Classical Text (= Lindsay [1904], Volume 1)

6 *mihi* [*mi*] **25–26** *ita me obstinate aggress*^{us} ^{e}*s ut non audeam* | *profecto percontanti quin promam omnia.* deleted [bracketed by Lindsay: dreadful doublet of 23–4] **32–33** DEM. *quid istuc est? aut ubi istuc est terrarum loci?* | LIB. *ubi flent nequam homines qui polentam pinsitant.* deleted [ruins 34–9] **65** *obsequentiam* [*obsequellam*: attested for Plautus, but metrically impossible here; Gratwick (2001) argues for the (unattested) word *obsequelia* with *liberius* at 64] **77** *obsecutam* [*obsecutum*] **85** *uxor tua suum* [Mueller, see Lindsay p. xiv: *huc uxor tua*] **108** *i bene, ambula* [*fietne?* :: *ambula* Fleckeisen] **133** *pernicies* [*permities*] **146** *nil . . . nil* [*nihil . . . nihil*] **201** *disciplina* [*discipulina*] **205** *longe aliam, inquam,* [*linguam*] *praebes nunc atque olim cum dabam* [unmetrical doublet of 204, perhaps an attempt to ease the metre] **217** *assuescunt* [Reiz: [*aues*] *adsuescunt*] **219** *itidem* [*itidem hic*] **224** *id est* [Camerarius: *est*] **230** *tune* [*tene* Camerarius] **235** *uti* [Camerarius: | *ut*] **247** *?experiri?* [*experi* Skutsch] **252** *igitur inueniendo argento ut fingeres fallaciam* deleted [intolerable doublet of 250] **263** *hoc auspicioque* [*eiius pici* Goetz and Loewe] **266** *quod* [*quom*] **306** *istuc* [Brix: *hoc*] **308** *audacter licet* [*audacter* :: *licet*] **324** *potitur bonum* [Valla Pius: *patitur bonum*] **358** *dic* [*dice* Ritschl] **360** *exasciato* [*exasceato*] **364** *essent uiginti argenti minae* [*a. e. u. m.* Fleckeisen] **366** *promiscam* [Palmier: *promissam*] **395** *conueni. sed* [Ussing: *quom uenisset*] [**482** metrically incredible] **484** *nosmet* [*erum nosmet*] **492** *alter est Athenis* [Bentley: *Athenis alter est*] **505** metrically dubious: *matris expers imperiis* [Brandt: *e. m. imperio*] **509** *matri* [Bentley: *matris*] **547** *ulmorum* [*ulnorum* MSS of Nonius p. 400 Lindsay] [**549** "whips" doesn't belong with the rest of the torture kit?] [**552** metrically dubious, del. Bothe] [**556** metrically dubious line] **613** *certum* [Lachmann:

mihi certum] **694** *monedulam* [*monerulam*] [**714** metrically impossible]
733 *ted* [*te*] **758** *amicae suae* [Gulielmius: *amicai eum*] **785** *post si* [*postid*
Lindsay] **826** *narra.* PAR. [Leo: PAR. *iam iam*] **855** *esse me mendacem*
[Seyffert: *me esse mendacem*] **897** *reuenias* [Ritschl: *uenias*]

Differences from the Sarsina/Urbino Text (= Danese [2004])

6 *mihi* [*mi*] **15** *ut alias* [Leo: *item ut*] **65** *obsequentiam* [*obsequellam*] **77** *ob-
secutam* [*obsecutum*] **85** *uxor tua suum* [|| *uxor tua* ||] **105** *quid uis* [Vahlen:
quid tum Niemeyer] **133** *pernicies* [*permities*]**146** *nil . . . nil* [*nihil . . . nihil*]
176 *mihi* [*mi*] **193** *mihi* [*mi*] **201** *disciplina* [*discipulina*] **205** *longe aliam, inquam,* [*iniqua*] *praebes nunc atque olim cum dabam* [unmetrical doublet of
204, perhaps an attempt to ease the metre] **213–4** *neque . . . neque . . . neque*
[*nec . . . nec . . . nec*] **217** *assuescunt* [Reitz: *aues adsuescunt*] **219** *itidem* [*iti-
dem hic*] **224** *id est ab re* [Camerarius: *est ab re* ||] **230** *tune* [*tene,* Camerarius]
235 *uti* [Camerarius: *ut*] **247** ?*experiri*? [*experi* Skutsch] **255** *te recipis* [*recipe te*
Scaliger] **263** *hoc auspicioque* [Goetz and Loewe: *eiius pici*] **266** *quod* [*quom*
Nonius p. 212 Lindsay] **275** *hercle liber opera* [Reiz: *hercle* | *opera liber*] **300** *ted
expendi* [*te* | *expendi*] **306** *istuc* [Brix: *hoc*] **308** *audacter licet* [*audacter :: licet*]
324 *potitur bonum* [Valla Pius: *patitur bonum*] **352** *med esse* [*me* | *esse*] **358** *dic*
[*dice* Ritschl] **360** *exasciato* [*exasceato*] **363** *mihi* [*mi*] **387** *nostris* [Gulielmus:
nostris [*aedibus*]] **395** *conueni. sed* [Ussing: *quom uenisset*] **418** *mihi* [*mi*]
453 *mihi* [*mi*] **496** *mihi* [*mi*] **501** *mihi* [*mi*] **505** *matris expers imperiis* [Brandt:
e. m. imperio] **507** *mihi* [*mi*] **509** *matri* [Bentley: *matris*] **510** *neque . . . neque*
[*nec . . . nec*] **547** *ulmorum* [*ulnorum* MSS of Nonius] **556** *collegai* [Seyffert:
collegae] **557** *ad* [Merula: *est ad*] **560** *tuo* [Guyet: *tuo* [*nunc*]] **581** *med esse*
[*me* | *esse*] **613** *certum* [Lachmann: *mihi certum*] **614** *tu* [Fleckeisen: [*mihi*]
tu] **633** *med ad* [*me* | *ad*] **656** *interior* [Bothe: *interioris*] **676** *mihi* [*mi*]
687 *ted an* [*te* | *an*] **693** *med aneticulam* [*me* | *aneticulam*] **694** *monedulam*
[*monerulam*] **698** *in me tam indignum tantum* [Bothe: *tam indignum dic-
tum* | *in me*] **700** *hinc argentum* [Lindsay: *argentum* ||] **712** *mihi* [*mi*] **733** *ted*
[*te*] **758** *amicae suae* [Gulielmius: *amicai eum*] **785** *post si* [*postid* Lindsay]
826 *narra.* PAR. [Leo: PAR. *iam*] **841** *mihi* [*mi*] **846** *mihi* [*mi*] **855** *esse me
mendacem* [Seyffert: *me esse mendacem*] **873** *ille operi* [Lindsay: *ille opere*]
905 *mihi* [*mi*] **908** *Artemona* [Havet: gap marked] **940** *i in* [*i* | *in*]

Commentary and Analysis

$$\Rightarrow 1 \Leftarrow$$

Killing the Plot

16–126 Somewhere in theatre Greece . . . Father enlists Slave One to swindle Mother and fund Loverboy Son

Finessing the plot, in line with the prologue, paterfamilias sweeps away the preliminaries (52–3):

> I already know it: that son of mine. Love. Sex.
> With that whore from next door. . . .

Son 'fessed up—cashflow probs (74–5). A brace of slaves are assisting son; now pater wants to join the team, and be as good a mate as his own father once was, in his day. Cash to hand son to hand hooker? In a word (= *breuest.* 88–91, 96):

> Now to get what I want from you in a few words.
> my son needs twenty minae cash, immediate.
> See it's there ready right away.
>   Where on earth from?
> You swindle *me*. . . .
>   · · · · · ·
> Any way you can: me. Or wife. Or slave Lizard.

For this play brings you the novelty neurosis of "Father who would befriend Son" (50). He is matched with another first: the archetypal Cunning Slave (255, *ingenium uetus*) who *won't* cheat Master, as he will put it himself (256–7, *caue tu idem faxis alii quod serui solent*), with wordplay between *serua* and *serui* to point up the dissonance: "Serfguard master"?—What *could* induce a "servant" to "preserve" a master?[1] This aromatic agent, Libanus (p. 143), is going to be shoved out of his limelight, when his predatory mate gets to play *Asinaria*'s angry hombre, in character as mock-sadistic steward (pp. 147–8, 152–3).[2] But the *real* twist will be that Mater is going to find that she has stepped into the vacant shoes of comedy's usual tightass, Father (62–83; esp. 78–9):[3]

> ...Mother keeps tight and taut rein on him,
> the way *fathers* habitually do....

This because Mother rules the family.[4] The money is mummy's; she brought it with her as a bride. She has an agent of her own, too, slave "Lizard," so being a woman does not cripple her reign (85–7: *dotalem seruom; argentum; dote imperium*). Nobody's noticed this for twenty years or thereabouts— all so that we can be there, Today, when the worm turns, and pater fights back. For, he says, his own . . . son. Through, he arranges, his slaves. One and Two, as I shall call them, to make a point about anti-~~heroics~~.

"Almost everything about Roman dowry is ambivalent."[5] Not least for registering where *Asinaria* is coming from, it is best to regard the whole subject as far too touchy for this bone of contention to be *explicable*. In her comic realization as pantomime shrew,[6] The Wife with a Dowry was a fantasy for Athens who has become a spectre for Rome.[7] "Cashing out" the trouble she poses to patriarchal command (*imperium*), to family and gender structures, is exactly where this comedy *points* us.

So, here we are, nailing a plot, in the soap "Athens" of Roman theatre. In with my Anglo-American slang I shall be using a touch of irritant *franglais* to keep Plautus' nicely annoying "Graecolatin" in view—grit for the pearl, I'd like to think. For this is where Roman scriptwriters take Athenian originals and do them to death. Just for fun, they pin more or less suitable new names on the players, still Greek, but now stuck with the whole range of connotations of "Greek" in Latin. In "Lizard"'s case, the name *Saurea* is an eyesorea that will be trailed before us all over the script (85, 96, 264, 347, 353, 359, 368, 372, 383, 399, 417, 431, 464; and in the recap at 584). Until it dawns on us that we are not going to . . . have the pleasure . . . of meeting . . . the real thing. So "Lizard" *is* his (nowhere quite paralleled) name.

In Greek slang (no surprises here) tyrannosaurous Σαύρα *could* spell "Willy" (too), so more than fit to serve his mistress,[8] and that *could* be the innuendo gag at 374, where Leonida "swaps names." On the other hand, the ill-omened name-change in question there is *from* Lionel "Leonida" (as 368 puts it) and *into* "Lizard," so it (also) fits to have Libanus threaten to "de-Lion-ize" his comrade—if he so much as lays a real finger on him in pretend ferocity (literally nominal but no less painful for that). In no time at all, Libanus will be precisely misdescribing Saurea to the courier, *because accurately describing leonine Leonida,* as "Lean-jawed, rather tawnyish, etc. etc." (400–1: pp. 147–8). So "Little Leo" makes a good name for *this* Slave in a 'Urry (*seruus currens:* 265, 740). His unslavelike name is otherwise used at 58, 101, 566, and 665 (where he collects a row of *animal* names: 667).

[NB For *Libanus:* p. 197; *Demaenetus:* p. 213; *Philaenium,* 53: pp. 137–8 (and see Index, s.v. *Asinaria:* names, mentioned; and: names, of the characters).[9]]

The scene for this comedy, will, as usual, be a street-front in this "Wally-wood" Athens (pp. 139, 231 n.13). Here we face two front doors, fitted out with stage porches to help involved eavesdropping scenes to work (pp. 207–10). One belongs to a stripped-down nuclear family: a *paterfamilias,* both senior and ageing, and married to a dowry, which handed his wife control of the family finances. Their son has hooked up with a working girl who costs. She is under the control of her mother (or "mother," maybe),[10] and they live "next door" to our Family du jour.

Madam will tell us that in this self-satirising world "we purchase *on Greek credit*" (199).[11] Lying for all he is worth, the ruffian slave posing as the ferocious slave in charge of their household will brag that "There's no one else *in today's Athens* that they reckon gets so much credit, as me, right and proper" (492: cf. p. 140). And the play's bore we shall love to deplore can't imagine how his contractual effort to programme cheating out of the hustler is invalidated *by being drawn up in Latin,* when he sets about limiting her to "pure Attic *diction*—and no word of aporia: none" (792–3: cf. pp. 171–2).

Yes, thanks to Greek culture, Romans can laugh *at* Greek culture. In Plautus' lifetime, they were taking on the Mediterranean cosmos of the successors of Alexander the Great, and cleaning up. Fast (world supremacy in less than a lifetime).[12] Theatre was one case of the spoils of empire going down a treat in the backyard of the new "barbarian" superpower: if backward Romans were prepared to see and hear themselves as "unGreek [so non-players in civilisation]" (11, *barbare*), they *also* preferred to lump all their new provincials together, forever, under the nickname of the aptly undistinguished Γραικοί of Thessaly, rarely rated as Hellenes by Hellas!

Knock knock, "Who needs Greek?" :: "Roman pantomime does."

One smart watchword of "theory" patter tells us that "comedy" depends on the irruption of otherness, and Graeco-Roman culture needed at all costs to other any eruption of their slave populations. Empire rocked Rome, destabilized by importation of Greek ways along with Greek plunder. Cultural shock, as well as exhilaration, accompanied both the re-vamping of upgraded housing (marble columns to frame polished studding at the front door: 425–6) and the re-structuring of expanded staffing (a specialized domestic steward, *atriensis,* would provide an interface between master and his dealings with the outside world, would take over bursarial duties, and supervise the domestic slaves—seeing to it that "shit gets fetched away from the front doorstep": 424). Even basic food and drink became . . . service industries (pp. **149–51**). The new cosmopolis crawled with "Greek" ~~human~~ chattels, and their attendant phobias. Plautus puts them on show in his show (p. **152**).

Plautus makes the slaves his powerhouse, our fantasy pledge of "wit, fun— a gas" (13–14). They are jokes as well as jokesters, and, they let us all know, owners are jokes too—hopeless when (we/they) try to play jokesters, and helpless when (we/they) lose (our/their) sense of hum . . . anity. Of course today's pair of agents aren't going to *need* their Get-Out-of-Jail-Free card. Ultimately, Master promises, he will bail them out of trouble (106–7). But, no he won't. Not just like that. If mater *is* in loco patris (79), *she* will be judge and jury of *that.*[13]

So we watch and wait, while the slaves put on their show. To see *how far* Father means to befriend son, *how far* to hit back at wife (pp. **153–4**). He can explore the underside of resigning power in his household, exploit for all it is worth resignation to powerlessness; he can pick himself to play on his underlings' team—son and slave agents, plus player-manager. But master will still carry the can for the lot of them: all will be on his head. His favourite surrogate agrees to fill his shoes (*patro,* 114), but *he* has promised. And the reckoning must come when The One Who Wears the ~~Trousers~~ *finds out.*

Disequilibrium between pater and mater materializes in terms of clout when command of cash kicks in. What's new? But when husband lashes out at wife, and she has power, that isn't right, so *she* must pay with the play. All's well because all ends . . . badly for her. *We* know; she must find out. When master joins his slaves to plot against mistress, conjugality is undermined. Pitting his agents against hers only shields the marriage just so far. At the death, they must face each other: he has messed up; she gates and punishes her jackass-husband-slave. But this hurts *her*, too. The theatre knew it from the start. Disempowered males are just castrated mules. Clap if you agree (p. 214).

There is room for (a) play within these dynamics, but that's the logic of the ~~plot~~. What, then, will be our treat in watching how it all works out? Wife has been set above her station, so her subordinate has been raised to intolerable equality with husband: her slave even has a subordinate of his own (433–5, his favourite: p. 150). Husband degrades to the level of his subordinates—son, and slaves. His two slaves steal her slave's part. Watch how families breed interpersonal complications, for that's what they *are*. Farcical—says Farce.

Demaenetus has done his own introduction. Everything's started so well, too. The only way now is up, and then down: "At first . . . he seems like the kindly, supportive, and tolerant father. . . . In fact, Demaenetus is a hypocritical old reprobate."[14] "Four fifths of the way through the play, the plot of Plautus' *Asinaria* takes a sudden and surprising turn . . .; suddenly, at line 735, without warning, comes the startling turn . . .; so extraordinary a transition . . .; the change in the character of Demaenetus, which appears as the critical discontinuity in the play, is in fact a secondary phenomenon, a function of an alteration in the plot."[15] Demaenetus "begins to enjoy his role a bit too much, to go too far with it."[16] So will Demaenetus wind up deteriorated, degenerate, or true colours showing? Is(n't) the "Father who would befriend Son" plot *designed* to feed us suspicion?[17] How far shall *we* go: when undone matrona, at the kill, suspects the old man has been lying to her about all those business dinners "through the alphabet,"[18] giving her that stuff about "exhausting days at the office," and stealing her things so she's been "torturing innocent maids" (864–7, 871–4; 888–9: p. 134); is this even *half* enough to accept the "suggest[ion] that this is not the first time Demaenetus has gone astray, [or] a more sinister implication: slaking his lust on Philaenium has been his goal all along"?[19] Still, *Asinaria* is about the play in *Asinaria*—there is plenty of scope for *deciding* how (much) to ham it up, as you like it (pp. 170–2).[20]

This is already true of this plot-laden curtain-raiser. The informational load of these scene-setting *senarii* (p. 118) is relatively high. But if the "LIB–DEM" dialogue serves as a work-horse for sense, that doesn't exonerate it from serving up a work-house of nonsense. Far from it, *Asinaria* already tears it up, to "improvize." As ever, Plautus "makes a mess of Comedy. More, his theatre makes a mess *with* Comedy."[21] Love it for that. To be sure, in terms of the argument, the very first lines uttered in character made it indelibly clear that pater's role turns on the instrumentality of his investment in his only begotten son (and refugee self). Here is how the hombre services his homicidal repulsion at the spousal virus—his missus-omatosis (16–22):

> So. As you will want for your one and only son
> to outlive your lifetime, out of harm, outlasting,
> so be my witness, by your status of elder,
> and by that woman, the one that you fear, the wife,
> if this day, as regards me, you tell me anything false,
> that said wife of yours shall outlast your span of time,
> and that in her life—your life shall fall to the plague.

This is muscular Latin,[22] a cameo of Roman *seriousness* that moulds sense to sound to modality so as to play off the difference-within-parallelism that binds a family nucleus:

between *sicut* . . . , *ita* . . . , and *ut* . . . clauses:
the son's tuom . . . tuae ~ the parents' tuam . . . tuam
and the redoubled rhymes superesse . . . sospitem et superstitem ~ ted -
testor per senectutem . . . per- . . . tu metuis ~ superstes . . . pestem op-
petas; uis . . . uitae ~ uiua uiuus.

Mighty murderous stuff, this, drawing us our "dramagram" (cashed out in the "fight to the death" finale, esp. 886, *uita uxoris annua,* 901, *periisse cupio,* 905, *uxoris mortem:* 911, *mortuus est Demaenetus,* p. 170). But this slave voice leads us on, too, through sole reference to "boy" → minimal once-over for "self" → repetition trauma for "partner" phobia:

. . . unicum gnatum tuae |

→

. . . per senectutem tuam |
perque illam, quam tu metuis, uxorem tuam |

.　.

. . . uxor . . .

.   .   .   .

. . . illa uiua uiuus . . .

The rhetoric informs *us*—those who overhear—how power in today's *domus* will triangulate. That *is* the burden of this clearly enunciated appeal for actor and (so) audience to mark these words: there should no more be collapse of distance between father and son than between husband and "that wife"—the *ma* in *ma*tron*a*. And this means: that's just what there *will* be, and the script is telling us how to align ourselves plot-wise.[23] But the *fun* of the entrée scene lies in its verbalizing of slave-master relations. In its "dialogism," *as such*.

When they strike up, (imaginary) lost ~~words~~ between the pair have preceded their audibility to us. "Enter already chinwagging" is how plays do start. The first page of a first act often just gets the players strolling to centre-stage with by-play, to focus and hush spectators. And yet, from (before) the off, proxemics strike up their silent choreography of social roles in interaction. To all appearances, this slave takes it upon himself to speak before being spoken to, to address master—owner and head of house (*senex*)—without asking permission or giving the courtesy of an appellative, and to presume to pronounce openly the presumption that master will like both the filial bonding and the marital enmity expressed. The rhetorical move in the exchange is, no doubt, a token of deference—*appealing* tô master, mobilizing *his* deference, in the name of all he cares for and against. All the same, within this carapace lurks . . . —cheek.

The anastrophe (the preposition postponed) in *med erga*, 20, shunts forward this forward slave. "The existence of such dialogues . . . embodies a kind of toleration of 'answering back,' a temporary, conventional suspension of the master's expectation of obedient silence and of his power to enforce it."[24] At the heart of the elaborated formalities, the point is aggressive confrontation that smuggles in asseveration—in the shape of oblique *death threat against master*. "Tell me no lies [Speak up, I want the truth and I want it] right now [or else—]." What a nerve![25]

This must be one *scared* slave. If master doesn't blow his top, the pair of them must be on close terms. (Is this a round in the family wars about to begin? "Have *they* been here before?") Master plumps for the reading "pomposity = anxiety." He takes the pushy pressure on the chin, and encourages slave to spit it out (23–4,[26] 27–8):[27]

In God's Truth, huh? I see that I am under oath
and obliged to speak up, whatever your question.
So right now. What is it you are seeking to know,
speak up. So far as *I* know, I'll make it so *you* know.

The routine repeats, in fewer words, so greater urgency; adding in the
comic cue "this is no laughing matter" (29–30):

I beg, lordy, don't mock, but answer my question.
Watch it, no lying to me.
                         Why don't you ask your question?

Later on we shall have an action replay, seen and told the way the slave sees
and says it, when he fills in his assistant agent (alone together to plot) and
wakes us up (all together to overhear the(m) plot: 362–4):

See, today the old boy took me off to one side, away from home.
He threatened me and you: we are both going to be over-elmed.[28]
if there aren't twenty minae of cash for Argyrippus by today.

This is *not* at all what master told him.[29] But it *is* what master *did* to him.

He'd thought he was for it. Frog-marched to the place too phobic to
name—the workhouse (= the mill).[30] When master good-as-fills in the
blank, slave makes him take the dreaded words he spat out and "spit
them *away*—hawking up, right from deep down the throat, all the way
to death—." "Watch out for trouble, ok"—"Oh no, not yours. Your wife's."
"My reward for that is you'll have no cut in the fear" (38–44).[31] The slave
takes us somewhere else, filling any space left by the vacant plot, so that we
can taste the script. Verse and worse, it's a nasty bit of work to get rid of
repressions on, an excuse for bad manners in public, offensive body noise.
A horror show played for laughs: yukkh!

This was the wind-up to that heralding of the missing plot, where cliché-
busting pater tells that he already knows all about son, slave agents, and
her next door (52–4, 57). A pair of founding formulae for the play introduce the revelation. Argu(ment)ably, they both tune us in to *Asinaria*:

(1) YOU WISH. It's time for slave to be at master's service. His reaction
is to hope master's "wishes all come true" (*di tibi dent quaecumque op-*

tes, 45: pp. **164–5**). The rest of the scene unfolds master's will: to buy son's love, make a killing from the family's own resources. No anger, coercion, or threats. Rather, slave pushes his luck—even buttonholing master *by name*—to extract that lifeline in case of a scrape (104–7):

LIB	Whaddya say, Demaenetus?
DEM	What do you want?
LIB	If I happen to get in a trap,
	will you buy me out, if the enemy cut me off?
DEM	Yes, I'll buy you out.

This move contrives to name Demaenetus for the *only* time in the first act. The handle will be bandied around by his two agents and the "courier" (344, 349, 354, 382, 392, 452, 479, 488, 580), and appear in both Argyrippus' filiation (522) and when dad is pronounced dad meat upon his exposure (911). We shall have to wait till the play is over before we can *know* why he got stuck with it. By then, we shall have decided what Father wished himself, and how *we* wish to relate to that (pp. **214–15**).

Meanwhile, now that slave is master's agent, he gets cocky, and comical: nothing and no one to fear, no harm can come: for master has made a clean breast of it in making his plea (111–13). Minds, and morales, have met, for master "promised" a safety-net (*promitto tibi*, 97), and can himself now rest easy, knowing this slave never breaks a "promise" (*quod promiserit*, 122).[32] But will bankrolling son for his jellyroll bring master his heart's desire? Why then, in cementing solidarity with (less-than-) alarming master, did the two of them trade so heavily on their shared hostility towards wife-and-mistress? (16–22; 43–4; esp. 60–3, *uerum meam uxorem, Libane, nescis qualis sit? . . . ;*[33] 78–9; 85–7; 95–7; = *hostes,* 105–6) Solidarity generated by this unanimity in wishing amounts to a bid to fold spectators into the drama. *Asinaria* drums up well-wishers with its . . . maleviolence (p. **213**).

(2) JUST ASKING FOR IT. It took *ages,* not "no time at all," to get slave's muffled question out of him: "Where are you taking me—not *there?*" Then we skip the real questioning, from master: "What's afoot, why didn't you tell me?" Instead, we face a trio of (suspended) rhetorical questions: "Why *ask* you, why *menace* you, why *get cross* with son?" (47–9, *suscenseam*).[34] This novelty puts a question mark in slave's mind: "Now I *am* fazed. What's this? Going where? . . . I *am in the fear.*" (50–1, *in metu* | ~ 44, *in metu* |) Quiz-

zical and farcical stuff, but also an undercurrent of ~~menace~~ runs through
the exchange, however roundly in denial.

It must be a brute assumption that even to *mention* "grilling, threatening, getting cross" should be enough to put the fear into a slave and a slave
"in the fear." Could a master's assurance reassure a slave? He came in scared
and imploring good faith. It must be a brave assumption that so far he has
gone along with master, and *his* assurance has reassured *him*. But master
could be fetching him to that (unmentionable) hard place between a rock
and another rock (31).[35] As the gloss he will give agent Two makes explicit,
when the plot thickens, the flak could see them "over-elm-ed" if they take
on the duchess and fall foul of her, or her hard-man agent (p. **222 n.28**).
Anyhow, own up: a master could always change tack. Just like *that*.

Comedy plays incorrigibly on this cruel edge: the promise of violence in,
and on, the air. Thus for master to order slave agent to "strip a nude," is for
him to order slave agent to "fly without wings" and "fish the sky, hunt mid
ocean with nets" (92–3, 99–100): he *could* be about to come out with something as dangerously impossible as "stealing a robe from the Mrs." (884,
929–30, 939).[36] Coming after *maximas nugas agis* (91, "You're talking utter
nonsense"), it is *also* to "order slave to strip [master] nude [sc. for scourging . . . ?]," and *that* constitutes cheek-and-a-half. "Plautus is careful finally
to let us *off the hook*, to defuse the *threat* of too much reality. But he never
quite lets us forget . . . that the true *stakes* of the comic conflict are different from that they appear."[37] No wonder that "imploring" unobtrusively
threads (fear) insistently through the script: *obsecro*, at 29, 39, 411, 431, 473,
608, 672, 688, 740, 851, 926; note the asyndeton *supplicabo, exobsecrabo*,
etc., 246 (the latter a ἅπαξ ["hapax," i.e., nowhere else, in extant Latin]).

Meantime, in our other home from home, next door, cash rules: between
madam and customers. On the other hand, here is a mother working a
daughter. *Couldn't* money and respect align this mother and child? Whore
and her "special" client will protest this, in the name of love (or "love"?).[38]
Does respectability through the wall *earn* any more respect? *Shouldn't* matrona align money and respect in her dealings with *her* family—her child
and husband (her men)? Whatever, father should control his family with
money and respect: but denied one, he jettisons the other (and plays the
lad). His subordinates keep faith with him, but this unmoneyed alliance

runs wild, heading straight for comic disgrace. Homing in, so everyone can get their kicks. Next up, madam will open up *her* world (chapter 2). Scenes alternate, so that (shorter) sketches centred on the bordello (chapters 2, 4, 6) will frame the antics in the family plot, until the gap closes for the finale (chapter 7). That is the play's design (chapter 8).

> Notional leveling keeps appearing on display in dis play.
> Between disempowered powerful and empowered power-
> less. In one portmanteau word-and-a-half from Plautus:
> *argumentum.*

❧ 2 ❦

Drive a Hard Bargain

127–152 Loverboy's lament
153–248 Loverboy spars with Madame: a deal is cut

The comic stage yokes together society's house of decency and society's red house. As paterfamilias takes the part of his loving son, they bid for a stake in the turn-over of the one-girl "brothel" through the party wall. Uptown and downtown interpenetrate and threaten a merger. Assets for sharing. It will be left to *matrona* to reassert the difference. But it will be left to the audience to make a final assessment.[1]

Money rules *both* outfits. What of desire? Comedy tests the world that insists on coupling carnal pleasure with civic degradation, when it fills the reservoir of energy that drives the strategies of masking, repression, and sublimation on which the family is founded. When conjugality buckles, its need for desire, affection, and affirmation is (traditionally) exposed through alignment with the sex factory. So long as the product supplies disposable toys for absorbing adolescent testosterone at the city limits, it provides the community with its other *system*—the object lesson in othering, denial, and obliviation. Taking to heart the existence of sentiment, caring, and generosity in the exploitation economy of sexual ownership of expendable females will spell taking to task the home of propriety for failure to monopolize human values. Defamiliarize the *domus,* and there shows up the money-go-round of a *sexless* (de-pleasured) powerhouse.[2]

It will dawn on us. That's why today's cash-plot heist of "self-swindling" gets under way as morning comes up. Master fetched out slave for kickstart. Then it's off(-stage) we go, to the mall (the forum: pp. **183–4**):

- to kill time (= master at the bank: argen*tarium* |, 116, and, last word in the act, argen*tarium* |, 126: in this redoubled echo, hear the "Starting-

Point of the Plot" [= *Archi-bulus*, in Plautin, 115, *consilia+exordiar*] that images "Cash-as-Ass": a*s*inari*a*m)
- to magic up the embezzlement (= agent One, off to . . . snooze a while. We can relax, too—and let the playwright fool us: pp. 143-4)
- to stumble into the miracle of a Courier, fresh in town, who fetches along, to *mother's* agent, just the sum required (= agent Two, in earshot at the barber's: to all appearances, slave stubble sat cheek by jowl beside free, and no fuss showing: p. 148)

Mean time. Out on his ear, a youth is turfed in a heap onto the street, now last night is done and dusted, as per payment rendered; rooms are cleared, as ever, come each morning. We can only assume that this is the problem child whose confessions we just overheard at one remove. Before he is gone, some of us *may* have our doubts about this:[3] we can have this salty specimen come across as less wet than "the average comic adulescens"—more self-reliant, if the worse for wear.[4]

Later it will transpire that he was a sassy alter ego, a boy who is now sucked dry but has no oddball pal of a pater to turn to, and squeeze for a sub. I relegate documentation of this (formerly the chief) critical crux of *Asinaria* to a whopping footnote or two[5] because I am sure that Plautus does fool with his audience here: it's no great feat to trick spectators in this theatre, in fact it's a built-in option, because (say it loud), *in the absence of names, a mask for a part such as the* adulescens amator *specifies the role, not the individual.*[6]

"Diabolus" will first be given his comic theatre *name* at 634, by when he is opposed to the Son, as his Rival (cf. 751, 913); Madame Cleäreta is *only* named at 751, in Diabolus' still-drying contract.[7] Thus the "[Diabolus]-[Cleareta]" scene is nameless, while its successor, the "[Cleareta]-Philaenium" scene, will name and shame the play's "young lovers":

- "Argyrippus son of Demaenetus," picked on and picked out formally as the john who is (not) special (522, cf. 542); first named at 74 (p. 161).
- "Philaenium," already flagged up as *meretrix* at 53. She will be named some more when the agents takes their chance to paw her (585, 623, 647, 680), when written into the contract so only Diabolus can paw her (753),

and when Demaenetus takes his chance to throw for luck, with his paws on her (905). Named, that is, for "Scripted Loving-and-Kissing" (Φιλέ-matic αἶνος: p. 189).

An obtrusive Roman touch in the scene even draws attention to this anonymity, where the hate-song revvs. up with imaginary threats to take madam and daughter to imaginary "triumviral" court, and turn 'em in—"naming names" (131–2): *ibo ego ad tresuiros uostraque ibi* nomina | *faxo erunt.*[8]

Now, when an irate lover's fume follows an irenic father longing to be in those beginner's shoes once again, this sets up the prospect of bouleverse-ment within the "masculinity" roles: *senex/adulescens* and/or/= *pater/fi-lius.* Soon we'll see.

Right away, sparks fly. Jack the lad starts up a hate-song, bending our ears as in arias throughout Plautus' oeuvre, but this one subsides after just a dozen astringent lines,[9] and to our astonishment, in recollection, this snatch will prove to have been the script's solitary lyric (in cretic tetram-eters: pp. 119–20, 183).[10] The monologue then settles down a bit, but still keeps up the uproar, painting a plaintive picture of the establishment be-fore success in bringing out madam. She will trade aspersions, lay down her law, and bargain over future pricing. The play is going to look toward dinnertime, toward din-time. Tonight, a family meal and a sex party, in here. Hee-haw. Here is where *Asinaria* bares teeth, first to last.

The sap is collared, his credit has run out. Cloth ears thinks he can turn back their clock—his custom raised this firm from "filthy rags and crusts" (punsome *sordido . . . pane in pannis,* 142). It's not the hooker's fault, it's the brothel-keeper's (147):

> She does what you tell her—obeys your command. You're mother, you're
> own-her.

The threats, the insults, fetch mother out "at length"[11] to teach how like, how unlike, her gaffe is to next-door's version of matriarchy. Insults run off her duck's back: hear her out. Have her say. She doesn't mind saying; it's part of her job—P.R. *She* is the independent woman, her own boss. Repu-tation? When you got nothin', you got nothin' to lose. Each syllable clinks a donation (153–5: a blazon of spondaic verse without resolution):

Never a one of your words, not for dosh in gold sovereigns,
can a buyer unload from me here, should one appear on the scene.
The verbals you wrong us with are twenty-four carat gold, pure cash.

This is the point. Provoke mama to stand up for free trade, fair trade. Capital on the nail, in currency named for ex-world-beating Macedonian royalty, named Φιλίππειοι for élite "equestrianism" (p. **236 n.12**). You want, so buy. Insults register here as bids. "Boycott" and "sanction" spell bluster and suction. Terms and conditions are, business as usual, that the highest offer gets exclusive hire—until credit expires (165–6):

Take her home solo, if you'll forever *pay* solo, on demand.
Your promise, this, forever. Just one condition: long's you pay top whack.

Market forces apply—supply matches demand (172):[12]

Par for par payment. This is equity rendered: service for fee.

The law of electric lady land. The role of madame: Κλέ-αρετή ("Our Hero-Simply the Best of her Kind"). She is her function, her duty, *her* version of mother's pride (*officium meum*, 173).[13]

The duet and duel of Madam and Client already give each other as good as they get, *verbally* speaking (158–70):

in portum ~ portitorem . . . portorio
solus solitudine . . . solus si ductem . . . numquam ~ solus . . . si semper so-
    lus . . . semper quae poscam dabis ~ datis ~ dandi . . . quod poscas
numquam . . . expleri potes ~ numquamne expleri potes
remisisti . . . remittam.

Perhaps this *adulescens'* adoption of maritime imagery for his shanty of a tirade itself serves to inflect him as something of a "generic" mannikin for the role—left pretty well where Plautus found him, in Athens-upon-sea (134–5)? The ocean notion is taken up by madam (157–8), after the outcast crystallized the house of sin as some "haven—with harbour-duties to pay the harbour-mistress" (*in portum ~ portitorem priuabo portitorio ~ porti-*

torum simillimae sunt ianuae lenoniae, 158 ~ 159 ~ 241). Both customer and retailer know how to talk their talk, as one talks disillusion and the other talks enterprise (see below). What price "love" . . . ?

Roll up, then, boys. The shop is open, it's today already. The haggling starts high: "you want her for free? You can('t) have her for free" (193–4):

> If one-twenty minae are paid me, cash, counted out in my hand,
> then, out of esteem, I shall grant you . . . tonight . . . free . . . for a
>   bonus.

Now let's get real: madam is the financial world's expert witness, closest Comedy can come to the mall. She has "eyes," not in the back of the head, but "in her hands," "credit" is a matter of "trust," and so the proverb ran, "One witness with eyes is worth ten with ears."[14] Roman business ran on *fides,* and so did Roman life:

> The Old Man is on oath from the start, his first words invoked *Dius Fidius*
>   (23: pp. 131–2).[15]
> Madam disdains *Graeca fides* (199: p. 127).
> What if *fides* is withheld from the one trusted by master? (458; cf. 583)
> His faithful slaves exult in their "perfidy" to others, licensed or not: *Per-*
>   *fidiae,* 545, *confidentia,* 547, *fidentem, infidelis,* 561, *infidelis,* 568, *fidelis,*
>   573; cf. 584, 586, 608, 611, 614, 617, 621, 667 (*bis*), 676, 772).[16]

More. In the course of these recriminations between madam and ex-client, the play is focusing in on the terminology of "give and take": *do* → *accipio* → *ducto* = *amo* (164–72: focused by the redoubled pun between *mo-dus* and *modo,* 167, 169 ~ 168, 170).[17] Haggling over sex is *Asinaria*'s game. Haggling over money, then; haggling over power. In Madam's world, you want bread—buy it from the baker's; pay for wine at the wine-shop (200). Sex is product, everything is for sale. Dowries say wives, too, are "a sell-out" (cf. 87). Comedy plays all this as The End of Antique Rome, where the *only* credit was faith, when folk "baked and brewed" at home, and new-fangled luxury imports (such as Comedy) couldn't help a paterfamilias crack up.[18]

Take it or leave it, comes the final offer (229–31, 234–40):

BOY   . . . Say, what do you reckon fair to pay you, for her,
                for her to go with no one else this year?

Mme   For you? Twenty minae.
                Plus this condition: should someone else fetch 'em first, it's bye
                bye you.

                . . . .

BOY   I have funds to pay what you demand. And I'll pay, but on my
                terms.
                So you're aware: (1) she's to be my slave the whole livelong year
                through.
                (2) she'll, in the time stipulated, let no man near her but me.

Mme   Why, if you like, the slaves I have at home, I shall go and neuter,
                the men.
                For clincher, see you fetch a contract, tell us the way you like us.
                As you like it, what turns you on: load me up with conditions.
                Only—just fetch the cash along with you: I'll stand the rest,
                easy.

Fair's fair: can't say fairer than that. Like many other comedies, *Asinaria*
says it is very much concerned with "fairness" (*aequum*): when son comes
to father (82); client vis-à-vis madam (176, 186, 229); weights and measures
(303); on manners (354); son to father (837); teaching son evil (932). Here
fairness is talking: "Wanted, 20 minae," for one year's sole rights; for the
year starting tonight (230, 235 → 635, 721, 753, 848).[19] The challenge is on
for the young executive: to cadge, beg, or borrow the readies. "With interest," he vows, if need be (245–8). Off with him to the mall to play ear-biter.
It's getting quite crowded over there. And now the race is on. Carn(iv)al
cash-and-carry.

Now (we reckon) we have met the spectre of the spectacle. She has had
our ear (p. 208), and spoke her lines for *both* the play's mothers. If her
neighbour could see herself in her mirror-figure, she would know herself
loathed (= if her counterpart could say how she saw ruling her roost, could
she make herself loved?). As for her client, this trainee for Sex in the City
speaks for *both* the play's boys. This one's eyes are open; his counterpart's

are still full of moonshine. (*He* will despair of lasting till nightfall: 630.)
The mall we are not to see is one end of the deal—but the sharp end is
here, on stage: chapter 3.

Home is where the mart is.
Where money can't buy respect.

❧ 3 ❦

Funny Money

249–266 Slave One's wake-up call
267–380 Slave Two's . . . brainwave
381–406 The Courier arrives
407–503 The con's too convincing: Saurea's world

The slave agent pair split and share the role as counterpart doublets (cf. *alter noster*, 58). One promised to help father help son, but has so far only napped, asleep off-stage and now back on. Time to assess the potential of his part in the script.[1] He must save us from more excruciation by that horrid bully, Madam. So long as he's with us, so long villain, we have a hero. Plautus knows how to get us on *his* side: foment sedition in the stalls, then swoop. Time, too, to . . . lose the plot, *and* dear Libanus' part in it.[2] A second time, this play's over before it's begun. Like master like agent—only the nice guy is fall guy twice in a row.

One has snored through his big moment, snoozed it away;[3] early bird Two has already happened on a chance of funds to divert, and high-tails it home to share the wheeze, with his mates, young master or astute Agent One (270–1):

Seein' its on a par they drink with me, go whorin' on a par
now I've got this prize I shall share it with 'em on a par In part.

Between the two sllaves, him-'n'-me, "as one," they'll llay an almighty favour on their masters—father-'n'-son (*suis eris ille una mecum pariet, gnatoque et patri*, 283; *in commune*, 286).[4] Just as tight as tight'll make it, this is the *L-'n'-L-* team, of Λίβανος and Λεωνίδας, "Frank Incense" and "Leo Lionheart." To clinch *their* deal, they need to defraud master without defrauding master, as promised. That is, they need to defraud mater. They

143

will do that by defrauding *her* agent. They have already done this by splitting and doubling *between themselves, pinching Saurea the Lizard's role.*

The Steward will take no part, tread no boards. They do it for him. He stands in for his mistress, in the "male" world of money, the market, the mall, the household economy. But they now understudy him. He's only a jumped-up (= "upstart") slave: he's not beyond their reach, he *looks* no different, can be impersonated *without so much as a change of costume.*

One and Two combine roles, to come between the management and its purse-strings. They intervene between master and mistress. Her agent blocks master from the accruing and outgoing capital: now master's go-between agent is in one stroke of invention handed both the prospect of incoming capital as required to subvent the required expenditure, and the subsidiary agent who will allow him to play his own role of agent of subversion. (No time to lose, for it's already bath-time, for the stranger ashore who is soon to appear in our midst, 357).

So master's slaves "formally" supplant mistress's agent by literally taking over his role. One will defraud, not master, but mistress, by defrauding her agent. And his assistant *Two will be instrumental* in this. He will act getting his hands on arriving moneys; but then, the plan goes, allow *himself* to be "defrauded" by One, to divert the loot- needed to fund joint spillage by those strange bedfellow buddies, old-and-young master. But Two has already relieved One of his role as principal agent entrusted by pater with the job of dreaming up a wheeze: for Two has, without a second's or a second thought, already posed as agent Lizard, when he had chanced to meet Courier in the barber's chair (343–57). There: more plot hi-jacked, play missed, and comedy suppressed. Typical, of comedy.[5]

In walks loadsamoneybags. But this close-shaven washed-up Courier is cagey with his assignment. He will not be imposed on by any intermediary, so it will be a close-run thing. Neither master's agent, nor mistress's—real thing or impostor. His 20 minae wad is earmarked for master in person or not at all, since a stranger may as well be a wolf. These will be his *terms and conditions.* Both the con artists know the significance of the sum, and that there is no time to lose (364). So, then, "Why not just take him straightway to Demaenetus and be done with it?" is no rhetorical question (p. 151).[6] I'm game: because they know pater is *there,* but madam's doors are *here,* not in the mall, and a Diabolical client will arrive any moment waving a cheque (pp. 141–2). Because . . . —but this isn't what the shenanigans are *about.*[7]

They are about *haggling* (p. 140). For more is delivered than metatheatrics when "the trader expressly states that, *had Saurea been there, he would have handed over the money.*"[8] There's more than a slip "twixt delivery and receipt," just as there is here between paraphrase and text (396):

> argenti uiginti minas, si adesset, accepisset.

It's worthwhile to take stock, the way a real Stewart the Steward would (20 minae in it for someone). See it from Courier's viewpoint. He has corroboration between the barber-shop chance encounter and the slave's confirmation of the address. Plus the check between the slave's (leonine) physical description of the *atriensis,* the guy getting a trim, and his appearance at the rendezvous. Before his very eyes/ears he will get a thorough and thoroughly convincing, circumstantial, sample of accountancy from the accountant's account, plus the offer of a promissory signature of receipt. What more could a paranoid postman possibly want? Well, for instance, should *accipere* depend on "reception" in the house, formal admission through the hallway, from *atrium* to the bursary, *tablinum*?

The staff might not be able to wheel out master to meet and greet *mercator* in person, however far he's sailed, however politely he may have shaved and scrubbed; but with a bonanza like "20 minae," any securicorps worth their salt should expect to be taken in, and "made at home." With all those $$$/£££/€€€ on his person, he *can't* be too careful. The Roman public all knew perfectly well the sanctity of *hospitium,* in the pleasure of business as in the pleasure business. Plautus' public watches the terms and conditions for entry to two houses: (A) says "Come with money or don't come in"; and (B) retorts "Don't let them in, and you don't get their money" (p. 232 n.19). This is why One just made such a big noise out of answering the front door . . . before the bell could be rung. To stress exclusion, non-admission, at the threshold (382–91). On any account, "give and take" is more than straightforward handover, physical transfer (p. 140). There is a general pledge involved, to honour the system, and everyone's place in it. Even the slaves' conspiracy must play securely within the system. Safe delivery models for the insecurity in all this Security: money's never safe *enough* (no one's ever safe from money).

Rest assured, the play is neither cutting loose nor breaking its spine when, after many a grin, we suddenly learn that master will take mat-

ters into his own hands now he has these on the swag (735–6: pp. **161–2**).
In turning over and round every which way the fit between money and
power, the slaves will have blazed *our* trail to their owners' contest in
ownership.

They will also have brought us the "fun" we were promised. The inven-
tive jockeying between unbuttoned master and his old hand played emol-
lient diplomacy. By contrast, the verbal joust "Madam vs Diabolus" was
typecast abuse, crowing rhetoric (*oratio,* 204), then businesslike negotiation; "Madam vs daughter Philaenium" will be one-sided debate (*oratio,*
516: pp. **175–6**), bullying met by dumb resistance; and "Diabolus and Pal"
will play canny legislators ironing out loopholes, then insulted losers
turned whistle-blowers. In the finale, "Pal and Matron" join "Pater, son,
and their Philaenium," and verbal interaction disintegrates as the cast fly
their several ways. But the lion's share of the script, *all* the donkey work, is
assigned to the two agents from L-.

- First they fail to unload the courier (249–503).[9]
- Next they'll manage to overload the lovers (545–745: p. **163**, chapter 9).[10]

Playacting Plautin: here's how to whoop it up.
This is where mice play—slave agents, children, and that glorified runner, the Courier (another species of messenger, cash on express delivery: a
free version of The Slave in a 'Urry). One unrolls the ball (256–7):

> Serfguard master. Don't you do the same as other slaves normally do
> —applying talented brains to set up a swindle on master.

The omens indicate "elms" and "rods," inseparable from "sharing advice
and implementing a plan" (262, 264; 261). Enter Two, at full speed. He
brings swag (*talk* of swag, that is, *as if* in the bag), and . . . a pun (that will
fasten up the play: 849+850, p. **169**). If they catch the wave, they can make
sure that both big and little master are under their sway (285–6):

LEO   nostro de*uincti* beneficio.
LIB   "*uinctos*" nescioquos ait:
           non placet, metuo . . .

                    ~

LEO   bound fast by our good turn.

LIB   "Bound" he's calling some people
                                                    or other:
                    I disapprove. I'm afraid. . . .

Two would "pay off his own back 200-lashes worth of [swollen contusion,
so "pregnant"] bump,"[11] to meet One—he "carries his whole hoard on his
back" (*de tergo; in tergo:* "back/hide": 276–7). Agents One, Two make a
two-man army: so their greetings are a "verbal raid" (*uerbiuelitatio,* 307.
Of "whip, prison, chains, rods").[12] "You—bound (*uinctus,* 301), stripped,
weighted, strung up by the feet, handcuffed.". . . "Executioners" bonanza,
torture, itchy shoulder-blades. . ." (297–316: cf. p. **162**).[13] Two talks tough,
and One "has his own household . . . —back, too" (—*tergum,* 319 = a *para
prosdokian* [out of left field] "ouch"; cf. 321, *tergo*):

> Look, if a back must clear the bill, I'm game, rob the National Bank.

Toughing it out, enduring, lasting, suffering: paying for your kicks the hard
way. Set for the theme tune of obdurate *Asinaria* ((*ob-)durare:* 176 ~ 196;
322, *obdurabo, periurabo;* 573, 907). It is hammered home by the pun at 324
(itself offset and set off by the paronomasia [clanguage] between 323 and
324: . . . *fert fortiter.* | *fortiter . . .*):

> fortiter malum qui *patitur,* idem post *potitur* bonum.
>
> ~
>
> "Bravely endure bad," the sayin' would run, "ensure good thereafter."

In the play's strategy, brute slave "suffering" is the well of the(ir) humour
(*patior:* 240, 324, 375 *bis,* 378, 535, 738, 739, 810, 832, 845, 847, 907). Two
is going to put One through it, and tells him so, in no uncertain terms,
in order to carry off his impersonation of mistress's agent Lizard and con
Courier. So One is not "to get cross" if he gets thrashed, but "suffer, suffer, suffer" (372; *patitor . . . patitor,* 375, *patiere,* 378). He must "promise,"
and does (*promitto,* 377). Showing how to take it, suffer in silence however
little you like it, is the recipe for their second great scene, in which the
bitten bite back, as they work their victim and beneficiary into the ground
(p. **163**, chapter 9). This tailpiece is where the farce kicks in, for forcible
proxemic abuse all the way (esp. 373, *attingas:* pp. **237–8 n.29**).[14]
    So, re-enter Two *as Lizard,* with "a beating or two for *anyone* who meets

him in a stew," as One warns Courier (*uapulabit . . . | si med . . . tetigerit, uapulabit,* 404, 406).[15] Two has lots to live up to, if he's to live up to Lizard: One invents one bastard of a nonce-word in *Aeacidinus,* as he mock-glamorizes this comic "wrath": a match for Achilles' (grandson of Aeacus), through allusion to the first mad word of Homer's Iliad, Μῆνιν). These words do what they say, "filling up" ears with thundering "bad temper": *Aeacidinis minis animisque expletus . . . iratus . . . iratus* (405–6: *iracundia,* 451, *nimis iracunde,* 470, *irasci,* 472).[16] Stew?—We're promised an epic tantrum.

The opening complaint got us straight into the jumped-up accountant Saurea's world. Let's go there. Leonida *all but* tells us *he* was a client in the barbers' chair (343, *in tonstrina ut sedebam*). But it must be part of the odium attaching to *Saurea* that he would order Libanus to *attend* him at the barber's (408)—he *would.*[17] One, "Lizard" lies, failed to turn up at the barber's as per "orders": "bad look-out for back/hide and legs" (408–9, *tergo et cruribus:* 410; *imperiosus,* 416, *imperium*):

MERC>LIB	It's Commander O.T.T.
LIB>MERC	Ow, damn me. . . .
. . . .	
STEW>LIB	You whipping boy. Scoffed at my command, did you?

"A beating. If I'd got a whip . . ., blows for those hips of yours" (417–19, *uerbero . . . uerberare*). Here is the power of Mistress, the corporal version of Madam's verbal violence (cf. *imperem,* 422, 431):

Pow, you got it coming.

What a pain, the real pain of a pretend assault. One thick ear. Next, designed to impress courier into taking a "promissory receipt" for delivery of the stash (*repromittam,* 454), the mock-accountant runs a menacing audit, *ad nauseam,* of the latest transactions in the household budget. It needs "weighing up" and "counting out" (*pendo,* 460, *pro dictis . . . pendentur,* 483; *denumerare,* 453, *enumerari,* 498, *adnumerauit et credidit,* 501: p. 150).

The grosser it gets, the better the take-off? Lizard's first strategy was to impress Courier by intimidation of One: would it rub off on him, and *he* submit, and obey orders recounted at one remove, now enforced in his presence? Would *he* "rate Steward's word as worth all too little"? (*nemi-*

nem meum dictum magni facere, 407)[18] His *manner* is compulsive repetition, counting out the insult of disobedience in triplicate (*ut iusseram,* 408 + *iussi,* 410 + *ut iusseram,* 413 = *imperium meum contempsisti,* 416). His *complaint* is exactly this: he must "bark every command, not one thing once, but the same things one hundred times over" and, far from ever coming out ahead, he can't even "keep up with the work" (421–3). This is as "never-ending" as the drudgery that is never done (*semper,* 420 ~ *nihil est,* 427).

- Over and over and over, he lowers himself (| *iussin . . . ,* | *iussin . . . ,* | *iussin . . .*), to attend to each sordid detail: "shit, webs, studs" (424–6).
- The dedicated manager identifies with his noble pile: "gate, columns, doors" (424–6).
- He knows the chores of maintenance work as the grind of surveillance: "fetching and carrying away, knocking down from up high, elbow-grease polishing to a shine" (424–6).

Yes, this fun-ctionary *thinks* in threes, "just these 1-2-3 days past, I've assigned full time to the mall" (428). So how can he be in two places at once? How can he make money work double time out at loan for interest, and keep the home front at it (or, even, awake)? (429–30).

This is righteous wrath from the servant true, all that stands between master and a "pig-sty" (430). *This* is what raises his voice and his hand against the slacker (430–1: do*rmi*ti*s inte*re*a* domi, e*rus in* hara, haud ae-dibu*s* habi*tat*—*tinnitus,* Courier will call it, 448).[19] *This* conscientious rat knows those dirty mice "sleep" when *he* is away (as One bragged to us at 253: p. 190).[20]

The teamwork that follows is the *truly* offensive offensive. At any rate, it will be this that will make Courier move to leave, One to call a halt, and Two at last to acknowledge Courier's presence (446–51).[21] To induce Courier to join in, "Steward" plays deaf to the stranger, rudely weighing into his busybody routine of checking the latest in the household finances *in mid-verse* (432). This lion-tamer of a chartered accountant conjures up a heaving swirl of money going out, and money coming in. That is (louder): *money coming in,* get it? We fantasize a regulated hive with a ghostly cast of characters, four in a dozen lines (and one kept for later: p. 152). They tell us what a Saurea adds up to; at the same time, they sneak past us an impressionistic sketch of the whole episode, and of the play at large (432–45):

Olive, shipment. Quid pro quo. We meet first "Le Compte," *Stichus,* Steward's favourite, named for every orderly "row" of figures in the ledger. He would be Lizard's pet—his pet creation, the slaves insinuate. The version of himself that permits Lizard to put on airs and play at being Master to a Steward of his own: his trusted minion, and "deputy" self (*uicarius,* 433). The middle man safely "clears the bill, payment made," just the way Lizard should be doing, if you catch the drift, Courier (*rem soluit? :: soluit,* 433 ~ *solutam rem futuram,* 454; *datum,* 433, *dedero,* 439, *dedi,* 444 ~ *da,* 457, *duit,* 460, *daturum,* 466, *da,* 473, *dare,* 488). Two understands that Steward *would* see through the flattery, join in rather than object to the satirized self-praise, and still not give an inch or soften a second (434–5). *He* is already moving on to the next item. *We* are still taking in the other track—of Leonida's covert self-exposure! For *this* Saurea does know *this* deputy, stand-in for Saurea. *Extremely* well. "And," he can say with feeling and no need to act, "no there ain't a slave in master's house that's worth more than" this one "is" (435). Trust the slave: he's playing his part to the fool.

Sale of wine, payment. Quid pro quo. For Le Compte to receive, *item.* Another successful transaction. Yesterday's: coming close to here, now, *today.* This time, the cash-delivery is perfect: The customer—"Extraordinaire," *Exaerambus*—actually fetched his banker along.[22] Where he once took a year to repay credit, now he's so keen, he comes round to write a cheque on the spot (438–40). He comes round *here,* to *this* spot. Fetches the cash "home." Get it, Courier? This is how to satisfy a Lizard's aspirations (*sati^s fecit . . . fecisse satis. . . . sat agit,* 437, 440 ~ *facturum sati^s pro iniuria,* 497). To get into his good books, cough up: "credit" his "credit" (*credidi,* 439 ~ *credit,* 459, *crederes,* 462 (with Courier's punning retort, 463), *credi,* 493, *credam,* 494, *credidit,* 501, *crederes,* 503).

Payment for worksheet; unspecified. Sub-contractor "Le Coureur," *Dromo,* is half accounted for; the rest to follow. He has fetched and handed over cash; he will complete the hand-over. Get the idea, Courier, half way there yourself: "what about the balance, then?" (*reddere . . . redditum,* 441–2 ~ *reddam . . . reddam,* 455–6). Consider that *Dromo* names a(nother) "Slave in a 'Urry," his inventor's dummy of a "Runner."[23] As Steward, though, Two knows he'd be half-way toward saying "Runaway," in Lizard's sorea head— and so, still worse, a likely "Defaulter" (as Courier will threaten, 446; and "Steward" will bluff, 469, 488).[24]

Party goblets, out on loan. To be returned. The fantasy ends with a total fail-ure to collect, after two ticks and one half-and-half entry (pending). Ends with a *Roman* loan—no interest, this is what friends are for, caring by shar-ing (p. 143). What a Lizard can't abide, and that is what "we" cannot abide about *him* (445). Ends with a drinks party, not yet, or ever, over; broken up, when the hire arrangements collapse. Like Demaenetus'? That friend, and addict, of caring-sharing. A still worse thought: when "*Philo-damus* receives these goblets" in this false accountant's inventory, does the "joke" lurk that Plautus' Greek forerunner gets to guest in the Latin play, "Δημό-φιλος through the looking glass? Sickening "enough" to put Courier off the show? (446) And us? "Friendly-People," this stagey Greek (stage-?)name says—all "Crowd-Pleaser" and "Penchant-for-Vulgarity" (cf. p. 213)?

To match the opening assault on his fellow slave, a change of tack-tics turns One loose on Courier—"Disgrace to humanity! Pay him the cash, I beg, or he'll badmouth you,"—eggs him on some more: "Stun that huzzy or you're in trouble, your legs will get shattered" (473–4), before Two-as-Lizard assails him in person, slave or free no matter (478–9, 481–4, *ua-pula . . . ut uapules . . . uerbero*):

STEW>MERC	Get beaten.
MERC>STEW	Lord, you got
	it coming,

your beating. The minute I clap eyes on Demaenetus today.

. . . .

Sure and it's retribution will be mine. On your back.

STEW>MERC	Goddam
	you.

Retribution will be yours, executioner? On me?

MERC>STEW	Yes, plus

the penalty for your verbal abuse will be paid me today.

STEW>MERC	You what, whipping boy? You don't say, ball-'n'-chain?

In the end, the "vitriol" cancels out (*contumelia*)—"I'm a person as much as you." "P'raps, and yet . . . a man's a wolf, not a man . . . —to a man who don't know what he's like" (490; 493–5)—and Courier clings to *his* terms and conditions: no offence, "It was Demaenetus I wanted. . . . It's Demae-netus I want." In person. In person. (392, 452, cf. 488, 495–6). Accept no sub-stitute. None (466, 494–5).

Whereas Courier began convinced, or at least prepared to go along with the idea, that this *is* Saurea (*noli, Saurea,* 417, . . . *Saurea, oro,* 431, he pleaded), he ends by squaring up to this Steward in a Stew, and flat discountenancing him (*Sauream non noui,* 464). So, if the slaves went right, in bringing their brand of slapstick to the fore, where did they go wrong? Maybe Two got into the Lizard role *too* easily. His nastiness even puts off the Courier. Why should *he* join the long line of Saurea's victims? Why would anyone help *him?*

Tiering in domestic staffing *breeds* such fiends. The downside of modern efficiency, pyramid organization. Once, before status anxiety, these old-style slaves know, "a master knew his slave, the slave knew his master," and so it *is,* for them, but *not* for master and this Steward, as they lie through their teeth (456). The cuckoo slave is a stranger in his master's own home: "a wolf" in the fold (495); the Courier isn't the only one that knows Saurea well enough only to refuse to credit him (464). On the way out, the con man tries to lay one last ghost on Courier, and sends our way one last smuggled protest against the régime such a Steward imports to, and for, Rome (499–503):

Cash deposit. Payment made to Lizard, in person. By His "Éminence," *Periphanes,* "Transparently Honest and Known to be so on All Sides."[25] "From rosy Rhodes," as loaded a *mercator* from across the water as . . . present company. Man to man, master's absence notwithstanding, Steward (he emphasises) was treated to parity, as if . . . free, as if . . . master (*solus . . . mihi . . . soli,* 500). *He* "counted out-and-credited" cash worth *sixty* minae. Yes, *three times* (× 3, check) what Courier is carrying about him. Fetch to Steward now. The trickster boasts, all too truly, "*He* wasn't conned." Now Courier won't be conned, either. And both One, Two, and we know perfectly well, how true (502–3):

> if Courier had checked out Lizard proper with other folk,
> then sure he'd credit him now.

Not by handing over the loot. But by trusting that the take-off of The World According to Saurea tells true. His victims *do* know him well: the feud has gone on "forever" (420; cf. pp. **148, 232 n.21**). They are signing off by telling us plain that the best way to "check him out" would be to ask people who know him. "Others" like . . . themselves. The fiction doesn't work; the fiction works. What *Asinaria* doesn't say, it finds a way to yell.

So would One, "The Brains," have made a worse job of acting the ruffian Steward, but a better job of unloading the Courier? This is for a director to interpret, for audiences to decide. Two even pushes the role on to the logical conclusion, of disregarding the Courier's free status. And Two did not just do One out of his role as The Brains on the team; he gave his comrade a whacking which itself helped spoil the con's chances of coming off. In this clowning, it's obviously intolerable outrage for this slave both to wish he literally had the whip hand (418), and, as he assaults master's agent, to complain that he "must carry a club with him" (427, *cum fusti*): he here appropriates the righteous-rightful "stick" attribute of a master, an elder, a paterfamilias (*scipionem,* 124). And tells us so. This "ascendancy" will turn out to be the mould for what One and Two are going to put Loverboy through. Next.

The power of money for little master meant a ticket to ride, the going rate to make a happy hooker. The same power for not-so-big master meant his opportunity to . . . bring the house down. In protest at being ousted from *his* role as pater by mater. His primal scream, we could say, his existential Angst. His point in vowing to reproduce his own father's naughtiness was to work towards blurring his part with his son's, via their agents'. He invents a role where he could escape from his conjugal "castration." Where he could resort to playing (his own) father, to mask his infantilization, by playing it through.[26] But *his* plot is in resentment of expropriation by *his* imperious matrona (and her agent); whereas his son's plot is in thrall to appropriation by that other imperious mama, via her agent's money-spinning "services."

Asinaria will not forget that its paterfamilias could neither block nor facilitate his son *because* the wife and mother could do both: she thwarts him, just as the bawd-and-mother thwarts son—and daughter. Escape into second adolescence was futile abdication from wedlock, from the start. His declaration of solidarity with the chip off the old block was a blow struck within that framing feud with his better half. And *that* was about shame, face, shamefacedness. It will take a showdown between the heads of house

to shake down their blocked relationship. Seconds out. The feud materializes in physical struggle for control of power-as-money, but this can't settle
their *marital* feud. And the children are all grown up now. . . .

Is it about him?
Him and her? Him & son?
About them? Why choose?
In *American Beauty*—

❧ 4 ❧

American Beauty

504–544 The Sex Slave holds out on Momma

The One about the Asses began with unprecedented consonance between master and slave. Then it erupted in friction between manageress and client. It flipped the switch into comradely cooperation between slaves frustrated by resistance from the outsider. A mutiny now ensues, as another worm turns, caught in the toils of money, family, necessity. This time the protest is brief, almost as short as the plot. Embracing, in equal measure, the stigma of stubborn, helpless, renegade silence.[1] Mother told daughter "no," but this Jezebel's a rebel (505, 509):

> You're not minded of parting from mother's command, are you that way?
>
> . . . .
>
> So, *this* is tending Devotion then: shrinking mother's command?

There is no cushion from *this* iron lady (*matris imperiis, matri imperium ~ imperium*, 87, p. **126**). But it goes in one ear and out the other. Her good little earner even dares put in her oar: if the whore stops sculling, "the whole of the household grinds to a halt on you," mama. Up your creek (520). No. The child's version of home economics founders in disparity (525):

> Seductive words are gold for you? Posh talk will do for fees?

Just the same as the son's problem with gift and take—the other end of the stick: "not having the fees to match the talk" (*dicta docta pro datis*, 525 ~

non suppetunt dictis data, 56). But this flash of defiance is over before . . .
it's begun: as *her* mum rubs in, she was already "barred from the one she
loves," that loverboy son, who could pay only in promises—"I'll make sure
you are rich *if mummy,* his *mummy, dies*" (*promittat,* 528–9)—and now
even the moratorium on that is up.

We already met momma: the rod won't spare *this* spoilt child (532–4):

> So, now. If he doesn't fetch me 20 minae over here, cash,
> Our Lady, he'll be shoved outa here, showering us with . . . tears. Out!
> This is the last day the "funds short" cop-out will run. Not in *my* place.

Now for Cinderella's chance to dance. Between finance and ~~fiancé~~. We
must be ready to meet her favourite, and make up our own minds about
the ?love? in this love-affair. The play winds all its agitations around Philaenium, but she is put at its disposal rather than handed her own crafted
presentation of self: the experience of this "call-girl" stays discontinu-
ous to the end, fragmented by the multiplicity of parts, as The Girl is
called on to play in the colliding plots of the rest of the cast. She must
act her way through alienated torment: forever taken for granted—mar-
keted, parcelled out, swooned over, auctioned to the highest bidder or
syndicate. We cannot begin to tell *how she feels*—when she takes on
her clutch of boys, croons Tru Luv, lets fellow slaves One and Two, and
their lordling and master, all slaver all over her, press the flesh, paw and
drawl, let alone when, for the run-in, she finally joins in the general rush
of jeers at the old fossil and tomfool (**pp. 160–1, 163, 180–2, 229 n.9**).
"How [this] She *feels*" is all she means to her clients—unless her chosen
dreamboat john (client-and-fantasy-escape from the backstreet?) means
his (ten-a-penny? vaudeville? sempiternal?) pledges of "love." Some
body, not somebody—unless our production champions her resistance
to victimage, and drools over her personhood, or respects her professional acumen.[2]

But, heck, Mother knows best: romance without finance is a nuisance.
Second time around, the "interlude" at the brothel will link up with the
family next door. Son and Daughter come out together, to meet the agents

of Father & Son. They prequel the grand finale, where Pa will join in, and the link will feature . . . Ma.

> Yes. There are the problems of $^?$love$^?$.
> A prob for the Mr and Mrs, too.
> In amongst those of power, money, and parenting.
> Exclusive terms and conditions: tonight, this year, this life
> —with me and nobody else. No one. Maybe just one?
> And if she downs tools? And he won't playball?
> Now for Argyrippus. Hi ho, $ilver.

⇒ 5 ⇐

Beating the System

545–590 We're in the money . . . *and* We're so pretty, o so pretty . . .
591–745 Lovers' last gasp lament *and* Slaves riding high: Loverboy pays his
   dues

For a second time, enter the brace of agents, in cahoots and on a roll
(p. 146). In no time at all, they are back, One plus Two. First time around
in the donkey derby, in sped Two, to share his (aural-verbal) booty (*maximam praedam et triumphum,* 269).[1] So near yet so far. This time they are
in tandem. They bring the (actual-virtual) booty. Courtesy of big master,
who played along with Two's imposture as agent Lizard. They will share
the role of "courier," conveying terms and conditions, tied to cash hand-
over. Special delivery, to little master, from that close ~~friend~~, soon coming
too close for comfort.

Let's check it out. Mother's agent, Lizard, failed to substitute for her: he
lost his mask to his understudy, the stage-money income never incame
into her coffers, and with it went missing the queen's command of the
castle. She doesn't know it, but now she is on her own, and will have to
deal in person. In person. As for son, his agents have been rustled away by
his would-be special agent of a father, pulling strings behind-the-scenes
for all he's worth. Which is to say, still operating, despite himself, as the
Demaenetus that the world knows (the one who "knows" why he carries
the "knarled" stick," of the *senex,* emblem of his authority: scio . . . *me hunc
scipionem contui,* 124).

For, come what may, the paterfamilias *must* be azygous, solo, cock of his
roost: witness the real Courier, who refused all stand-ins, no matter which
or whose, master's or mistress's. The commander is no underling domestic,
but only as *that* Self can he commandeer the wife's power. Finally on his
own, in the finale. Fresh out of agents. Outed from playing son's friend and
agent, son's rival and (anti-Oedipal) tormentor, his bid to ham a substitute

identity by usurping son's self will collapse in face-to-face confrontation by the Mrs. Before, he missed her, by streets. Then, Mr. must meet The Wife in person, and will have to deal with it. On his own, clapped out. Then only the audience can redeem Demaenetus. Ultimately, it's in your hands: showdown at sundown (p. **215**).

Old master has played his part: *his* father had dressed up as a Ship's Cap'n to pinch his son a woman from a pimp (69–70). Now that comic plot called life is doing the rounds again, another generation, another tour. "This touch gives one an odd view of life, that it is a series of comic plots strung together, so that . . . a given man will first be cast in the role of a comic son, and then in that of a comic father."[2] *Our* father has himself played along with the wheeze that his agent Two was his wife's agent, Lizard, and relieved the Courier of the 20 minae (580–4).[3] In the com-nick of time, as those aspiring tragicniks, Romeo-'n'-Julie-baby, stare curtains in the face (594):

Your mother told me the day's over. Ordered me: time I went home.[4]

Still wet behind the ears, a second regular at the motel here bites the dust; "shut right out" (*exclusust foras*, 596). The script steps aside for a liminal moment's escape from the liminal moment's doom, pumping up the farewell hug "from here to eternity" weepie highpoint of "see you in hell" melodramatics. . . . [5]

The unbearably soppy tension builds under pressure from split-stage overhearing and overheard double dialogue.[6] And that is what bursts the bubble it creates, too. With a "boom-boom" slave joke for openers—first in a lovely long line of groans (619–20):

LEO>ARG	Goo'day, master. Hey there now, is she smoke, this *femme* in your arms?
ARG>LEO	Pardon me?
LEO>ARG	Because . . .[7]

But, at the same time, the daft havering-wavering pause here actually serves to stuff *us* full of Plautine thematics (597–602):

ARG	I'll stay the night, if you like.
LIB	Get him! D'you hear how he's showering out night shifts? So now

> he's a workaholic Moses, no less, working the daytime through,
> the way he drafts conditions for the nation to keep. Cojones!
> Any persons gearing up to obey *his* conditions, for a fact,
> they *shan't* ever do right, and round the clock, day 'n' night . . .
> —*shall* get pissed.

This tosh *fait un âne,* it triggers the work of the hyped-up stage business that holds (up) the comedy.[8] You see, the agents carry the cash. They learn where little master's up to, all "'Cos I love her and she loves me, she does" (631–6, *hanc . . . haec . . . huic*):[9]

> . . . her mother has chucked loverboy out of the house here. Me.
> 20 minae of cash have driven me all the way unto death.
> The 20 the boy Diabolus today told her he'd pay her,
> so she'd send her off nowhere but to him, for the whole of this year.
> You guys see what 20 minae got going? Their strength, their power.

The slaves begin at once to imagine what they could extort from Boy Meets Girl. *She* asks for all she gets, for triggering wish-fulfillment fantasy by hoping "The gods grant your wishes" (623). The slave's strategy of rhetorical smuggling strikes again when they name that dream,[10] and then fall straight into matey back-stabbing (cf. 42–3; 624–8):

LIB>PH	*A night with you'd do me, darlin'*—a jug of plonk, if my wishes came true.
ARG>LIB	Mind, not a *beep* from you, boy to beat up on.
LIB>ARG	I'm wishing for you not me.
ARG>LIB	Then say on what you like, ad-lib.
LIB>ARG	To whop *him* here a beating, lord.
LEO>LIB	Who would ever credit it? That from *you,* you pansy with a perm.
	You? Dish out a beat-up, when taking a whopping fills your lunchbox?

This verbal spray of insubordination whips up all the fun of the unfair, as heralded at the off (*uin erum deludi?,* 646, "Fancy a laugh at master?"

~ *lepus ludusque in hac comoedia,* | *res ridicula est,* 13–14, "wit, and fun in this comedy. This one's a gas"). But as they demand slap and tickle foreplay with her, "with loverboy in attendance"—yes, *present in person* (647), and inflict degrading role reversal with him, they do more than take liberties.

If wishes were horses (then slaves would ride). In a word—*that* word (671, *imperat*):

What it takes—"needs must"—command away

For the nice slave's nasty ride-a-cock-horse now *brands* sweet little master: this is his "baptism," named Ἀργύρ-ιππος, "Cheval-Argent," as the élite youth turned from future "knight" into élite beast of burden by the necessity of carrying off the loot he crawls to win: *Argyrippus . . . argenti,* 74–5, *Argyrippo argenti,* 364, *Argyrippe . . . argentum,* 732–3. He is elsewhere named twice as Philaenium's special client (522, 542), hand-in-hand with her (753), once by Father (833), and once in the Pal's prediction (917). Unattested in Greek culture,[11] the name *Argyrippus* speaks out as loud as any *Carry On* or *Life of Brian* speaking moniker. The moment of his humiliation, his "passion," simultaneously climaxes the tease and foreshadows what sour big master is going to do to him tonight when his playboy house-party (*con-uiuium,* 834) will commandeer the bunnygirl and make her boyfriend, looking daggers, sit up and beg (841: p. **212**):[12]

ARG	Ow, just watch me smile.
DEM	*I wish my ill-wishers . . .* —would smile *that* smile.

The *fun* "fun" died after the doublet agents dropped playing dog gods—granting the boy his nirvana, "the handy 20 minae cash, so I can pay them her mother" (725; 731):

That's enough fun out of him, I propose.

Perfect timing, but here's the rub (732–6):

LIB>ARG	. . . Your father ordered us to fetch *this* cash here to you.
ARG>LIB	Great timing, spot on. You've fetched it right on the dot.

LIB>ARG	In here there'll be 20 minae, good 'uns, we did bad to get 'em.
	He told us pay you them *on fixed terms and conditions.*
ARG>LIB	What's that, please?
LIB>ARG	You pay him his fee: the night with her, plus party.

Like servants, like master. So son must sit and (with us) watch his ~~best-friend~~ father climb into his role, mess with his girl, Ms. Storyville (Φιλέ-αῖνος: p. 189), and insist on making it a threesome. Dear daddy bear's already sneaked round into the wrong house, waiting for those lucky losers / unlucky lovers to join him, and party on. Someone's going to eat someone's porridge, sit in his chair, and a crowded bed awaits. High time the agents left us. The finale will be between the big guns. My pitch, however, is that our double agents' Big Number is where *Asinaria* earns, and uses, its spurs. Accordingly, I give it the once over here—and come back for more in chapter 9.

We come in at the double. Only our twin association of agents can list their citations—"roll-call-of-honour" and "dossier of criminal records" rolled into One plus Two (*uirtutes = malefacta,* 547, 556, 558 ~ 567). These upbeat brothers sing antiphonal pride. In rebel music self-portraiture, back-slapping slave-style. You name it, "we" have been there (548–51, 557):

> Us up against whips 'n' branding-irons 'n' crosses 'n' shackles
> 'n' fetters 'n' chains 'n' cells 'n' hog-ties 'n' legirons 'n' collars.
> Plus those passionate daubers, with our back for intimate canvas,
> ?who have routinely inscribed for us scars on our shoulder blades?
>
> . . . .
>   . . . What hero braver than I, for suffering blows?

The assortment of tortures in ascending order of hysteria piles in, leaving us with "16 strongmen: 8 heavy birchers, plus 8 equipped with flexi elm birches, reduced to so many zombies by tough-guy you (*pendens aduersus . . . ualentis uirgatores,* 564–5; *uerberatus . . . , tua duritia . . . , ulmeis . . . lentis uirgis,* 569, 574–5; cf. *scapularum . . . ulmorum,* 547). But on this occasion these stubborn critters aren't here to suffer anything of the sort. Instead their assignment is to play fully endorsed "Courier(s)" and as such (we have just learned, the hard way, from them) *they* have the whip-hand. As their elelmentary jeering at the lover's "Solonian" legislation for night life insisted (597–602), they are the ones (the One-Two) who are in a position to impose *terms and conditions* of their own, and this in and through the very act of delivering the *terms and conditions* mandated to them. (Told you there's more to handing over money than handing over money: p. 145.) They will decide just how much suffering to inflict. For *this* scene, the pair of tantalized would-be recipients of the transfer will be at *their* mercy. For the moment, *some* of the power of all those paper noughts is at *their* command. And these assailants will talk the hind legs off a donkey, co-stars in "The One About The Assets."

No, master Master cannot have the money. His "agent" can. He can tell Ms mistress to ask nicely, so he must, and she must (*(ex)orare*, 662, 675 *bis*, 686, 687, 707, 740).[13] They won't let him load, they will let her implore.

Moreover, lover will pay over the cash to beloved, so he is in fact *her* agent go-between, and she is in fact his little mistress, who can deliver the fee to big mistress, as *her* agent-and-courier, as the money finds its tortuous way to its destined home, in the mock materfamilias' pocket, at her command. For this replay of the last scenario, then, the girl gets to compete with her other half. They audition for the roles of special agent One (soft-spoken *Libanus*, fragrant Frank Incense) and under-assistant agent Two (raw-tempered *Leonida*, Spartan Coeur de Lion, there starring as mock-Lizard, agent Three). And this is the comic prompt for the associative juggling of roles between our refined mentors in torture, too.

First Two forces boy down on his knees and grabs girl in his arms ("You lug me by the *lugholes*," 668, *prehende auriculis*).[14] Then One—as boy pimps gal with "Sure, there's none better than him, and no, he's not a bit like this thief" (= Two, 681: *non similem furis huius*)—takes his turn ("You must make me a crawling snake—give us a double two-forked *tongue*," 695; *uicissim*, 682).[15] Of course they are in it together, tweedling and needling the couple, "alike":[16] the question is (not), which is the courier, and which the sidekick? Who to turn to (669, 697; cf. *in partem*, 679):

| ARG>LEO | Kiss you . . . , *her,* you whipping boy? | |
| LEO>ARG | | So just how insulting did that look? |

. . . .

| ARG>LIB | Hug you, executioner? | |
| LIB>ARG | | Just how insulting do I look? |

'Dee put on his show; now 'Dum takes his thoroughbred for a ride. They are quits and we need to quit. ("Dusk" will descend upon us, soon Diabolus will spring the plot, our brevity will belie itself: *conticinno*, 685.) The satisfaction of devising *satis*-faction is a key challenge for any comic funday: the boy tried to call "Enough" (*iam sat est*, 707 ~ 446),[17] "You two've had your fun," and finally moves to stop them playing their victims off against each other by *jointly* addressing them (*quoniam, ut est libitum, nos delus*istis, 711 ~ 474: p. 151). As one, the two slaves respond by competing in hyperbole.[18] One plays the god "Salvation," so the other plays the rival attraction "Fortune In Your Favour." This is the boy's chance to regain control, and win by a neck. Pagan gods need worship and worshippers at their assizes. Pagan polytheism was neither henotheist nor monotheist, so you "*can* praise" one "deity *without* slating" a second (or at least you can tell yourself this, and try). *Both* can be "better" and "*Both* are good"—and, as always, both can prove it, by "bringing good"—and handing it over (718–9).

So the trap is sprung. Godhead is the limit case of praise. You can't blame Plautus for cashing in that running formula of blessed wishes. Gods grant prayers. Our t(w)in Santa Clauses One and Two will answer and respond "turn and turn about" (*uicissim*, 722), and that is the wish of young lovers and play lovers alike (720–2, 722–6):

LEO>ARG	**opta id quod** ut *conting*at **tibi uis.**
ARG>LEO	quid si optaro?
LEO>ARG	**eueni**et.
ARG>LEO	**opt**o annum hunc perpetuum mihi huius operas.
LEO>ARG	impetrasti.
ARG>LEO	ain uero?
LEO>ARG	certe inquam.
LIB>ARG	ad me adi uicissim atque experire.
	exo**pta id quod uis** maxime **tibi eueni**re. fiet.
ARG	quid ego aliud **exopt**em nisi illud cuius inopiast,
	uiginti argenti commodas minas, huius quas dem matri.
LIB>ARG	dabuntur, animo sis bono face, **exopt**ata *conting*ent.
	~
LEO>ARG	Wish to get what you want.
ARG>LEO	What if I do wish?
LEO>ARG	Yes, it will come true.

ARG>LEO	I wish for *her* services through this whole year round.
LEO>ARG	Look no farther.
ARG>LEO	You don't say?
LEO>ARG	I certainly do.
LIB>ARG	It's my turn. Step up and try me.
	You wish hard that what you want most of all will come true. So be it.
ARG	What else should I wish hard for? Gotta be where the dearth is complete:
	the handy 20 minae cash, so I can pay them her mother.
LIB>ARG	Yes, they *shall* be paid, be of good cheer, your hard wishes *shall* come true.

So it is that two gods are assuaged for the price of one year with one girl. Such luck! But first, there is the small print to assimilate: one night, one party, to *start* the year, with Father playing Child to the Man. At the symposium, "wit and fun" will play, "for a gas," a riot of ex-ploding naughtimess-morass-nausea-noise-nemesis-missus.

Open, sesamus.

⇒ 6 ⇐

Stick to the Script

746–809 Pal writes a contract for rival Loverboy
810–827 Loverboy's Pal will snitch to Mother on his new rival: Father

Once more in the play, someone just missed the wave, and must play catch-up. Diabolus the other (half of the) young lover (role) is too late. Ha! The play's least favourite son, this earwig you mustn't let burrow into your mind and laser the fun in you, has taken too long to write his own script, and now *Asinaria* has him beat. He brings an agent of his own, hustling to the stable-door and bustling away when the horse has already bolted.

Just when the rest of the cast thought he'd beat them to it, he missed the boat. He doesn't know how far we've come through the comedy, he's still using an intermediary when the others have used theirs up, and the gloves are off. And reading off a contract between client and callgirl makes an obvious way to *start* a comedy.[1] "Diabolus himself comes up with the next play (to tell Demaenetus' wife, line 811), but the writing must be left to the parasite (820–27)."[2] In the end, his Pal will try on another "contract," for another day and another comedy. He would like to broker another way to fix the year: a 50/50 split, a trilateral bargain (915–18: p. 170). But this isn't how they see the draft they think they are finalizing, to settle once for all (year) Who Gets the Girl. It's *meant* to wrap it up (746–7, 749–50, 802, 809):

DIAB   *All right.* Show us. The contract you've scripted, between
       me; playmate; madam. Rendition of conditions.

     ·   ·   ·   ·   ·   ·   ·   ·   ·   ·   ·

PAL   I'll see madam shudder, when she hears the conditions.
DIAB   *Action*—Lord, a transmition for me.

     ·   ·   ·   ·   ·   ·   ·   ·   ·   ·

DIAB   Lovely script from you. Real pro of a contract.

. . . .

DIAB   *Just love those conditions. Sure do.*

These smart asses, they've seen to all the ins and outs. Each and every last *i*
and *t* are dotty and cross.[3] In the line of duty, the draughtsman must mime
banned mouthwork for our benefit (794–8, *sic . . . , simulat, sic*):

> "Coughing: if she happens to start, she shall not cough, such
> that in coughing *so,* she snakes out her tongue: at no one.
> Item: suppose she does *ham up* a snot-runny cold,
> she shall not make like *this.* You shall wipe her lip clean
> rather than she openly fakes a kiss: for no one."

We'll stitch up Mme Maman, with a penalty clause banning her from
"joining in the wine" and using the rough edge of her tongue ("fine: 20 . . .
—days off the booze": 799–802). And we'll stitch up Mlle Aimée, with a
ratio (parity) of "as many filthy nights" with Diabolus "as nights she says
she wants clean" (806–7).
        No hitches (752–5):

PAL   "Mme *gets* the fee of 20 minae, cash,
                for Ms Storyville to be with him both night and day
                this year's duration —."
DIAB   "—And with no one else, either."
PAL   *Stick that in?*
DIAB   *Yes, stick it in. See your script is clean and clear.*

No glitches, either, in case she gets wise and plays the system against
itself (786–90, *ne . . . commoveat → moueri*):

DIAB   I don't want her having a prop, and saying she's barred.
PAL   I know: frightened of quibbles.

A n-n-nod's as good as a wink to a blind horse (784, *nutet, nictet, adnuat*).
No ~~quibbles~~. ~~Puns~~ verboten. ~~Tricks~~ proscribed. Etc., Etc., Etc. "The parasite
and Diabolus [are] as much the enemies of *ludus* as any agelastic *senex*. Note
that Diabolus is also afraid of the power of other poets/artists. He particularly fears writing and painting" (761–4).[4] He fears that the courtesan will

behave as a courtesan must, playing men off against each other in all the age-old ways specified in the contract: in her element, as party-girl. She fakes, just like a ~~woman~~, in the very next scene.[5]

Odd-man-out Diabolus (first *named* at 634) has sleepwalked his simple path thus far. Now he finds he is in Plautus' farce, and plenty of company. Straight back out of the brothel he bursts. Second time around. Now, though, Madame is nowhere. So—at (the) last—bring on Mrs Mum, to fill her boots. Tell on pater. Use agent—leave Pal—to finger the old man, and play *Diabolus'* advocate. For this is the baptismal moment for the dullard Rival: ὁ διαβάλλων tells us, he's "The Snitch," not the *amator*. His role was to obstruct and hinder. Now he unblocks and effects the dénouement. He *does* wind up writing the script. One second he was winding us up, then out he pops from the brothel, and in a flash *Asinaria* is done and dusted, and the Pal's agent will get the play wound up. He plays Father's nemesis on behalf of his *alter ego,* the Son, takes the revenge that the Boy won't (get to) dare for himself.

All that's needed is a knock on Mother's door. Then there'll be "trouble and strife" (824, *turbas, litis*), what boils up, here on stage, into a "battle" royal, way beyond "strife" (912, *hoc gliscit proelium,* 914, *hi dum litigant*). A Final Act (it brags) to die for: Dad's comedy goose is well and truly cooked (935).[6]

> To come together, fall apart.
> Nothing is revealed.

7

Rotten Rhetorics

828–850 Dad's party swings
851–941 Mum fetches him home

The girl's parent had expelled her "lover," then mama expelled her lover—
the trick she loves and who loves her. That good child was a good(time)
girl scolded. Now the boy's parent has bought his way inside those same
coin-operated doors, and means to impale him with the sight and sound
of him sharing a couch with the hustler he loves and who loves him.
This good child is a good lad scolded: he too must grin and bear it, some
more—love his "~~friend~~" of a father, and smile through the hours to count-
down (847–8):[1]

> You'll endure this one single day through. *Because* I've handed you power
> to be with her for a year, I've come up with cash to fund loverboy.

The son's papa-enforced *pietas* matches in detail the mama-extracted *pietas*
of Philaenium ("Devotion": 831 ~ 506, 509). Even his forced smile-through-
gritted teeth humanizes the brothel: "walls had smiles," never mind ears,
back when it was fed money (207, *tum mi aedes quoque arridebant*). What
comes of a father favouring his darling son. Empathizing has turned out
worse than oppression. Worse than any tantalizing tortures dreamed up
by those fly slaves to work their cash-machine. "Bound . . . fast," indeed
(*me . . . tibi deuinxti*, 849+850: cf. pp. 146–7).

For the boy, relief is not at hand. The evening breaks up in a confusion
of tongues, a morass of split-stage double dialogues,[2] as matron watches
askance and hears husband torment naughty son, cheat on her, promise to
rob her wardrobe to keep the lap-dancer sweet, wish wife dead—and soon
too—, and answer son's question—"Pa, do you love ma?"—with "What, *her*?

Me? I love her right now. For . . . — not being here." Compounded with the reply to "How 'bout when she's here?": "I long for her—dead" (899–901).

She *is,* of course, here, to hear jack make an ass of her. And so this will cost him. "With interest" (902). *His* life (910–11: *salue-salutis-mortuus*).

Payback time sees a welter of tit-for-tat spite as mum chases dad off home, leaving boy and girl to head back inside. For now. (As they say, it's not a house, it's a home.) Maybe our applause can stop dad's drubbing dinning in our ears, but restoration of "parity" is in the offing for the lovers, anyhow. Down to earth with a bump—"mañana," as Pal dangles another twist of the knife (915–18):

> . . . I'll bring Diabolus to the manageress, with 20 minae
> to pay, so monopolizing *her* will be on for him, in part.
> Argyrippus will be *biddable,* I hope, agree to
> share with him, enjoy her alternate nights with Diabolus.

Once Father-who-would-be(friend)-Son butts out / is butted out, there will be just two lover-boys to fight for the one . . . part. Would *they* mind teaming up, 50/50, like those winsome slaves, One and Two? (916, *in partem:* p. 143) This conciliation will only mean getting real and formalizing the triangular situation that obtained when we came in . . .

So reads the plot[us]. But fine-tuning in sextalk and violence is the linguistic bearer of the "play" that opens up within the characterology of *Asinaria*. Its madam is "mother" (or mother) and owner of *meretrix* (*lena, era,* 147: p. 127). But the girl is and is not, *amatrix,* and her favourite *adulescens* is either her love or her living, or he is both. This son may just be making the old old mistake of "first love," immaturely falling for the call-girl and calling this phase "love" (he is). And he may be put in the impossible position of his father's compulsory voyeur so we can mock-drool at the limits of "sophisticated" elasticity in interpersonal relations (we will). In any case, the "affair" is made to keep us guessing, wondering where to put ourselves and what we think of the play's director (when that role, trust me, is ours).

Similarly, we know that *matrona* is an *uxor dotata* (898: wife on the warpath tells us she is, p. 181), and paterfamilias a *decrepitus senex* (863), and ultimately the *cuculus* in the love-nest (923, 934).[3] But is she a "shrew" or "witch" or "hag," or a woman who loves her man? Shall we join in with the baiting? "Demaenetus is not in a position to grant his son the money, for it is his well-endowed wife—this expression is meant in the literal sense—who controls the purse strings."[4] Does "the promise of slapstick comedy embodied in Artemona's *matrona* mask rescue for comedy a scene that has veered dangerously near the tragic"?[5] The dramatic point is—*how* true do you want to make it? If, "in her case, too, there is no portrayal of pain or spiritual anguish,"[6] then what is the point of the mocking snitch twisting the knife the way he does? (856–7, 858–9):[7]

MRS   I had always thought he was a good guy—best of the lot—and
             loved his wife.

             ~

PAL   Now you must know he's a bad guy—worst in the pot—and
             loathed his wife.

Likewise, I'm sure. Is her husband a "wally" who tries his hand at master-minding a personal triumph at everyone else's expense, a "nut" who thinks you can mess around with second childhood without getting everyone's fingers burned, a "git" who can't handle having a girl in his lap any more than the next spectator could, or is this a "bloke" going through his late middle-age crisis? (pp. **129–30**)[8] Are they stuck with a problem neither they nor anyone else can handle? What is this fun making fun *of,* and *with*? How much is written into the script, pinned to the tale, and how much is up for grabs, between cast and producers and audience?

A good deal of the play foregrounds getting the language right, as the cast tell us they are trying to find the right words and get the words right. Neither attending fornication class nor drafting a formal contract will do it for Diabolus (222–5; 751–808), whereas improvisatory sleight of tongue works a treat for agent One: "I meant your wife's death, not yours" (43); and for agent Two: "How much do you reckon you weigh stripped?—I dunno.—I knew you didn't know, but *I* know, because . . ." (299–300).[9] These two can't help it: it starts off a simple dialogue ploy for gaining the upper hand, so that slave is plain incapable of telling master "yes, you're right" without an instant comeback (54–6):

DEM   Is it as I say, Libanus?
LIB   You're on the right track.

	That's it. But a pox has gone for him, something chronic.
DEM	What pox is that?
LIB	Not having the fees to match the talk.

But, as in a real farce, outside theatre, it all winds up just as complex a stew of cannibalized rhetorics as the old stager Flatfoot ("*Plautus*") could make it: "soap," as we say.[10]

Where we came in was pressurizing master to tell no lies—not to get close enough to the [m✳✳l] and its [w✳✳ps] even to speak the words (16–30; 31–38: p. 132).[11] Madam then comes on as an impress of language: first rule for tinsel-town Bordelloville is that in her line of show biz clients' abuse is gold dust; second fact is, their threats are so many tongues wagging (153–5; 162).[12] She tells true with wordy—generic—*lectures* cooked up on fish and fowl (178–80;[13] 215–25[14]), outrageously *encrypting the play* in paragrammatism, and telling us so, into the bargain: *uel patinarium uel assum, uerses quo pacto libet* (180: listen!). She acts out the young pup's antics, studiously souping up the amator dramatics of bawdeville ecstasy (181–5, *studet* → his charge, 210, *meo de studio studia erant uestra omnia*).[15] She painfully puns (illicit use of lingo) *lectus illex* (221),[16] and assiduously assonates *oratione* uinnula uenustula (223: *uinnulus* ἅπαξ).[17] It is all one flurried flourish of specialized power-knowledge (*disciplina*, 201),[18] and her unworthy pupil has *lots* left to learn, and *not* forget:

non tu scis? . . . perdidici istaec esse uera (177 ringed with 187)

~

non tu scis? . . . haecine te esse oblitum, in ludo qui fuisti tam diu?
. . . discipulum semidoctum (215 ringed with 226–7).

She comes up with a prize *verb. sap.* (a word to the wise), on market terms and conditions for the down and out. As follows (203):

uetus est: "nihili coactiost"—scis cuius. non dico amplius

~

Old's th'ills: "Credit limit zero"—you know who gets that—say no more.

"A different rhetoric," observes the victim, who must supply the missing word, (the word for his own powerlessness) (204), before he mortgages himself into blank debt, money or his life (*nisi illud* perdo *argentum*, pereundum *est mihi*, 244, cf. 637, *qui non perdo pereo*). Shut out; shut mouth; shut down: "shut doors" (241–2).[19]

The cultural pragmatics of slave subjects take over the balance of the play. One stages a nifty show of his credentials as Cunning Slave, putting the mockers on his own prospects. His first words send his own sense of self-importance up, as a triple rhyming take, of ascending length, metrical virtuosity, and stylistic level, turns the heat on . . . himself (258):

unde sumam? + qu^{em} intervertam? + qu^o hanc celocem conferam?

~

Where'll I take it from? Who'll I send the wrong way? Where'll I . . . point
   my yacht?

Quick as any (word for) yacht (i.e., *speed*boat: *celox = uelox* in Plautin), Brains is there in a flash. For those who can read the signs, there are signs everywhere. They are clearcut, solid (plain, spondaic, unresolved verses), first giving a green light any which way Libanus likes, ad lib., with unanimous consensus on all sides, optimum conditions for counsel from any council (259–61):

*imp*et - rit^{um} *in - augur - atum* ^{e}st: = quouis - admit - tunt *a - ues*

   +

*p*icus - et *cor* - nix ab - laeua, = *cor*uus - parr^a ab - dexter - a

   +

*cons*ua - dent. cert^{um} - hercle ^{e}st - uestr*am con - sequi sen - tent*i - am.

Too good to be true? His next word just has to be "But . . ." (*sed*, 262), and his last words will foretell truly that they foretell "ob-struction" (*obscaeuauit meae* falsae fallaciae, 266 ~ *fingere fallaciam*, 250: p. **190**). As Brains guesses, this play isn't big enough for the both of them (himself and Steward: 264), and worse still, his own yacht (part) has been scuppered, cut from the script. In the meantime, he takes a bow. With a cameo to rethink the power-pack of Roman augury, first trusting the birds to shape his planning,[20] "but" then at once seizing on the elm tree tap-tap-tapped by the woodpecker for his master sign:[21] *for this interpreter*, "elm" spells "canes," just the way "birch" spelled "cane" in not so long obsolete English English (259–64, cf. 315, and p. **222 n.28**). Enter Two, toting his verbal "booty"—the chance to turn words into a syndicated

cash prize (269–71, 294). His breathlessness makes him a stern challenge to One's power to read signs: "Must've burgled a house, *if acting
in character*" (272). "Spoke the word 'bound'—'bound fast by our good
turn', but, all the same, ugh: 'bound'" (*nostro deuincti beneficio.—"uinc-
tos" nescioquos ait: | non placet*, 285–6). Looks for "a partner in crime"—
ugh—it's an instant omen when someone "shivers in a sweat" (a second
time, | *non placet*, 288–9).

A rap—rat-a-tat-tat of tit-for-tat flyting in slave Latin from the torture-
block—yokes the team (296–307: *uerbiuelitatio*, p. **147**). Beyond in-group
insults, it featured a riddling sport with the knowledge of ignorance, for
joker and straightman sidekick (299–305):

LEO	quot pondo ted esse censes nudum?
LIB	non edepol scio.
LEO	scibam ego te nescire, at pol ego, qui ted **expendi**, scio:
	nudus uinctus centum **pondo es**, quando **pendes** per **pedes**.
LIB	quo argumento istuc?
LEO	ego dicam quo argumento et quo modo.
	ad **pedes** quando alligatumst aequom centum**pondium**,
	ubi **manus manicae** complexae sunt atque adductae ad trabem,
	nec de**pendes** nec pro**pendes**—quin malum nequamque sis.
	~
LEO	How many pounds ya think ya weigh in ya skin?
LIB	—*Shucks* I dunno.
LEO	I knew ya don' know, but sure I do 'cos I'm the one that weighed ya.
	In ya skin and bound you are way up at 100 pounds, weighed by feet.
LIB	How d'you work that out?
LEO	—I'll tell ya on what basis how it works out.
	Once a fair level 100-pounder has been strung up tight to the feet
	when the 'andcuffs hug ya 'ands in their clasp pulled up right to the beam,
	ya ain't way over, ya ain't way under . . . bein' a no-good thug.

Way beyond the reach of civility, this multiple assonance verges ponderously on sense before tipping over thunderously into—horrendously bathetic nonsense.[22] The correct response to this just has to be monosyllabic: "*Up yours,*" and the impressive reflex: "That's your legacy from Mme Slavery" achieves closure in parity: a draw with honours even (306: *uae tibi*).

When the courier arrives, One perplexes him by answering the door before it is knocked (382–91). He "knows" all about (not just the sale of asses, but) the Courier's mission. The other thinks he'll "know," from One's description of "Lizard," if the "Lizard" he met *was* Lizard (*scio*, 398; *iam scire potero*, 399). Enter Two-as-Lizard, as arranged, and we are treated to the underlings' version of what a vicious slave overseer feels like from where they stand. Their ask is to show the bullying sadism only too convincingly to the free neutral: he is appalled. Yet from a managerial viewpoint, it's plain to see, as well, that this maniac is setting the staff demanding standards, applying himself energetically to painstaking vigilance down to the very last detail: kicking ass, "this repulsive, *nauseating,* stuff" (*iam hic me abegerit odio suo,* 446: p. **181**).

So the slaves run smack into the mailman's special delivery mentality: he knows he will never accept *any* assurances as "knowledge." "He'll never hand his parcel to anyone *problematic*" (*nouit . . . sciat ~ non noui. ~ nosce sane. | ~ sit, non sit, non edepol scio . . . ego certe me incerto scio hoc daturum nemini homini,* 455, 456; 464–6). This draws the heat onto the Courier, but he won't be faced down, and the ploy of forcing One to insult him actually alienates him from the plaguey *pair of 'em* (473, *malum hercle uobis quaeritis*).[23] They reassess the situation, and decide it's as well to call it quits—"We're all of us human." "Agreed . . . But I don't know you, and an unknown human is a wolfman, there's no knowing." "I knew you'd . . . apologize. . . . I know you would if you could" (490–503, *scilicet; ignoto . . . non nouit ~ scibam . . . scio pol crederes*). Stalemate (503, *haud negassim,* the Courier's last assinarian word: "no." p. **209**).

For interlude, madam tries to overpower her recalcitrant moneyspinner by browbeating and pulling rank. This Academy is alma mater for Whores (*praecipis . . . praeceptis,* 507–8: pp. **150, 179**). But *this* pupil of hers has learned rhetoric by *plying* her profession, and counterattacks (*dicacula . . . amatrix → accusatrix,* 511, 513). Mother demands her right to reply, and turns scold, summoning up the rhetoric of invective (*pars orationis,* 516–18; 521–34). Daughter has surrendered, pretends to seek counsel, before a final appeal (*mone* . . . , *sine me,* 537, 542). But mother understands that she's not even pretending she isn't acting submission, but rather she's smuggling in a protest, delivering an unspoken ultimatum, and mutely telling her mind(er)-controller where to get off: this is "impudence" passed off as "obedience" (543–4).[24] The tussle of wills makes for a gripping sketch of civil oratory slumming it; but the clash is also a clash with the slaves' sparring sessions that it divides. It all makes for a sandwich of acting, interacting and overacting.[25]

Now the agents have their head: now they have the bread. In a matching riot of ebullient lists and repetitions (esp. *ubi* . . . clauses: 561–4: $\times$ 6; 568–74: $\times$ 8),[26] bogeys and fantasias, their triumphant duet mixes up the Roman empire with the Roman vampire. As one, the pair spoil high-and-mighty heroism with celebration of their own murderous tolerance of pain and terror. Their lives are no better than the fate of captured enemies of the state: so much for their recognition as fellow human beings, let alone equals, indispensables, or even superiors, as and when it suits unseated master, his immature son, or visiting stranger. Owed to joy, the travesty hymn starts by dedicating its savvy self to lying propaganda in its own idiom (*Perfidiae laudes* . . . , 545, another pretend deity, trumping master's first words, *per Dium Fidium,* 23: p. **225 n.15**). It ends by slapping itself on the back (try it), for this has been a quintessential performance of the real spirit, not the fictive elation, of Slavery (577):

> How *apt* for you and me both, couldn't be better. *Just the ticket* for our
> talent.

The slaves' fun-packed campaign of revenge on the young master is at hand. As it begins, they are set free to comment on the lover's discourse with impunity, for in theatre asides get no comeback. As soon as dammit, Two comes up with a brash assertion that money doesn't talk, it swears. Taking a leaf out of his own creation, the mock-Steward's book (418, pp. **193–4**), he underlines, once for all, that in this (word)play the brass—the ass—brays loudest (588–90):

LEO	. . . attatae, modo hercle in mentem uenit,
	nimis uellem habere perticam.
LIB	quoi rei?
LEO	qui uerberarem

asinos, si forte occeperint clamare hinc ex crumina.

~

LEO ... Ooh-la-la. Just popped in my head, lord,

I really do wish I had a pole.

LIB Oh yeah, and what for?

LEO To beat up on the asses, happen they start yelling from the money pouch here.

Now the metaphor's out of the bag. Cash it if you can.

The doves come out to bill for their one last time and to coo double-suicidally, as the accompanying sound-track of sarcastic commentary pauses for the cameo: asses to asses (598–602; 606–15). First reaction is to give pity—second is, the offer is withdrawn: "*Highly-strung* lovers are beaten hollow by *slaves strung high*. This they *know—they've been there*" (616–17). Not before time, the dare-devils burst their bubble, and join the crowd: four's company. At once, they burst the sweethearts' bubble, and ruin the mood. They enforce comedy (619–20):

LEO>ARG	ere, salue. sed num fumus est haec mulier quam amplexare?
ARG>LEO	quidum?
LEO>ARG	Quia *oculi sunt tibi lacrimantes, eo rogaui.*

~

LEO>ARG	Goo-day, master. Hey there now, is she smoke, this woman in your arms?
ARG>LEO	Pardon me?
LEO>ARG	Because your eyes they are watering. Hence my question.

The guying starts right away: first him, then her (621–2, *perdidistis ~ perdidi*; 623–4, *uelitis ~ uelim*):

ARG>LIB+LEO	"You've lost—"
LEO>ARG	"You can't lose *what you never had.*"

. . . .

ARG>LIB+LEO	"The gods grant your wishes"
LIB>PH	"*A night with you'd do me, darlin',* a jug of plonk, if my wishes came true"

The word draws blood; is retracted; and the sword turned aside to internecine laconic laceration (625–8, *uerbero ~ uerberare ~ uerberes . . . uerberari*):

ARG>LIB	Mind, not a *beep* from you, boy to beat up on.
LIB>ARG	I'm wishing for you not me.
ARG>LIB	Then say on what you like, ad-lib.
LIB>ARG	To whop *him* here a beating, lord.
LEO>LIB	Who would ever credit it? That from *you,* you pansy with a perm.
	You? Dish out a beat-up, when taking a whopping *fills your lunchbox?*

By-play where slave-drubbing merges in punning innuendo with sex-banging, for *uerbero* as noun/verb indicates either active or passive role in both these forms of whopping assault: "Ass-whipped"/"I whip ass, beat up on." [27] Then the boy's attempt to advise the agents is ceremoniously put down with a thud (641):

Master. You should know not everything's just as sweet to everyone.

As it appears, these grown men know about lovers; as far as you can tell, lovers don't know about anything. "So you do what you advise us to do." Leave the talking to us (644, sua*uia* . . . sua*ue* . . . , sua*des*). Here the firm determines to twit (torment) their better, not elder. Their victim(s) must try to outslave slaves, *to* slaves, in slavering lip-salve (her), as well as slobbering lip-servility (him). Until they are brought to their knees, and have plain had enough.

As we know, these hardmen are(n't) kidding. They systematically take apart the superiority complexes of social standing, as far as possible utilizing irreducibly basic choreographies of bodily subjection. Kowtowing, bended knees, rough ride, and genuflexion. As they make master crawl, they whip his ass, until dobbin can't hack it. [28] Only when despair sets in, from "head to foot" (from start to finish of the scene), do they relent (728–30):

LEO	I was head of today's *gold strike.*
LIB>ARG	I was foot.

ARG   How come both head and foot of *Act Three* are lost
                                  from sight?
                I can't understand what you're saying, I can't know why you're
                playing.

As comic luck would have it, however, their worst trick comes when they
stop playing tricks. Now we see that they were understudying Big Master
when they hammed up that wish for "a night with you . . . , darlin', and a
jug of plonk" (624). For *they* came in knowing at the "head" of the Act what
none of us could. (Don't shoot the messenger.) At its "foot" here, we find
that Big Master's terms and conditions are what you might expect from a
guttersnipe slave (736): "the night with her, *and throw in a* party."

The twist, of course, is that this is pater getting as far inside his son's skin
as he can. So the agents holding his carrier-bag were actually out there,
before Little Master, taking off Big Master taking off Little Master, all too
close to the life and the bone. In return, we are bound to find that, as re-
juvenated lover, father will put on a better imitation of his comic slaves'
imitation of himself than of his boy's performance as juvenile lead.

Manewhile, out comes the alternative juvenile lead for his moment in
the spotlight. Diabolus is funny because he refuses to be anything of the
sort. He knows every nook and cranny of the *ars amatoria*,[29] and in com-
mandeering pleasure erases it. He comes on stage with the script, turns
performance into reading-over, writes in a last-minute "insertion" of one
more "exclusion" and an eleventh-hour "deletion" of a "prohibition" (754–5;
787–91). He brings contract backed by cash, trumping Madame at her own
game, of scheduling the traffic in sex with The Babe (504–8, *interdictis . . .
praeceptis,* 522–3, *uetui . . . | compellare ait contrectare, colloquiue aut con-
tui,* 536, *non ueto,* 544, *dicto:* 747, *leges pellege,* 749, 809, *leges ~ lege,* 166, 231,
234, *leges meas,* 239, *legem:* the play's *own* contract.[30] Cf. Argyrippus' *leges,*
600–01, and *licessit,* 603; Demaenetus' *legibus,* 735).

But . . .

Straight in he goes . . .

And straight out he comes.

In a trice, what a turnaround (809–10, *sequere intro.—sequor.—sequere
hac*). His "poet" (748), the "Pal" who drafted this legalese verse (it *is* verse—
in *Plautus'* script), had been nailing all of us with his tangle of tedium.[31] So
the bores held up the play, and as a result damned up momentum for when
the floodgates are to burst open wide, and grant us all relief (release . . . ,

relapse . . .). As he leaves, Diabolus the angry young man lets his agent take over (*ne mone,* | *ego istud curabo,* 826–7), for their snitching will release matron's tsunami of wrath.

Here at last the debauchery we've been waiting for comes out into view, disgorging the inside story—mythical Roman orgy, for three: "bodies adjacent, his and hers, lolling on the dining divan" (831, 833, *haec nunc mecum accubat, tecum accubat;* 843, 845, *istaec est tecum; aliam tecum esse*). Watch the spoilsport show us the matrona watching the paterfamilias hard at it ogling and canoodling—will she accept the evidence of her eyes? The pillar of society a faceless rutting satyr—beyond the pale, beyond recognition (879, *accubantem, amplexum*):

> You could, I suppose, happen you catch sight of your husband installed
> with crown, hugging playmate, if you saw him . . . —could you tell it is him?

The live-sex-peep-show starts from the promised clinch of "hugging" getting out of control (882, *quid modi . . . amplexando*), and moves straight to hardcore oral gluttony, with booze plied from the son's side, to right, and the girl's side serving up simultaneously, from left field, "sweet, sweet kisses . . . breath to die for." Some turn-on for the wife, instantly hot to land killer kisses of her own . . . ! (891–5, 903, *sauium . . . suauiorem; osculatur; oscularier; osculando;* cf. 940. *sauium*) Funny thing, sex in marriage. (Perish the thought, good folk in the audience.)

But this is a family show. In front of the children. At his benefactor's party, son must (not) knuckle under. He acts letting it show that he's trying not to let it show, but of course he is trying to do just that. Just the way that the girl put up resistance to her parent's pressures. Except that she was pleading for just a window for love, whereas he is not pleading for anything, because that is the term-and-condition for him to be in a position to buy that very window. He just has to get through tonight, as agreed, and they'll win a year's uninterrupted bliss for two. The play between politesse and repression hits the heights here, as son kisses ass in the very act of laying bare the dynamics of the present love-triangle (842–5):

> Certainly, I know why it is, Father, you credit me blue over you:
> 'cos *she* is with you. And yes, too, *shucks,* tell you the godhonest truth,
> Father,

this scene hurts me bad. No, not that I'm not passionate for you, all you
want,
but I love her.

As anticipated, this puts dad in a tight spot, as his ugliness is flushed out
for all to see (846):

at ego hanc uolo.

~

Well, *I* want *her,* I do.

Specifically, the ugliness is flushed out for matrona to see. This is her cue
to enter, and re-think, coached by the informer, who is no way lying, he
knows her husband's wickedness, and plays himself appalled by the ex-
posée (*filio sciente; accreduas; mendacem; rata; scito; uera; ratus; uerum
hoc facto sese ostendit*, 853–63). He knows she'll make her husband's life a
fatal misery, sure as eggs, and knows how to poison her mind still more
with a spray of denunciations (*ego istuc scio;* 869, *censen tu illum hodie
primum . . . ?*, 887).

This is no time to develop any sort of characterological dimension,
as the finale carves up the niceties, the roles shear off in their several directions, and the cast lob at each other fragments of used script. When
Demaenetus makes one more "promise," to "steal from the wife" for another young lovebird, "on his wife's death within the year" (*promisit*, 930
= 884–6; cf. 939; and 901, 905), we have heard it all before (*promitto*, 97;
uxorem . . . circumduce, aufer, 96; *usque ad mortem—uxoris*, 42–3). Master
is now the one reviled as in areas of the play where slave abuse has bandied
the insult "Executioner!" around (il)liberally (*carnufex*, 892 ~ 482, 697).
"Kissing" and "cursing" cross swords again (892–903, 940 ~ 669, 687, 697).
Ditto, "Do not mess with a dowried wife" (898 ~ 85, 87). The fun will cost
plenty—"with interest" (902 ~ 248).

Now *She* "can't endure it" (907: pp. 147, 195). *He* has "killed the girl with
distaste," where once the agents "repulsed the courier with distaste" (*odio:*
921, cf. 927 ~ 446). He "divines right," where once one slave "divined" to
another (*hariolare:* 924 ~ 579, cf. 316), and wants her to "huddle—over
there" (*abscede paululum istuc*, 925, cf. 939 ~ *secede huc . . .* , *concedite huc,*
639, 646), before he is reduced to "beseeching" the Fury (*obsecro*, 926: last

not least of these in line: p. **134**). He is the "cuckoo in the nest" (923, 934, *cubat cuculus, cuculum . . . , male cubandum* ~ birds hunted [215–16, 881] or portentous [259–63], and lovebirds [666, 693–4]). "Is it right for a father to shower *those mores* on son?"—as he'd heralded (932 ~ "I am resolved to follow those *mores* of my father," 73; *largirier,* 932: *largus,* 533, 598). His last words turn abuse on the slave-girl: "Climb a cross" (*i in crucem,* 940 ~ *cruces,* 548). Mumma's "good boy" sucks up to her (931): *his* last words (lies) are an "I told you so" (938, *dicebam, pater, tibi . . .*):

> I told you, dad, not to go against mum.

Five used characters in search of another author have done their Plautin best to mix up so many strands of comic-civic discourse, in a welter of paltry re-cycled slivers: ensemble.[32] First the avengers spy on the revels, overhearing a nightmare of "distaff distaste" from matron's old man (*osorem uxoris,* 859: pp. **171, 222 n.31**), until *he* backs the wrong horse by betting with the girl's lovely name for good luck—and *she* bursts in (905–6; 907). The snitch cleans up the plot and clears off; the witch harries the cuckoo from the nest; she fetches along the *right* formulaic verse refrain, so we can all help stow the toys back in the box for another day (921–5, **210**):

> surg^e, ămator, i dŏmum. |

The unanswerable shooing of anything any male might try to say in the first half of *any* trochaic *septenarius* (p. **119**). More conclusive a tag to join in with than any "Look behind you!" in any panto of ours. To give themselves an out, too, the girl fires a couple of gibes at the old boy's back, then takes her boy and the play on home. Yes, this party's *over*.[33]

Take a bow, everybody. How good was that?

Say no more.
Applaud us.

⇒ 8 ⇐

"It's a gas"

Space, Movement, Verse

A Plautus play works a helical pattern of spatial and metrical dynamics, its verse spins to-and-fro between the two stage-doors (metre: pp. 117–20). That's why they are there (pp. 134–5, 136). Now we have read through *Asinaria*, I shall focus directly on its stagecraft and stunt values.[1]

Key

A   the "family" household
      Demaenetus, Artemona, and Argyrippus,
      Libanus, Leonida, Saurea, and all
B   Madam's house
      Cleareta, and Philaenium
C   the Rival and his crew (his home is off-stage: 827)
      Diabolus, and his Pal

A1: conversational *senarii*, 16–126, continuing those of Prologue, 1–15:
    Father and One came out of their place and headed for the mall. Intimate conversation threads intricately through and between verses. This acts out rapport.[2]
    We'll meet again, but they won't. Not where we can watch them at it.

C1/B1: singing cretic tetrameters, 127–37 (overreaching half-way into one parodic excrescence, 133, the choriambic tetrameter [with ionic a minore third limb]: pp. 120, 224 n.9).[3] Then stand-off wrangling in Plautus' most common metrical form, lively recitative trochaic *septenarii*, 138–248:

That (d)ejected lover will join the men's club at the mall, to beg or borrow; madam pops in and out of her house.

Both will be back. But the anticipated re-match will not come off.

A2: the trochaic *septenarii* carry on, **249–380**. Broken by the arrival of the man with the money: iambic *septenarii* from **381–503**:

The One comes from the wings, joined (hotfoot from the mall) by the Two, who will copy One's round-trip to the mall and back, before Courier arrives from the mall, and the trio eventually leave together for, yes, another visit for each of the three of them to the mall. When One sent Two off to tell master about the courier, Two dashed there-and-back in a trice before reappearing as himself-playing-Lizard-looking just-like-Two (367, 379–80 ~ 403–7). One guessed, more prophetically than he can know, that Two "must've burgled a house, as is his way, and woe betide the guy that got so casual about watching the door" (272–3).

No house-door turned a hinge *here,* since One "saved his mate the door from a beating," to spare Courier the trouble of knocking (382–91). Lizard, "Three," runs the household rota, as mama's *atriensis,* so his impostor Two berates One for neglecting chores around their portals (424–6). One and all needed Demaenetus, and he, mind, is in the mall.

The walk-on part of Courier will have done with it there, and b. off.

B2: more trochaic *septenarii* for Madam's second scene, continued from B1: **504–44**:

This repeats the mood of Madam's first cameo, except that she emerges from her house in company, and, instead of ejecting her inmate, comes to tell her she will be ejecting a second gigolo strapped for cash. She binds her verbally, hand and foot, and leads them both straight back, together physically if not by mutual consent, into their house.

Madam will not reappear.

A3/B3: more iambic *septenarii* for the slaves' second big scene, **545–584 + 585–745**:

This is a repeat from A1, in that One and Two come on simultaneously, very much together, like Master and One. Only they come *from* the mall (as they did in A2, except that then they arrived separately, but left very much together). Eventually they disappear into their house.

And they will not reappear.

B3/A3: neither mood nor metre is broken by the arrival of the kids without the money, for all the pathos-bathos of their duet with voice-over (591–5, 596–7, 606–615: **585–745**):

One and Two are joined again. Only, not by that rock, the Courier, but by those all unknowing mugs, the play's Son and Daughter.

The audience-on-stage first overhears, and then hears, that a second loverboy is a "chuck-out" (594–6, *domum ire iussit; hinc exclusust foras;* 632, *hinc me amantem ex aedibus eiecit huius mater*). So for a third time, those brothel doors have swung open to let out a pair of inmates; and expelled their second ejected client (as in B1). Only, this one will be ~~reprieved~~, and he will go back where he came from, together with the daughter, who will go back inside again, bound fast to her companion (as in B2). Only, this time, about as together as you can get.

They still have it all to play for.

C2: prosaic halting *senarii* for the rival and his simpering pal, attempting to re-start the play, only this time directing it their (negative, unfunny) way; these two are so dull, dull, dull, that there is no differentiation by change of metre from their double act as chartered accountants, to their reappearance, agitato and masterful, respectively: **746–809 + 810–827**:

Diabolus the rival loverboy brings on his Pal plus that proposed contract (238–40: p. 141). Which naturally controls rights of access in terms of "lock and key to the door / girl" (759–60, *fores occlusae omnibus sint nisi tibi. | in foribus scribat occupatam esse se*). They are in pushy mood; they bring their terms and conditions; they *must* have raised the 20 minae, somehow, at the mall (245–8: pp. 141–2). So it is in line with madam's terms and conditions for the behaviour of her door (it opens to Greeks bearing gifts) when the pair simply walk right through it without standing on ceremony, or knocking.

Tumbling straight back out again (**810–827**), they split up, the pal to do the snitching, Diabolus disappearing off home (for good). No music for these anti-comic villains, still (we just said), even though they've stopped reading the dry-as-dust contrick (Moore (1998) 250–1).

A3/B4/C3: after two more *senarii* of preparatory directions to seat and settle the party, 828–9, Father has his brief moment on top, as he tortures Son, in the play's only iambic *octonarii*, **830–50**. These longer lines are great for quickfire dialogue interchange, which calls for precision timing around the full Roman cast (pp. **170, 182, 230 n.2**). This is broken by the arrival of matrona, bringing more trochaic *septenarii* to join those of both madam's scenes, so as to dominate proceedings to curtain-fall, **851–941**; for they even run on through the extra- or para-dramatic Epilogue from the cast, **942–7.**

The Pal must've pushed straight into his second house in a row. He went to fetch matrona; he fetches her out to spy on the scene next door.

Job done, he will slip away, go join Diabolus, with a compromise plan for consolation.

This mother is on a round-trip, and will return home, but with husband in tow. Forcibly leading, not led, (un)together, and bound fast for eternal, adamantine, conjugality. Meantime, Son and Daughter double-act exit and reenter, for the second time, at her place, together as anyone can possibly get.

Only, still with it all to do, and no time to do it. Fresh out of plot.

Such are the directions for traffic through *Asinaria*. Two trajectories, however, are outstanding, and they stick out. One of them is more than filled in, the other one is much more of a blank. Let's see if Plautus messes *this* up (= "LISTEN!"):

(1) We know the astounding sight that awaits matron at hers next door. She both pays a visit and does not. She marches over, but does not have to barge her way in, as Plautus' party contrives to spill out onto the street,[4] and things hot up and boil over. *How did her dirty old man come to be in there?*

We last *saw* him ever-so-carefully underlining (to agent One) that he would wait in the mall, at his friend the banker's (**116–17**: with that apt, if elsewhere unattested, name *Archibulus,* "Archie Plotter": pp. **136–7**). Two swept off to tell pater that his agents are going to try to fool the Courier into handing over the loot to Two-as-Lizard (**367–9; 378–80**). In the event, One and Two took courier there to find big master, and carried off their ruse with his assistance (where we couldn't see it: **580–4**: "what a funster our old boy proved to be . . ."). One and Two then got to play courier to little master. He "needs" father, so dad can have his pound of flesh, and then deliver Ms. Dora Adora to son, for a year less a day. Son will send Two to fetch Pops—but, no: Two knows the long and short of it already.

Dad must've told him (them) this was what he was going to do, when they unloaded the courier with him; and now, we are specially *told*, pa has gone and got ahead—so far ahead, he's been having to wait for everyone to catch up (especially us).[5] Plautus has bulged the "wit and fun" of those astonishing stand-out scenes to the point where there's barely time to tell us, once more, that there's no spare capacity to spend on this "brief" ~~plot~~ (741–5):

LEO>ARG	He's been inside for donkey's years.
ARG>LEO	Well he didn't come this way.
LEO>ARG	Through the alley,

that way he came, round through the garden, on the quiet, so no one'd see him

come here, none of the household. Afraid his wife'll get to know about it.

The cash—if your mother knew what happened about the cash—

ARG>LIB+LEO	Whoa! Sh—

don't put the mockers on it!

LIB>ARG+PHIL	In you go, quick.
ARG	Farewell, you two.
LEO>ARG+PHIL	Make love, you two.

(2) At the end, we shall watch son duck back into madam's house, with his lass, at least for the moment. Earlier, he had gone back into madam's house, on *her* terms and conditions. For he ended the scene of his humiliation *with* the bargaining power of the cash (745). It was lack of that which had, *first* time round, got him "thrown out" of the house for lack of funds (between 545 and 585). *But when and how did he get in there in the first place, so he could be bounced out on his ear?*

Out trot Jack and Jenny, for their swansong, parted by mother's exclusion order (585–6):

LIB	Wait a mo'.
LEO	Whassup?

LIB   That Philaenium coming out from inside,
              Argyrippus alongside?
LEO   Zip your mouth, it's him. Let's listen in.

The boy *could* have been in there all the time, including when that Rival who coulda been Argyrippus (the one we must've surmised *was* him) got himself ejected and dismissed (B1: 127–248).

[That would've been precisely the sort of case of "three's company," where "two" had been "a crowd," that Diabolus' Pal is ultimately going to suggest for the love-triangle compromise we shall never deliver on (i.e. "every other night," 915–18). In spirit, too, that is indeed the shadow that the first ejection scene does put over the rest of the play, the hold it has on its repetition, only with Argyrippus co-starring (B3: started at 532–4; proceeding at 585–615; interrupted by 616–745). And this is what will put on hold that after-shadow, the would-be third rival, the other could-be Argyrippus: namely, Father. For the other mother will come over and eject *him*, too, from madam's establishment. Lasso him, back in harness, on the road. Lover-boys all have this coming.

Any spectator, though, would *prefer* Argyrippus to have gone in *after* the rival's expulsion. One at a time makes very good fishing, and madam only seems to have a string of the one girl.]

But (if you listen to me) *Asinaria* does tell us how come we shan't ever *see* Argyrippus walk in that door, past that sign "Strictly for hire."

Sure, the front door opens wide to all who can pay the entry fee. On the other hand, discreet patrons, like that ageing would-be Argyrippus, could always use the alley-way. But in the case of the one and only true Argyrippus himself, however, the point is (madam tells us) that he keeps slipping through madam's terms and conditions. Spatially, by worming in there.[6] Verbally, with his promises, his procrastination.

The reason why madam trooped her daughter out (for B2: 504), and promptly marched her back in again (545), was to tell her (and us) that the game's up: "today" is the end of the road for Argyrippus. As we heard (532–4):

So, now. If he doesn't fetch me 20 minae over here, cash,
Our Lady, **he'll be shoved outa here,** showering us with . . . tears. Out!
This is the last day the "funds short" cop-out will *play.* Not in *my* place.

So mother brings her outside *because Argyrippus is inside.*[7] Madam at once piles in (504):

Am I really powerless to tame you to obey when I say no?

She warned daughter *not* to talk with that Argyrippus, son of Demaenetus, *no* physical contact, *no* conversation, *no* eyeballing" (522–3: Φιλ-αίνιον = "*Loves-talk,*" *dicacula,* 511). But instead (526):

You go and love him, go and chase him, go get him summoned to you.

So, yes, the boy *can* be a back-door man, just the way his father will do it, when he has a go at making like a kid on the block again. (Only, papa will be a kid who is armed with the cash needed to open the bordello door and the bawd's girl's legs both.) But the boy has a trump card all his very own (penniless, but not penisless): his Pretty Woman will not abide by madam's terms and conditions, not when it comes to *this* lover. Because he's special, he's The-One-That-I-Want (ooh-ooh-ooh): "I love him, mama . . ." (. . . *cum illo quem amo prohibeor,* 515).

Now, since agent One can already tell Two, when he first arrives hotfoot with his bombshell news, that "Big master's at the mall, but little master's in here (viz. at madam's, not *domi*)" (328–9, *ubinam est erus?* | *maior apud forumst, minor hic est intus*), we shall reckon that Argyrippus has got in there between C1/B1 and A2 (viz. between 248 and 249).

The rival lost out, noisily; now the protracted "wit and fun" of all those failed attempts of One and Two to set up and con the Courier is about to begin (329–30, *iam satis est mihi* | . . . *mitte ridicularia.* | *mitto*). Agent One comes into his own *as* "*agent* One"—he has been that since before we came in, before (we heard) the son leaked (and finessed) the plot to father (57–8, *tune es adiutor nunc amanti filio?* | *sum uero, et alter noster est Leonida*). Now between his mall-bound exit (after A1, at 117) and his reentry from the wings to start off A2 (viz. at 249), the rival has been ejected (= C1/B1: 127–248), and "A couple of hours have elapsed."[8]

Agent One immediately makes a point of telling us so, in no uncertain terms, as he gives himself the wake-up call, seizing the moment to play the novel part of "Cunning-yet-Loyal-to-Paterfamilias' slave"; only then to find that his role in initiating the plotting (as he will next ascertain *from*

Two) has been cut by the finessing of the plot, and its preemption *by* Two:[9] 249–51, 253):

> Well, lord, Libanus, you best get on and wake yourself up now,
> and plot a trick for organizing a bash at the cash.
> It was yonks ago you split from master, and went off to the mall.
> There you slept like you're on vacation, through to this hour of the day.

"Much time has elapsed" formulae tell us that *some ~~plot~~ has passed us by.*[10] Argyrippus' prime agent is privy to the boy's whereabouts (who else?), and *he must've met him off-stage:* a not very funny thing happened on the way to the mall. Or back. This is how One knows that Argyrippus is "inside"— where "inside" must mean "inside *madam's*" (329).

So Argyrippus will be at madam's between 248/9 and 584 (and so knows precisely that Diabolus is out there fund-raising "on a vow to fetch the 20 minae per annum whack today," but has *not yet* brought the dosh to madam and reserved the merchandise: 633–5; *iam dedit argentum? non dedit,* 638). And mother's blood will boil, she will be good as her word, and force the issue. Her last act in the plot will have been to show this second loverboy the door, finally: asap (viz. between 544 and 584).

The next time this happens, the other mother will lose *her* rag, and exercise *her* ultimate command over *her* household. Mme will take her loverboy, the old boy, inside, like a child. *Amator!* Meantime, their son is moving out, and moving in with a partner, not unlike a daughter transferring to set up home with her man.[11] Only, not even in a hotel, but in a brothel.

> What is an *uxor dotata* (for)? Otitis?
> Someone has to keep the aspidistra flying.
> *Plus d'un âne qui s'appelle Martin.*

❧ 9 ❧

Beastly Lives

591–745 (reprise) Have the whip hand, get your own back

neque ego homines magis asinos numquam uidi. ita plagis costae callent.
quos quom ferias, tibi plus noceas. eo enim ingenio hi sunt flagritribae.

~

I never ever saw worse human Eeyores: the way blows have hardened their
ribs.
Go give 'em a whack, the one to get hurt'll be you. They're whip-busters by
temperament.

Pseudolus 136–7

These are, as a matter of fact, the only "asses" *or asses* in the rest of Plautus
beyond the seven mentions in *Asinaria*.¹ They belong to the brothel-keeper
Ballio (= "Beater," from βάλλω; and (?) "Prick," from βάλλιον²), who is
driving out of doors his battalions of servants, soon to be joined by les
girls. They will wake up their ideas or "be mottled" by lashes. These "blow-
bearing anthropoids" beat me and *this* (= whip) in "hardness" (*duritia; pla-
gigera genera hominum*), but their "hide" isn't harder than this "rawhide
(= whip)" (*tergum . . . terginum*), so do say, "Does it hurt? There, take *that*,"
any slave despising master" (*doletne? em sic datur;* 133–56). Have it.

Now when Louis Havet, the French Latinist nearest to *Asinaria* and dear-
est to my heart, imagined the best comedy we can have lost when the
Attic ΌΝΑΓΟΣ, *The Donkey-driver,* degraded into Roman (*fabula*) ASI-
NARIA—*The One about Donkey-driver* or *The One about Donkey*[s], for
centrepiece extravaganza he conjured up a comic *muletrain* driven by an

191

exotic Macedonian: so how many panto-donkey pairs would you like to
see lugging loadsabullion cross-stage apace?[3] This would certainly make
for echt Roman ostentation (Macrobius, *Saturnalia* 1.6.29):

> Asinae cognomentum Corneliis datum est, quoniam princeps Corneliae gentis,
> empto fundo seu filia data marito . . . asinam cum pecuniae onere produxit
> in forum, quasi pro sponsoribus praesens pignus.

> ~

> The nickname "Jenny" was given the Cornelii because the head of the Corne-
> lian clan bought a farm or gave his daughter to a husband . . . , and brought
> into the forum a jenny with money for load, to serve interested parties as
> tangible pledge.

I shall now follow Havet's lead, only forget Demophilus' play, and assert
that this is exactly what clown *Plautus* brings us. Would you believe, a
mule-train *in a shoulder-bag*—a "neck pouch" (*crumina*, 590). As it were,
Asinaria in a hold-all.[4]

Yes, master fetches slave out to the place "where rock grinds rock" (31:
33–4):

> . . . In the Ironbongo-Clubbery Isles,
> . . . where dead oxen assault live human beings.

Welcome on stage. The donkeys we'll see and hear today will be actors
playing slaves playing slaves.[5] Busting their ass this way (we said, p. 178)
will be done by those beasts of burden, the agents. Their deal is that, whatever the terms and conditions, they suffer beatings, whether or not it ever
gets them anywhere, or saves their going there. Inured, stubborn, hardened to it, these ascetics carry the can for one and all. Master lays his commands on his slave, and heads for the bank. Agent Two charges in, like the
proverbial speedway team of "four white . . . chargers" (279). He's looking
to hook up with his mate, and "share the yoke" (288, *adiungat*). He "bears"
and "shares" that (verbal) booty (*maximam praedam et triumphum . . . adfero*, 269, etc., etc.). For both of them, "loot" means a step toward buying
freedom—by suffering (277, 321):

> . . . He carries all his *Aladdin's cave* on his back.

.   .   .   .

Look, *if a hide's needed to square the bill, I'm game for robbing* the National
Bank.

The burden of the play is simply this, so "LISTEN!" (*taceo*, 332: 334–7):

LEO	Remember an Assyrian dealer buying them Arcadian asses off our household steward?
LIB	I do recall. So what is it comes next?
LEO	There. So. He's only gone and sent the cash to be paid to Saurea for them asses. The young guy's just got here, and he's fetching the cash.

"Carry cash for asses" (347, *ob asinos ferre argentum*). "Cash for asses fetched"
(269, *argentum afferat . . . pro asinis*). "20 minae of cash. . . . | What's it for?
Asses . . ." (*argenti uiginti minas . . . | qui pro istuc? asinos . . .*, 396–7).[6] Run-
ning a household is all about this *quid pro quo* (*pro uectura*, 432, *pro eis*,
437, *pro iniuria*, 497). The slaves, as we heard tell, can't open their mouths
without b(et)raying how large back-scarring beatings and back-breaking
toil loom in their lives. They congratulate themselves on surviving, they
brag of their weals.[7] In their skins they know how close life brings them to
these donkeys, their alter egos (339–42):[8]

LIB	. . . You must be meaning *those* donkeys— clapped out, gone lame, the ones with their hooves worn right down up to the hocks?
LEO	That's the ones. They once used to hump here the birches of elm for you.
LIB	Got it. Same ones carted you off to the farm, bound fast.
LEO	*Perfect* memory.

Enter the bearer of the shipment. The slave stops him "beating down his
mate, the poor old door . . . —super-sensitive to the approach of any [bi-
ped] kicker" (382–91, *calcitro*, usually of a horse, cattle or, of course, ass—
human or animal).[9] Once a slave rigs up as a super-slave (we felt it), he
lashes out, verbally and corporally. Treats his fellow slave as a whipping
post (418–19):

STEW   . . . Wish I'd got a whip here in my hand—

MERC>STEW   P-lease, do

be calm.

STEW>LIB   —so I could give those hips of yours a good scour, so toughened
to blows.

All the bullying—of the free stranger as well as the slave associate[10]—only
makes Courier obstinate, and dig in his heels stubborn as a mule: *this*
messenger, in his merchant's cloak (*chlamys,* according to the MSS), sig-
nifies money, he *is* the cash he bears. The muletrain of three trot off with
the loot to find the guy (who should be) in charge. Next door, madam is
having problems curbing *her* stubborn beast of burden, unruly daughter,
assiduous worker, and money-spinner (504, ~~mansuetem~~; she breaks the
rules, takes *dicta pro datis,* 525: pp. 155-6). When the slaves return, it is at
a canter.

Now *they* are the money bags, swagger in their step, and congratulate
each other on their histories of crime and punishment, "suffering blows
bravely . . . , 8 strong birchers . . . , taking a beating . . . , 8 strong lictors
equipped with flexi elm birches" (557, 564-5, 569, 574-5).[11] When these couriers decide to eavesdrop on The Lovers, instead of badass Lizard wishing
he had his whip about him, a re-verbera-ting idea strikes agent Two (the
former mock Lizard. 589-90, *uerberarem*):

LEO   I really do wish I had a pole.

LIB   Oh yeah, and what for?

LEO   To beat
the *a$$es* with, happen they start making a racket from the
shoulder bag here.[12]

The slaves assent. "The pain of Love's Torment is nothing to the pain of
Slaves' Torture—they should know—they've tried it" (617-18). With which
lacerating point, they burst the bubble, with more verbal reverberations of
beating upon beating (626-8). Little master has learned the power ascribed
to money; the slaves proceed to cash this in. For 20 minae, they'll ascend
from slaves to freedmen to patrons (and he'll move down from master to
patron to client, 651-2: 653):

There's 20 minae here, inside this money-pouch.

The "gas" in *Asinaria's* bag of tricks comes between this tantalizing news and the eventual hand-over (732–4):

LIB>ARG   . . . Father ordered us to fetch *this*
                        cash here to you.
ARG>LIB   Great timing, spot on. You've fetched it right
                                                    on the dot.
                    In here there'll be 20 minae, good uns.

But if this will be the Son's reward for taking his beatings like a human donkey, the suffering's still only just begun: with the money comes the blow of Father's terms and conditions. So has the poor boy really learned slave phlegm? (738–9: how facile in fact is *faciet facile?*):[13]

LEO   Will you endure it,
                                                            Argyrippus,
                    —your dad hugging *her* tight?
ARG   *This*'ll ease me into enduring it.
                                                    Easy.

For the last Act, Son will be forced to perform the slave's shtoom part for Father at least as well as the slave had for big Master in the first Act. He is bound to "suffer it," must indeed acknowledge it out loud, only to be *told* he is told to (*perpeti . . . perpetere*, 845, 847: p. 147). He must at all costs play up to his tormentor's mood: join in with the party, sweet wine, sweet talk, love, be of good cheer, wear a smile, be glad his wishes have come true, and thank him for the chance to say thanks for the chance to say so (830–50: 850):

Ow! Doing that bound me to you, fast.

This may not earn him much, though he will have the last word in the drama, and when he does leave, he'll leave invited inside into the motel asylum with the floozie. And he does duck the play's sting in the tale of revenge, which unfolds when the wrath of comedy's losers ignites with Diabolus' outrage (810):

Me? Suffer this? Keep mum?

and erupts with killer matrona's fury (907):

> non queo durare.
>
> ~
>
> I just cannot endure it.

That's why mama will never make a comic hero: she has rights to assert. She is in command, and in the ascendancy. She *has* money, so she doesn't need it. She has power, so isn't treated as cash on legs. She is the boss, so isn't hardened to suffering. No chance of *her* grinning and bearing it, gritting teeth and wearing a smile, tickling the torturer's ears and bragging of the traumas out of earshot.

She had no business showing up at asinine *Asinaria* and pooping the party. She had no part to play—other than to part the assembled company. The whirlwind whistle-blower She. Has been (t)here all along, on their back, athwart every lap-eared Roman husband (*auritum-maritum poplum*). The invisibly audible Reality Principal, as in Ariel: "Thou liest" (if you know Shakespeare's *Tempest*).

Imperium. Command is on display in this tempestuous play. Command—command the house, the stage-door, entry/exit. Open for money. Money for sex. Sex money, sexy money. The bank will pay XXXX to the bearer on demand: cash it out. Do the donkey-work. Put your back into it and a shine on it. Whatever it takes. Scars and stripes. Choking words. Down on the knees. Straight up a cliff. Obeisance. Slave away. Enslaved to slaves. We all are, they know it. They could explain, but cannot. That would be plain silly. In our minds as in our ears.[14]

There's a lot to put up with. Money makes donkey-work for its bearers and beneficiaries alike. For the slaves, this is one more chore to put their backs into: portering, first Two, then the other, One (657–63, 689–90):

ARG>LEO	Do put your deposit here. Check this pouch here. Plain flat on my neck.
LEO>ARG	You're my master, I will not have you shoulder this burden for me.
ARG>LEO	Why don't you liberate yourself from labour, and stick it on me?
LEO>ARG	I'll be porter. You, as befits an owner, go ahead, unladen.
ARG>LEO	Hey now.

LEO>ARG	Whassup?
ARG>LEO	Why don't you hand it here to flatten my shoulder?
LEO>ARG	Her—the one you will hand this to—tell *her* to beg and plead with me.
	Where you told me to check it, slopes on the vertical plane. That's flat.

· ·

ARG>LIB	Dear Libanus, my patron, hand it over to me. It's more fit someone liberated hump a load on the street than a patron.

Askew and aslant, agent One is here dubbed *Libanus,* not just for "Lebanon" and "frankincense," like many a Greek slave, but for "Liberation" from "labour," and undubbed ~~Libanus~~ for *libertus.* Plautus' pleasure principle puts plenty into ad libbing with the name (*ubicumque libitum erit animo meo,* 110, cf. 711, *ut est libitum*).[15] On one side he is the softie binary for toughie Spartan Leonhardtsen (627 ~ 681): *Libanum . . . libentiores . . . quam Libentiast* (268: a comic pretend deity); sacrifice is due to Λίβανος (712–13). On the other, he is the comedy's free spirit: *Libanum . . . liber* (274–5); *Libanum libertum* (411, cf. 689–90). In Plautus' day, the middle of Mars' month of March *could* make an aptly Marsy Gras moment to stage *Asinaria:* Republican Rome had celebrated the year's traditional puberty rite for its *adulescentes,* the granting of the *toga uirilis,* then—at the Liberalia: *libera lingua loquemur ludis Liberalibus* ("We'll lloose lliberated llingo at the Lliberalization Festival (of Bacchus)," Naevius, fr. 27 Warmington).[16]

[Libanus is also named at 35, 54, 60, 64, 249, 287, 312, 408, 616, 629, 677, 683, 707.]

Libanus' "neck" is, besides, the right verbal place to "check" luggage, *collum/collocare.*[17] The jokes make it "plain" that the jokes are about "plane": *plane/plane.* The slapstick slippery "slope" in play acts out social status. It will be the creative matrix for the double satire on master Master ahead, which deserves an encore, and second thoughts, and is about to get it. In the neck—check.

First, the heir apparent is forced to kneel before the knees of "his" brave slave. To worship the legs of every human carthorse that ever lugged lumber (339–40):[18] "You must be meaning those donkeys—clapped out, lame, and with hooves worn down up to the hocks?" (670–71, 674–8):

LEO>ARG	And yet sure you'll not carry it off, unless knees get a massage.
ARG>LEO	What it takes—"needs must"—command away, massage 'tis. Pay what I beg?

. . . .

LEO>PHIL	. . . If this was mine, this day you'd never plead with me, and me not give it. Better you plead with *him*—he gave it me, to keep safe . . .
LEO>LIB	Cop this, p-lease, Libanus.
ARG>LEO	Ball-n-chain, have you dared make fun of me?
LEO>ARG	Lord, I'd never've done it if . . . you weren't so . . . bad at massaging knees.

This is Agent Two's bag, he makes all too convincing a budding actor of Mastery. He invented the humiliation of grovelling below the knee as a typically sadistic punishment for a non-existent crime, arbitrarily triggering a groundless complaint at imaginary shortcomings of Slavery: "nice try, boy, but you ain't getting nowhere" (678). Agent One takes up the baton as he cops the holdall with the stash inside. First (we just heard tell) he reprises the refusal to permit Sonny Jim the token sop of "portering" (689–90). Then, hey up, he invents a rhyming humiliation of social elevation, riding high on the back of the workers, weighing heavy on the necks of the underling downstairs.

Once firmly astride the saddle, the new boss shows (encore) *he* knows imperious, ten-a-penny cruelty inside-out and upside down. He comes up with a sarcastic barrage of running complaints, taunts, threats, and final dismissive insult of bogus disssatisfaction—trumped-up, acted up, imitated to the life. To "carry off" the cash, the Badly Drawn Boy is going to have to stoop to conquer. He must "hoist" his inferior, the trash *he* will trample through their lifetimes long. Whoa there, steady up; this is assuredly, lord, one of the highpoints and at the same time one of the lowpoints of Roman theatre (699–710):

LIB>ARG	uehes pol hodie me, siquidem hoc argentum ferre speres.
ARG>LIB	ten ego ueham?
LIB	tun hoc feras argentum aliter a me?

ARG	perii hercle. si uerum quidem et decorum erum uehere seruum, inscende.
LIB	sic isti solent superbi subdomari.
	asta igitur, ut consuetus es puer olim. scin ut dicam?
	em sic. abi, laudo, nec te equo magis est equos ullus sapiens.
ARG	inscende actutum.
LIB	ego fecero. hem quid istuc est? ut tu incedis?
	demam hercle iam de hordeo, tolutim ni badissas.
ARG	amabo, Libane, ohe iam sat est.
LIB	numquam hercle hodie exorabis.
	nam iam calcari quadrupedo agitabo aduorsum cliuom,
	postidea ad pistores dabo, ut ibi cruciere currens.
	asta ut descendam nunciam in procliui, quamquam nequam es.
	~
LIB>ARG	So you'll give me a ride, lord, today if you'll hope to fetch this cash.
ARG>LIB	*Me* give *you* a *ride*?
LIB	Gonna fetch this cash off me some other way?
ARG	Lord, I've had it. If it is fit for owner to give slave a ride— climb on.
LIB	Shit happens. Here's how the overblown undergo subdual.
	So stand ready, the way you used to as a kid. Know how I mean?
	Pow, that's the way. Get going. Well done, no horse is as smart as you, horsey.
ARG	Climb on right away.
LIB	I'll do it. Hey up, what's this? How you going?
	Lord, I'll take some feed away if you don't highstep à grand galop.
ARG	Please, Libanus, whoa there, enough.
LIB	Lord, you'll never plead a yes today.
	'Cos now I'll use the spur, and drive you straight up the slope, at a trot.
	Later I'll give you to the millers, for torture there at the races.

> Steady, so I c'n climb down now on the slope, though you're
> one bad 'un.   710

The imposition on master steps up: "carry" → "hump" → "give a ride" (*fero* → *porto* → *ueho*).[19] Putting him through his paces deals another "blow": *em sic* (704). If you will, a physical smack on the rump just to steady the ride for mounting, the injury before the insult added in the verbal pat on the back, "Good boy," which precedes the instant switch-round "Gee up" that marks the off: *hem quid istuc est?* (705: with aspirate). Plus immediate threats if the pace isn't exactly right.

This—ow—is how it feels to be sat on, and any steed that wants to unseat the rider—"Whoa" (706)—needs reminding who has the whip hand. New boss, same as the old boss (we don't get fooled again). The slave knows how to act tall in the saddle, he digs spurs into his beast so as to drive him full-tilt up to the top of the hill, before at once forcing the inevitable ride back down again. Verbally, threats turn dressage into deliberate working to death. Workhorse slaves know exactly where they are headed.

As things are, their end is that workhouse, the m**l, where society finds the staff of life, but knackered animals—horses, asses, humanoid vehicles—find a never-ending round of grinding toil, pain as bad as any fiendish punishment devised for slaves and criminals, and every hour of it a flat-out rotary race to oblivion, hauling ass (709). Worse than bizarre that "This is the earliest literary reference to an animal-driven mill that has come down to us."[20]

That lies ahead. Immediately, the jumped-up jockey knows an exquisite torture to inflict on a mount: pulling up to dismount on a downhill slope. Riding begins and ends with commands, to "Stand ready" and come to a "Stand still." Slavery amounts to a lifetime of "standing by" (*asta*, 703, 710). There is no escape from that ascent, the "slope" of social standing (*aduorsum cliuom . . . in procliui*, 708, 710 ~ *procliue*, 663). "Climbing on" meant backing up, halting, and make pony stand ready, steady, wait for it (| *inscende*, 702; | *inscende*, 705). "Climbing down" means a noisily sadistic kick in the teeth in the form of another effortless bogus complaint. No, horsey isn't the "Good Horsey" he was patted for in the paddock. He should be ashamed of himself; fancy winding up as one more four-footed also-ran who don't make the grade: "You're one bad 'un" (710: note the assonance):

*descend*am *nunci*am *in procliui*—quamquam *nequam es.*

The banter between the foursome of fellow human beings began with pity felt and instantly retracted by slaves toward lovers: "the pain of Love is nothing to the pain of slave torture—they should know—they've tried it" (617–18, *O Libane, miser est homo qui amat.—immo hercle uero. | qui pendet multo est miserior*). Losing a patron for the future is no loss to the slave—he can't lose what he never had (621–2). The juvenile lead needs breaking in to get real, his self-pity just has it coming (629–30):

> How you guys' fortunes leave mine far behind in their wake, Libanus.
> For this day I shall never live till evening.

No wonder the slaves put their heads together and go on the offensive. Right away, "20 minae" up slaves in the ascendant to freedmen to patrons, and down boy from master to patron to client (651–2). Agent Two then enforced supplication. Agent One took over, and made himself a second patron, outstripping the ascription of that daft name of his (689–90):

> Dear Libanus, my patron, hand it over to me. It's more fit
> someone liberated hump a load on the street than a patron.

When he enforced equitation, little master thought it was the pits, and told the world why (701–2):

> Lord, I've had it. If it's fit for owner to give slave a ride—
> climb on.

This provokes an outburst from the high and mighty One, a triumphant yelp which marks the equestrian event as the centrepiece of *his Asinaria* (702):

> *Happens all the time.* Here's how the overblown undergo subdual.

All this was set up by the attempt to unload the Courier in the last show-down showpiece, where the truculent violence of that slave steward rode roughshod over social stratification (*non decet* superbum *esse hominem seruom*, 470, *tun libero homini male seruos loquere?*, 476). Now, in the sequel, the role of principal boy bears for a second the whole load of class-hatred for society en masse: give untermensch his head, and he'd make sure pride goes before a fall, *sic:*

super → sub-.

About as likely outside farce as the chance this nonce-verb has of ever catching on in Latin (*subdomo* is a ἅπαξ). It would mean turning boasts into beasts, hosses and asses into bosses and posses. Worse, this is the excruciating moment when "carrying the cash" choreographs ultimate humiliation of our prince charming into "carrying the trash." Getting mounted means standing still while the creature from the bottom of the pile takes advantage of his chance to play Mr Big, by messing around with his mind as much as his body, his memory as well as his bottom (702–5):

ARG	Climb on. . . .
LIB	So stand ready, the way you once did as a kid. Know how I mean?
	Pow, that's the way. Get going. Well done, no horse is as smart as you are, horsey.
ARG	Climb on right away.
LIB	I'll do it. . . .

Our young lover was once a boy and was treated as a "boy" (*puer*). But "boy" also means "boy" as in "slave" (*puer*). According to this smear, boys were used to being treated like slaves, and that means putting up with having to stand by patiently while being mounted astern—from the rear. Playing piggy-back games with dobbin is innocent; the slave's fun innuendo of passive buggery for master Master is not.[21] The infantilization of superior breeding assuredly completes the comic game set and match:

slave → beast of burden → boy → defenceless child victim → bum boy.

Whereas the expulsion of the *adulescens* from the bordello was a formulaic shouting-match of irate degradation, swearing to tame the household by dumping it back in the gutter where he found it (138–45, esp. 145, *reddam ego te ex fera fame mansuetem, me specta modo*, cf. 504, *nequeon . . . te . . . facere mansuetem . . . ?*),[22] Sir Slave Knight's crossing of sexual with status subjugation knots together Plautus' nadir and zenith of carnival subversion through extraordinary comedic hyperventilation.

All good thinks come to an end. The slaves are finally brought down to earth by being elevated to heaven. Ultimate satisfaction takes the form of

ascension and obeisance, and the opportunity to play One god off against
another god, Two (712–16):[23]

ARG	*You giving me the cash?*
LIB	Yes, if you stand me statue and altar status.
	sacrifice an ox to me here like a god: for you, I'm Salvation.
LEO	You just shoo him away from you, master, step my way on your own,
	the orders he gave for himself, stand me them too, down on your knees?
ARG>LEO	Which god am I to name you?
LEO>ARG	Fortune, yep, Fortune in Your Favour.

To be sure, this denouement caps the theme of heartfelt supplication from
a believer that runs through the whole encounter: prayers for salvation
from cruel fortune have accompanied salivating rituals of self-abasement
(*salue*, 619, 623, *salus*, 648, 656, 672; cf. 911; *sospitor*, 683; *serua*, 654, 688, cf.
256, *and* 17, 911;[24] *uostrae fortunae*, 629,[25] *supplico*, 682, 715).[26] If (spurred
by the puns *ut est libitum . . . Libanus*, 711, and *statuam . . . statuis*, 712)
we thought that sacrifice to Lord *Libanus* ought simply to feature *frankincense*, we have missed the religious conversion of the governing metaphor of servitude as donkey business for tetrapods of every rank: for the
extortioner's demand is that an *ox* be the immolated victim (713). Bovine,
equid, andrapod—the story of human culture.

The invocation of these twain divinities creates the transition to the
topic of wishes, not horses, and so to the play-off between One and Two:
with the last words in the scene the girl presses the button: "They're awmighty good goddesses, both of them" (719). Her first appeal to the slaves
who hold the mastercard had been to beg Two (665):[27]

Don't *unyoke* us, we are lovers.

Between these interventions, Philaenium has been played off against Argyrippus by the uppity slaves, and she has been played off between them,
too. The quartet of bipeds move in and out of teaming up as a pair of
quadrupeds.

In terms of theatre somatics (you heard), when the two slaves stepped aside for a pow-wow, so both were in it together, they turned down the boy's encouragement that "it's sweeter to chat in a clinch," on the grounds that *they* can do without that, but *he should certainly take his own advice* (639–44).[28] So the lovebugs wrap themselves around each other again, while the conspirators plot their mutiny, just as they had when making their saccharine "hope to die" vows and wishes, and so induced the slaves to break cover and break up the schmaltz (613–15):

PHIL   My mind's made up. I'll do to myself all that you do to yourself.
ARG   Oh honey's sweet, you are sweeter.
                                              Sweeter than life to me,
                                                   you are.
              Let's have a hug.
PHIL   Oh yes please let's.
                                              Wish we can get buried
                                                   this way.

It's the "eye-stinging" hug (remember?) that the slaves can't stand a moment more, as they encircle the babes (619–20). It's the girl they crudely go for, after putting the boy down (623–4 ~ 621–2). This first verbal-reverb of an assault puts master Master's back up, while his slaves back down and bicker (625–8: 625):

Mind, *not a beep out of you,* whipping-boy.

This is the provocation that launches the running aggravation that aims to come between the lovers.[29]

First off, Two demands that the girl's pleas move beyond words, and get physical (662, 664–7 ~ 668). For his turn, One puts down His lead, and demands an ego massage from Her—"loving or kissing?—Both!" (683–5 ~ 686–8). Boy ups the ante, and so does She: "I'll do what you want, just give us the cash" (692). But (we saw), no more than the back, the neck is never far from slave thoughts (657–63). Next this slavering slave wants *his* whack of kiss-ass flattery, topped by *his* piece of ass, a milli-second of "necking" (694–5 ~ 695–6: 696):

Make me a collar of your arms, hug me tight all around the neck.

Both lovers need practice at buttering up "master." They let their merce-
nary drive *show,* calling the couriers "treasure, supply-line" (655) and "eye
of gold, gift and glory of love" (691, *aureus, donum*). Neither "lover" needed
any coaching in how to treat a person under their command who played
up. It was the young man's own fault that his protests prompted his exquisite humiliations (669 ~ 697–8):

ARG>LEO	Kiss you, her, whipping boy?
LEO>ARG	So just how insulting did that look?
	~
ARG>LIB	Hug you, executioner?
LIB>ARG	So just how insulting do I look?
	No you won't speak such an insult against me and not pay for it . . .

The slave duo had from the start seen how to bracket the couple to cause
the maximum hurt. They'll single out the girl, so that her sucking up to them
will provoke the boy into provoking them to massive retaliation (646–8):

LEO	. . . Like some fun with master?
LIB	Sure got it coming.
LEO	Want me to have Philaenium give you a hug, *in front of him?*
LIB	Lord, I fancy that.

The plan—"Cuddle her till he's a laughing-stock" (679)—imposes its shape
on the scene to the end, where "beg" and "suck up" turn into those twin ge-
nii of Salvation and Favouring Fortune, once the boy has made his double
wish for "a year of her to himself" plus "20 handy minae" (720–25). The
drama turns on this logic of "linkage": where the courier would not release
the funds to the agents "Unless Big Master is present" (*ero praesente . . . ,
ero . . . praesente,* 455–6), the slave successors to his role insist on "A hug
from the girl while Little Master is present" (*praesente hoc,* 647). The
money lubricates the circuit of desire in which the lad must let the agents
make a pass at his lass so that he may buy her body for himself, exclusive.
This is exactly what his father means to lay on him, momentarily, as slang
puts it. Buying love, he bought the girl, and bought his son, enslavering
over both of them.[30]

Boxed in by money and family, unlike the rival who gets to share venting the displaced Oedipal venom with the other surrogate figures of Jocasta-Clytemnestra-matrona, and her parasitic pal,[31] poor little lover must at once grow the patience of a slave. He can't pull it off. But (recall) the whole idea that love is misery was scotched from the start: the slaves as usual know better. Accordingly, as will not elude anyone in the audience, revenge on the person of his lordship is only skin-deep. They treat Argyrippus as horse, not ass.[32] Going weak at the knees, the slaves talk the girl's billing and cooing into verbal fantasia,[33] but the boy's torments are confined to (mere) portering, flattened shoulder, kneeling, and the saddle, not the real thing, the slaves' back/hide/neck/legs, beating, breaking and blows, whips and hooves worn up to here. . . . In parallel, the girl *says* "She'll do anything, for the dosh" (692). But there is not the slightest risk that anything but token, momentary excruciation will be imposed on the prince and his showgirl.

> As you like it.
> As you were.
> God-man-beast.

A Right Earful

Audience as *Asinaria*

As well as eyes and spectacles, playwrites make audiences need ears and ear-trumpets,[1] as much as slaves and children (64–5):

> Parents the world over, Libanus, will take their kids,
> *if they'll hear me out,* and do some favouritism . . . .

This includes everyone in town. (= "Keep your ear to the ground!: all of us are [in] this play.")[2] *Hearing* is reading out [loud]. It is [not] heeding, [dis]obedience, trying to attune, reaching for the intonation, following along a rhythm, indulgence; and it is overhearing, sneering, snooping, spying ready to snitch, and give the game away. To mention "hearing" is to command people—to suss, and lend 'em, out. This is how the play functions, and it is what the play, as such, is about. This re-wind chapter is devoted to listening when *The One about the Donkeys* tells us to. Let's listen. Hard and easy.[3]

(1) Back at the start, the slave heard himself booked for master's agent, not condemned to the mill. As they split, agent One found control passing over to himself. Pater calls twice through the distance: "You listening?" (*audin*, 109, 116).[4] To ask and (absolutely vital, this, did they but know it) to tell whereabouts they'll be. Master can't (over)hear the asides: "I'll be *anywhere I please*"; and, the future holds no fears (110–13: 114):

> *Why, you'll be no big deal for me, if I pull this off.*

Slave's lobes would have burned if he'd stayed to hear master out, singing his praises (118–26. *m- m- m- m-*: 121; for 124: p. 158). He didn't.

(2) Client's voluble volleys drew Madam out in the street. They trade ear-fuls. Her "Scram" calls his bluff, "Wait, wait, listen" (*audi*, 228–9). He is given terms for an assignation; they are non-negotiable; the door slams.

(3) We begin the Courier scene "with" agent One. We are privy to his re-actions as he overhears soliloquizing Two's asthmatic crowing, hell for leather. He does love to hear himself talk. The late arrival needs a silencer fitted, as well as a break: his tongue is his "patron" (290–2), the top of the voice is needed for him (296), but questions must be calm before he as-phyxiates himself (326).[5]

At last they meet, in pomp and fatuousness (cue messenger of tragedy: *quod adfers aures expectant meae . . .* , 331–2):

LIB	What's that you're fetching? Mine ears are a-g-o-g.
LEO	Focus your mind. You'll know it, I'll know it, fair do's.

= "Pray hush" in the theatre, no pin must drop in this otoscope for Rome. We must all bear with plot exegetics (*ausculta*, 350):[6]

LIB	What next?
LEO	So listen *up, and* you'll know.

Courier goes to knock (i.e., kick) at the door.[7] We're waiting for him, and get in first, with "Basta! Don't beat down my mate the door, with your kick like a mule!" (*ohe, inquam, si quid audis*, 384; *uerberarier*, 387; *calcitronem*, 391). We watch the matinee rehearsal for the scene, then overview the two agents' attempt to method-act Courier off the stage, minus payload.

For Courier's benefit, Two-as-Three fakes splenetics at One, until he risks earache nauseating him out of town (446–8):[8]

```
LIB>ATR                                              heus iam satis tu,
                 audin quae loquitur?
ATR>LIB                           audio et quiesco.
MERC>LIB                                    —tandem opinor.
                 conticuit. nunc adeam optimum est priusquam incipit tinnire.
```

~

LIB>STEW	Hey,
	enough's
	plenty.

You hear what he's saying?

STEW>LIB   *I do hear. I'll simmer down.*

MERC>LIB   He's

hushed,

now's best to approach him. Before the tinnitus begins.

We overhear asides from Courier to us; between agents and Courier, and agent to agent, in our hearing; assorted asides meant to be overheard and—not.[9] This is eery drama, defamiliarized otology. Nothing works, everyone meets their asymmetric match: *exeunt omnes.* But just LISTEN: as sigmatism threatens to cut loose, and then does, the scene con-cludes (467–7; 493, 499, 502–3):

. . . supplicassis.

. . . tractare sese.

. . . molestus ne sis.

. . . .

. . . fortassis . . .

| fortasse . . .

| fortasse . . . percontatus esses

. . . negassim. ||

(4) Juicy Lucy *says* she's "a good girl: she (has to) hear mama out—and listen!"—cowed into serfdom (she *means,* in this parting shot of protest) with a flea in her ear for going astray (516–18: *audientem dicto, mater, produxisti filiam,* 544).[10]

(5) We begin the cash-undelivery scene with harmonies, One, Two, before Three, Four, the suicidal lovelorn, come on for their eavesdropping: "Zip your mouth . . . , let's listen in . . . , let's shut up and listen" (*subauscultemus; taciti auscultemus,* 586, 588). "You hear? . . . Put a stop to your chit-chat, so I can take in his" (*audin,* 598).

The slaves love 'em and leave 'em, stepping aside for a confab, a word-in-the-ear not a cuddle (619, 639). Hatch the plan to mock the Babes in the Wood: "Listen up, help out, gobble my words" (*auscultate,* 649).

Histrionics divide and link lovers, lovers and agents, agents and agents; the parting of the ways comes from the lad, who takes loot and lady indoors, with a "Whoa! Sh—don't put the mockers on it!" (*heia,* | *bene dicite,* 744–5).

(6) The prize bore, earnest Ernest, is not cut out for "wit and fun," and is cut out of it. Here hear his Pal read out the proposed contract for him, to give us "a(n ear-splitting, side-splitting) gas." "Listening to it will freak out madam.... You listening?" "I am. All ears" (*cum audiet; audin? audio,* 749–50). Resuming, to conclewd: "Hear the rest." "Speak, I hear you" (*audi relicua. loquere, audio,* 791).

The anti-dramaturgic otacoustic dollop of play-reading sticks out a mile after the sparky buzz of electricity just circuited round the stage. Hiatus-ridden and gagging, the monotone monologism of obsessional, myopic, legal Latinity sets us up for the imminent crescendo of consternation, invasion, outrage, closedown. How blinkered are we to the special(ly otic) FX of the let-down? Schadenfreude rides again.

(7) It's a bust, the script runs ragged (p. **181**). The rival's agent calls matron in to suffer heartbreak, fly-on-the-wall: "There's your guy . . . Let's catch birds from our secret (am)bush . . . You hear what he's saying?" "I hear" (880–1; *audin quid ait? audio,* 884) The eggshell "scene within a scene" structure implodes when she does, reeling at pater's lucky throw of the dice: "I can't endure it" (*non queo durare,* 907: pp. **181–2**).

Her world (and it *is* her world) falls about her ears, torn asunder: she must be hearing things. At the death [of dramatic intercourse], her along-for-the-ride "assistant" scrams, and jolly japes fray into so many loose ends of pandemonium astir, before dinnertime unwinds into throwback incantatory hounding, as the cacophonous bray of anti-marriage reels in our gelded hero (*domum,* 867, 897, 902, 937; *i domum,* 940; and the full—half-line—formula, at 921, 923, 924, 925, p. **182**: this time, we *all* sing):

surg^e, a—mator,—i dom—um. |

~

Up, lov—erman,—home you—go. |

M a t r o n a is only named at 885, when set on the warpath (and [by conjecture] at 908). No doubt Ἀρτεμώνη is a vengeful "A r t e m i s" who always gets her man,[11] and she makes a fearful Graeco-Latin paragram. As her tongue-lashing whips the comedy home, it's hard not to see her as the play's ultimate slave-driver. Prologue did tell us to listen to the play rename itself (10–12: p. **xii**): "... changed its name from the Greek name of the play." By the end, surely we'll see that *The One about Donkeys* turns out to be *The One about the Donkey-driver,* after all.

Even as we recognize the formulaic label [sc. *fabula*] *Asin-aria,* the Plautin will still tell us not to miss the inflection of *asinar-i-:* for an *asinaria* would be a (woman) "donkey-driver," and a *fabula asinaria* would be *her story,* too.[12] In Greek, for good measure, ὈΝΑΓΟΣ, *The Donkey-driver,* is "common gender," so *anyone can play, including the matron.* It is down to her that the plot can come about (now we know [*that* is] why she bought those donkeys in the first place), and now both Demophilus and Plautus "bring their ass" on-stage, and show it off: him, her, them, and us, asses, asses, and morasses. So, yes indeed, the change of title does make "such infinitesimal difference" (pp. **xii, 191, 219 n.5**). And that *is* "fun."

Res ridicula est.

The oldster's grouch was that he was displaced by mrs from his own home, her owned home. Finally he got his wish, to join forces with their son. Only, he joined them forcibly (843–9):

ARG
> ... and yes, too, lord, tell you the godhonest
> > truth, father,
> this scene hurts me bad. No, not that I'm not passionate for you,
> > all you want,
> but I love her. ...
>
> . . . .
>
> ... So you got your wish: I want my wish for me.

DEM
> You'll endure this one single day through. *Because* I've handed
> > you power
> to be with her for a year, I've come up with the cash to fund
> > loverboy.

ARG
> Ow! Doing that bound me to you, fast.

So far, so good: game, set, and match. The son got *exactly what he had coming.* Just what he had asked for, in the first place. An unstoppable reason for *not* asking your dad for any personal favours (*tibi . . . amanti argenti feci copiam*, 848–9 ~ *uti sibi amanti facerem argenti copiam*, 76). An emotional licking: "Ow!" (*em*: cf. the "smile that hurts," 841, *em aspecta: rideo*, with 431, *em ergo hoc tibi.*).[13] Gotcha (*deuinxti*).[14] Father does fuse with son, for matrona has made him into the third of daughter's would-be Young Men to be thrown out of mama's house and into the street. This is what the play made us, and told us, to watch. That little ear-tickler of a song-and-dance from the lucked-out "chucked-out" lover began there (*foras aedibus me eici?*, 127; *eicis domo*, 161). As Madam retaliates, she does as she says she does when she *says*, ponderously, how "The doors of a brothel open to fee-paying customers, but visitors who can't pay find the door shut" (241–2, *ianuae lenoniae*), and with that auricular-oracular keynote promptly *does* it, disappearing indoors, shutting up shop. That's the way, you can't beat it. Do your stuff, and beat it.

Now. Do it *your* ways.

> The lovers bang the brothel door behind them.
> Cue the whole cast to meet on stage to end it all.

Epilogue

942–947 Some curtain call: your applautus is appreciated

A Roman audience has been round the theatre block before.[1] Knows that an actor applauded is *also* a slave saved, from lashings of lashing. The lead *is* a mule, as well as today playing one, and his hide stands to suffer the tanning that the slaves playing the slave roles have bespoken as the story of their lives (p. **235 n.5**). So today's play bows out with a re-doubled plea to show appreciation, once for the slave/star, twice for the master/butt. The pitch goes: the good name (of) Δημ-αίνετος is at stake. *Omnes parentes* listening to him in the *auritus poplus* should stand up for him: "*Celebrity-Celebrated.*" In a word, as in eras bygone of participatory-solidary masculinist socio-politics, this civic theatre can still ring in our ears: "*Vulgaire-Populaire.*"

The play's Snitches saw pa "with his son, at son's girl's place, drinking the day long, robbing wife blind" (825–6, *cum suo . . . gnato . . .*). We produce our take on the orgy (literally) as we see it, then hear that they told Ma (what she least wanted to hear, and was bound to rise to), and she agreed, that pa was flipping his lid "with his son's knowledge" (853, *meo . . . filio sciente . . .*). We get to hear Snitch repeat the exposée—in the version "with his son alongside" (863, *cum filio | potet* una atque una *amicam ductet . .*). What gets her is partly that her mule is kicking in another stall (874), partly that "the pervert's perverting his very own son" (875, *. . . suum corrumpit filium*), as pa performs—confesses? brags?—for her and us to witness and judge ourselves (882–3, fateor, *gnate mi . . .* me corruptum *uideo*). Accordingly, *her* beef is that pater's crime is the disgrace of putting the—their—child on the receiving end of such behaviour: a Father to be ashamed of (932, *istoscine patrem . . . mores largiri liberis*). So far as *she* is concerned, this is a family play, about the desecration of the family. Look no father (862): *hoc facto sese ostendit.*[2] We remember, too, that Demaenetus told us, told Slave confidant, and told himself, that what he was doing was focussed on be(com)ing his son's beloved father (67, 76–7): *uolo amari a meis* |; *ego percupio obsequi nato meo,* | *uolo amari ʔobsecutam ʔ illius, uolo amet me patrem*. His idea was to buy his son's love just the way his father had his, and sod the shame (71–3) *neque puduit eum . . . beneficiis me emere gnatum suum sibi.* | *eos me decretum est persequi mores patris*). *This* father wanted to do same as *omnes parentes* (64). The epilogue offers a different line. Here, all there is to play for, apparently, is that this guy cheated on his wife, *for his own gratification* (942):

> . . . *suo animo fecit uolup.*

Qua farce, that is to say, *Asinaria* invites you to get real and resist sanctimonious clap-trap: it can look like the script's last word cues Self-Regard, pure and simple. Brackets off children from parents. For in the beginning, our clapped-out Father who ain't in heaven didn't just trot out The Plot. No, he was telling everyone with ears to hear, compellingly-compulsively so you know it's his truth, *exactly* what's driving his plane (67–77, 83): *uolo . . . uolo, percupio . . . uolo . . . uolo . . . , cupio* (cf. 84, *cupis . . . cupere*). In the end, *that* is Plautus' "clap trap": let's hear it for the Pleasure Principal. Put your hands together, for *uolup*'s sake (846):

> at ego hanc uolo.
>
> ~
>
> Well, *I want* her, I do.

The heart of the matter, she's a private dancer, do what you want (her) to do: this theatre imprint—this economy of pleasure—plays through its cityscape scenario of bawdello amenities to up the libidinal stakes of comic concupiscence (237–9, *si tu uoles . . . ut uoles, ut tibi libebit . . . nobis legem imponitio*, 737, *quae uolet faciemus*, 835, *amari mauolo*, 844–6, *quae uelis . . . uolo . . . uolo*). Let's hear it one more time: Plautine myth reinvests community in the risking of full selfhood to the velleity reserved for *pater* (*ego = uolo*).

As Niall Slater's fine tailpiece on "the Epilogue" marvelously concludes: "As Tinkerbell is revived by the audience's applause in J. M. Barrie's *Peter Pan?*"[3] Well, yes. And more "as"s:

> As a play, *Peter Pan* is above all famous for the moment when Peter Pan turns
> to the audience and asks if it believes in fairies. This is ~~merely~~ an extreme
> version of the demand of any play that, at least for the duration of its per-

formance, the audience should believe that it is true. . . . In point of fact it is too easy to give an Oedipal reading of *Peter Pan*. The father, Mr. Darling, is humiliated—he plays a joke on Nana the nurse (the New-found-land dog) which falls flat and then challenges the family: "Am I master in this house or is she?" . . . It is equally easy to describe the difficulties that Barrie had in writing, and especially in ending *Peter Pan*. . . . [T]he actors were all sworn to secrecy and . . . no one knew how the play was going to end.[4]

The *Assinaria* audience, too, can go home, go on to their party, dream the dream of having their cake and eating it. Walking the line between *uolup* | and *uapulet* |—"kicks" and "a kicking" (942, 946). As long as we are still here, however, the cast can tell us how *they* see the play. They have the nerve to tell us the old'uns are the best—it's been the old old story all over again, no surprises there (943, . . . *nec secus quam alii solent*):

What he did was nothing new, weird, or off the way other characters behave.

Pater himself had tried to end the play at his highpoint, the zenith of a top "Venus" throw, for rebellion, naughtiness, devilry, sex, frivolity, farce, "fun." Upon that death wish, for "Philaenium for me, me, me, and death for the old lady," he brought the house down (904–5: 906, to a cast of [invisible] cupid extras):

pueri, plaudite.

But in the end, it was always going to be our turn. *Your turn*. What do you reckon to playing Pensioner Pan and Tinkerbell?
Wallop.

Applause: Plaudits please.
If you believe in hoaries.

NOTES
BIBLIOGRAPHY
INDEXES

Notes

Prologue

1. For a couple of lively recent productions, see: (1) www.mun.ca/classics/masc/ asina (director: C. W. "Toph" Marshall, translator: Peter L. Smith, 3–7 March 1997), performed in the drained fountain in front of the University Library, University of Victoria, B.C., and keenly reviewed in *Didaskalia* 4.1 by J. G. Fitch (of UVic) (www .didaskalia.net/issues/vol4no1/fitch.html); (2) www.asscarpediem.it/carpediem in three acts (director: Antonio Anelli), 22 August 1998, at Basico, 28 July 1999 at Barcellona (Sicily), and 30 August 2000 at Terme Vigliatore.

2. In the [devilishly aposiopetic] form *homo homini lupus,* this stars in Bacon, in Hobbes—and in Freud's *Civilization and Its Discontents* (Wright [1974] 136 and n. 16).

3. Cf. Segal (1968) 116.

4. Victorious Rome did go to the theatre in the course of triumphal celebrations (cf. 545–76), but if there was a reason why Mars should "help" out on this play-day we can't *know* it (p. **197**).

5. *Demophilus,* playwright of 'ONAΓΟΣ, is to all intents and purposes lost to us (p. **151**). We know Atellan mimes of Pomponius and Novius were titled *Asina* and *Asinius* (Ribbeck [1873] fr. 226, 255; cf. Putnam [2003] 104–5 n. 10). *Asin-aria* should mean "The Donkey-play"—except that *asinarius* in Latin means "(male) donkey-driver."

"T[itus] Maccius Plautus" appears to be a jocose pseudonym connoting "Phallus the son of Clown [*Maccus* of so-called native Italian "Atellane" farce] the Mime-actor [where *plautus,* or *plotus,* = "flatfoot" = *planipes* = "mime"]" (Gratwick [1973] 83). Cf. p. **172**.

6. Cf. 942–7. For a *grex asinorum:* Tacitus, *Histories* 5.3.

The crier makes a noise, then sits down, and hushes: he is a model theatre-goer (cf. Gilula [1993]).

On the status of these actors and actor-managers: Brown (2002) esp. 235–6 (Jory [1966] holds that the *dominus gregis* is simply the owner of the slave actor).

7. *Auritus* of the ass: e.g. Ovid, *Amores* 2.7.15, with Henderson (1992) 31–2, on contempt imaged for slave Cypassis' scarred chassis; cf. Callimachus, *Aitia* fr. 1.31, on assonance, θηρὶ μὲν οὐατόεντι πανείκελον ὀγκήσαιτο; cf. Bertschinger (1921) 22, on Phaedrus 1.11.6, *auritulus,* and Putnam (2003) 107–8 and n. 24, on Horace's *Vinnius Asina . . . onus* (*Epistles* 1.13.2, 8, 12) answered by Augustus' *Onysius . . .* ὀγκωδέστατος (in Suetonius, *Life of Horace*).

One gain in asinification is "otacoustic amplification": *et aures immodicis horripilant auctibus* (Apuleius, *Metamorphoses* 3.24). Where "Neddy = Big Ears," as in areas such as Apuleius' spectacular-euphonious novel and Plautus' theatre-auditorium, the oral-aural terms and conditions of ancient textuality self-enact, as self-reflexive and self-echoing: see papers in Kahane and Laird eds. (2001), esp. Gibson, Gowers, esp. 77–83, "Ass's ears" (at 83 seeing the point of Plautus' *auritum poplum*), Henderson, Trapp.

Chapter 1. Killing the Plot

1. Cf. *serui quod seruati sunt,* Donatus on Terence, *Adelphoe* 181, Maltby (1991) 564; *Asinaria* 805, *seruus seruet.*

2. Thus the first act's sweetness and light preludes a line-up of noisily detonating temper in store—lovely bad manners, naughty verbal release (pp. **136, 145–6**).

3. I shall presume to give a different inflection to the play's metatheatrics from the "tale of failed improvisation" profiled by the pioneering reading in Slater (1985) 65.

4. I shall project onto the play family values that use but abuse those in the gutsy reading by Konstan (1983) 47–56, esp. 52, "The success of the son's affair is contingent upon the social integrity of the father . . . [who] must now, according to the conventions of this story, mend his ways and take up his proper position in his house. . . . His humiliation is intended to bring him to his senses and make him play the role, at least, of a Roman head of household." Theatre always fights its stock of narratives, whether archetypal, spliced, mutant, or decomposing, and I think reading for the plot sidelines the wind-up in Plautine farce.

5. Treggiari (1991) 323–64, "*Dos,*" at 323.

6. Schuhmann (1977) esp. 62; cf. Nisbet and Rudd (2004) 280 on Horace, *Odes* 3.24.19–20, *nec dotata regit uirum | coniunx.*

7. Rei (1998) esp. 93–4, and Vogt-Spira (1991) esp. 17–26 (who argues that *Asinaria* can have had no Attic original).

8. Σαύρα = "willy" (the one-eyed trouser snake): Bertini (1968), 159 on v. 85 (and 224, on v. 374).

9. Schmidt (1902) reviewed the Greek names in *Asinaria,* coming up with twenty-four, of which ten occur in other comedies as well as in Greek reality, eleven more turn up in Greek reality, and three more are unattested but standard Greek as name-forms.

10. Cf. James (2003) 54 on this *maternal* side of the *lena.*

11. I.e., no credit at all: cf. Freyburger (1986) 223 n. 560 (p. **238 n.30**).

12. The Greek historian Polybius took as long to write the whole story of Rome's reduction of Hellas to *Graecia* as it took the Romans to do it: as detainee and virtual hostage, then honoured guest, friend and counsellor, and finally (not uncritical) apologist. Reading the chunks we have left is our best link into metamorphic Rome from Plautus through . . . Terence (cf. Henderson [2001a]).

13. Wedlocked to frustration, *Asinaria* never leaves us in doubt of "the outcome," speaking through its slave curtain-warmer (84): *cupis id quod cupere te nequiquam intellego.* This show will be short 'n' sour (88, *uerba in pauca*), a psychological study (titter ye ~~not~~) of one underdog's bid to get real, just once (113): "you've *shown the whole of your mind,* in the course of speaking your plea" (cf. pp. **181, 213**). This draining psychodrama—

14. Anderson (1993) 79–82, at 81.

15. Konstan (1983) 47, 48–9.

16. Slater (1985) 64.

17. Henderson (1999) 38–66, on Terence, *Adelphoe,* at 54. This father-son ʾfriendshipʾ is the oddball in the grid of (a dozen) relationships studied by Raccanelli (1998). The father's father bailing him out of trouble (68–73) suggests to father that "permissiveness" *ought* to run in the family (cf. Borghini [1999]).

18. The names (faithfully inventoried by Schmidt [1902]) are an Attic "phone book"; all the same, they contrive to "start" with "*Archi*" and "Hello," "Hello-" in the first verse, and for the second, "Reclining" [symposiast] and *his* Graeco-Latin rhyme "Strange" (*Clinia-Dinia*) sandwich "Neigh-bour" and "Punchbowl" (*Chremes* and *Cratinus*), where the latter wears the legendary name of a classic Attic comedian, a match for the booming finale of *Demosthenes* (865–6). These facile Greek socialites pack in the "light" syllables after the grave entrée of *īt īn cēnam* (864, Gratwick and Lightley [1982] 131).

19. Sutton (1993), 86–96, at 91–2. Cf. 887: p. **181**.

20. I say this lightly, but I don't mean it lightly. Theatre scripts are for playing for all *we* are worth. Thus intrusive "stage directions" from the editor (that's me) would flatten the play there is to be found in the dynamics of Plautus' drama. The same cast can (must, in any case) produce a different take every time, by relating to one another, and responding to relations between the roles differently. Treat the script as a theatre of language, and *re-act.*

21. Henderson (1999) 3–37, on *Poenulus,* at 28.

22. Cf. Virgil, *Aeneid* 4. 314–6, with 328–9.

23. Mounting the scene-setting as dialogue means prejudicing (from) the outset. Paterfamilias + sidekick conspire to stigmatize/pass off matrona as The [deprivative] Enemy (of Comedy), *im-portunam atque in-commodam* (46), but even here the words approved as the instant truth of uncensored thought are in fact minced—masked/marked as *if* "involuntarily" released (46–7, *fateor . . .* | *posterius istuc dicis quam credo tibi,* cf. p. **213**). In production, you can leave her framed, as

stereotyped agelast, or stress that she *has* been framed, when she finally takes the stage to represent *her* victimage (pp. 170–1).

24. Robbins (1993) 53–90, "Impertinence: Servant in Dialogue," at 60.

25. Really, drama provokes more answers than questions. *We* can take the slave's compulsive [half-remarkable] question as *comic fiction* signalling "unconscious" deathwish (hence *dic obsecro hercle* serio, 29, and *caue mihi* mendaci *quicquam*, 30): the flight *is* heading straight for [purgatory], in the "mill" next door / the confines of their home / the pillory of comic theatre. Neither player knows that they have already boarded the plane . . . , in *our* spoof disaster movie.

26. In removing 25–6 (as [?] a later production's version of 23–4), Leo (1895) erased clumsy stage directions for the exchange (bold aggression, appreciated by receptive master). The master's finessing of any questions from the slave deflates all the fuss over the slave's ask about what master is asking of him: it was a set-up (*roges* |, *rogem* |, *rogas* |, 24, 29, 30, cf. *scire . . . scibo . . . scias*, 28–9).

27. For *fides* in *Asinaria*: p. 140.

28. In the Plautin lexikon of slavery, "elm" is going to spell "birch"—a scourging: 262, 341, 547 (?), 565.

29. "Libanus grossly misrepresents what Demaenetus did say to him v. 88 ff." (Gray [1894] 51, ad loc.)

30. Cf. Ennius, *Pancratiastes, Fabulae* fr. 382 Warmington, *quo nunc me ducis?*, presumably from another cowering comic slave to his *senex iratus*: *ubi molarum strepitum audibis* | *maximum*, with Wright (1974) 63–4. The t-r-r-rembling t-r-r-rips in short syllables (31, 34): *ducĭs ŭbĭ lăpis lăpĭdem tĕrit?* | *ăpŭ^d fustĭtŭdĭnas, ferrĭcrĕpĭnas insŭlas.*

In Greek, as it happens, a quern = an "ass," ὄνος, grinding on a μύλη, "millstone" (Moritz [1958] 10–17, "The donkey"; donkeys did not drive pre-Roman Greek mills, cf. p. 200).

31. Libanus' Latin coughs up expressive metrical gobbets that congeal into a word-icon for The Mrs.: *ag-ag*-usqu-exscrea . . . *age quaes-hercl*-usqu-ex . . . quousqu- . . . *r*-uxor*is* (43–8). Later *uxor* will coagulate into *osor* (859). How far will you go? Right down to the depths of the throat? Metapoemetically, this bit of over-acting hits the damned spot right away for the bitter taste of *Asinaria*'s gobbets of bad taste: *do not swallow.*

32. Neither "promise" need deliver: (master) "It won't harm you if you pull off this [swindle] today" :: (slave) "Then you can worry about something else of your choice" (p. 133). Promises are like pleas and wishes—conceptual and verbal precision rules (as in any contract). So are "threats," as when lovers match extremist pledges (604, 611). Comedy tells us we really *ought* to listen hard to just what does get said, or not. As in a real exchange (?).

33. Master and slave further conspire by vying for the lead (61, 63): *tu primus sentis, nos tamen in pretio sumus.* ~ *posterius istuc dicis quam credo tibi.*

34. ~~Suscensere~~ studs the play with wrath looming under erasure: 49, 146, 354, 372, 459.

35. Master joins in this topic to set the mood for today's script: meets his slave halfway by talking his talk. Capping Libanus' pair of nameless places with one of his own (31, 34, *ubi, ubi* ~ 35, *ubi*), he cuts all too close to the grain in grinding out a not-half-ways-bad sampole of scally-wag slave jive (336–7): pol *percepi* . . . pol*enta?*

36. This imagery preludes hooking client fish (178–80) and netting skybird clients with*out* nets (225). As meta-commentary, the script is also writing its own review—"What on earth? The tops in entertainment. Sheer, pure, utter, fantasy. Best since the loaves and fishes sketch. *Impossible* to miss" (90–100, *unde gentium?* | . . . *maximas nugas agis.* |, etc.).

37. Shershow (1986) 48–52, at 52, quoting *Asinaria* 615–7 (my italics). See Parker (1989) esp. 238.

38. On "the junior *meretrices* of comedy . . . who still believe that they can afford to integrate free love into their professional activities," see James (2003) 294 n. 56.

Chapter 2. Drive a Hard Bargain

1. For differentiation between the speech profiles of Plautine roles for women, starring *uxor dotata* as pecking hen, see Schauwecker (2002).

2. See the revisionary theorizing of comic taxonomics in Lowe (2000), "Dramatic Fiction: New Comedy," esp. 194–9 (I do not, however, see how "Philaenium can be Diabolus' sister," 193 n. 10).

3. You have to listen hard to get this crucial suggestion when quietly made by Hunter (1980) 221. The same sort of audience-trap is sprung in Terence, *Adelphoe,* where another prologue swallows its own plot, and sets up its Genial Father as "presumptive voice of the *argumentum*" (22–4): there the first act shows us a pair of fathers alarmed by the hot news that a son is stealing a girl from the town pimp; next thing we know, we see it happening before our eyes—except that at the end of the scene we are "oh-so-casually" given to realise that the boy was indeed doing the deed—but doing it *for* his little brother (Henderson [1999] 58, 61). In *Asinaria* the two lads share their part as (acknowledged) competitors and rivals, not (avowed) brothers and allies.

4. So Sutton (1993) 88, in my view on the right lines, despite over-reading 135 as literally meaning that this *adulescens* has "money . . . earned at sea," and those have been "the savings he has all but run down" (*relicuom,* 233–4. "Leonida," though, is *not* "another female slave in the household": ibid.). Rosivach (1998) 63–6, diagnoses "a long-term relationship with just one young man. . . . We may infer from Cleareta's threat to make her daughter available to another young man that up to this point [Argyrippus] has had exclusive access to her (195). . . . If this affair with [Argyrippus] is Philaenium's first. . . ." "The downfall of all the boys" (*adulescentum pernicies,* 133) is indeed madam's command over their wanting to have the girl for themself, and not have to share with each other (230, *ne cum quiquam alio sit*), and this is indeed the fulcrum of the plot, dictating the contract full of vetoes

on contact with Other Men (751–86, *passim*, cf. esp. Diabolus' amendment at 754) just as it frames the terms and conditions for Demaenetus' mutiny, and ultimately shapes the terms and conditions for the Pal's solution: a time-share between the two lads (916–18: pp. 140–1). Quite apart from unclearity how madam will deal with those 20 minae amidst the ruins of Demaenetus' deal with her, this is forgotten by Rosivach, who sees "the liaison between Argyrippus and Philaenium restored. . . . In time he will settle down. . . . Philaenium and Cleareta will probably fall back upon Argyrippus' rival Diabolus or some other suitably wealthy young man" (65–6).

5. Reassignment of 127–248 from the paradosis' *Argyrippus* to (the so-far-unnamed and unnamable Diabolus) *adulescens-amator* is vital to any reading of the play which is *not* after analyst dismantling: Leo (1895), 1, note on 127, Goetz and Loewe (1889 [1881]), 1: xxiii–xxiv, and (most forcibly) Havet with Freté (1925), introduction, *passim*. There you have it: "Havet bastardized *Asinaria*" (Phillimore [1926]).

Cf. Bertini (1968), esp. 57–9, on Havet's denial of Plautine authorship (which briefly celebrated the *Asinaria* with a [posthumous] volume to itself—by relegation to an appendage to the rest of the Budé series; but comprehensive coverage was soon reasserted: Ernout [1932]); and ibid. 48–56, "*Num Fabula Asinaria Retractata Vel Contaminata Ad Nos Pervenerit Quaeritur,*" esp. 48–9, summarising the reassignment of 127–248 from Argyrippus to the *adulescens* (Diabolus) (which need not be put quite so implausibly as in airier discussions such as Havet [1905] 94–5); *pace* Lowe (1992) 158–63, who refuses the ascription to (Diabolus), and claims that "Havet's theory is open to fatal objections" (160). Danese (2004) also supports, and fully documents, said ascription.

6. Of course this cuts both ways: p. 213.

7. The name occurs in one Greek inscription: Schmidt (1902) 360–1. Solin (2003), 2, 818, records one dubious Diabolus.

8. An obtrusive "elemento Plautino": Scafuro (1997) 455–6.

9. "I am a genre piece," starts the lyric (*sicine hoc fit*, 127: "The Forced Exit"). The first two lines tumble out as they yodel about tumbling out (of the house, as the singer is doing), as *promerenti optime* hoccine *preti redditur* indicates, while preparing the way for the exquisite rhetoric of the "halved" pay off line, *bene merenti mala es* ↔ *male merenti bona es* (so much for *his* unbalanced mind!). The next line picks up *mal-*, and "halves" again, with end rhyme: *at malo cum tuo* ↔ *nam iam ex hoc loco*, but surges off to inform the police, and bring the house down, before the number loses all control and bursts out into abusive curse in the name of every mother's son ever brought to a sticky end in every operetta ever performed (133): per-*lecebrae* per-*nicies* ↔ *adulescentum exitium*. Where sex-'n'-death meets the end of the line. Starting back over, the song resumes, having heard and understood the truth wrung from its momentaneous execration: "the sea is not the sea, you are . . . —and I, I am all washed up (134–5: *mare . . . mare . . . mare . . . mari*).

He has found that he was lost but now has foundered (135–6, *repperi . . . intellego*), and eases down from the falsetto at 138, in the course of putting distance between past and future, . . . *at posthac tibi* |. The elaborate vow of revenge blusters away (*bene feci → male . . . facere faciam, . . . faciam . . . faciam*, 137–40), and does indeed name this boy's destined function in the drama—avenging angel. Whistle-blower, or Snitch, in fact (p. **168**).

10. This is the cornerstone of the standard line that *Asinaria* was "*inter antiquissimas Plautinas fabulas compositum*"—and even "may be the earliest surviving Plautine comedy": Bertini (1968), 55, cf. Hough (1937), 35, Della Corte (1961); Anderson (1993), 121. But we all know donkeys *don't* sing—much.

Add (the clincher, this): it's . . . short (*breue*).

11. *tandem*, 151: i.e., the song and splutter so far has been more "background;" we're to treat the showpiece row that follows as bringing out where we can join in the showdown that just threw the Boy out on his ear. "Progress" starts from the marching orders at 228, *nunc abi*, with the boy's "Hold your Horses" postscript at 229, *mane mane, audi. dic*, and the promise of a comeback, plus contract and fee.

12. Madame acts this goose-'n'-gander point out by halving the verse "50/50" (171) | dedi equidem *quod mecum egisti* ↔ et tibi ego misi *mulierem*. |. But this is *also* where she moves in for the kill—invading the Boy's line, twice (at 173 she gobbles up three quarters of the verse), before grabbing the mike for her "defence speech" (*quid me* accusas . . .). Thereafter, just one outburst (204–14), and hardly a word in edge-ways (176, 187, 190, 195–6, 227), before peremptory dismissal (228, *nunc abi.* |) decrees "Prosecutor Dismissed!"

13. See Slater (1985) 59, "the *lena* is content to perform her part just as it is usually depicted in the arts—and says as much!" (= 174–5; cf. 186). The excellent reexamination of Roman prostitution by McGinn (1998) happens not to deal with *Asinaria*.

14. *semper* oculatae *manus sunt nostrae: credunt quod uident*, 204; cf. *Truculentus* 486, pluris est *oculatus* testis quam *auriti* decem.

15. *Dius Fidius* is realised by Plautus here, and rationalised by Varro (*De Lingua Latina* 5.66), as the deity that "must" lie behind the formulaic asseveration *medius fidius* (i.e., "So may D. F. [safeguard] *me*"). Freyburger (1986) 288–92, esp. 289 n. 278, considers the evidence, including a temple of Διὸς Πιστίου at Rome.

16. On *fides* in *Asinaria*: Lombardi (1961) 30–2 (and 29 n. 36 for the oddly "active" sense of *fidem habere* at 458).

17. *Accipio*: 87, 396, 469, 765, [772].

18. Pliny the Elder notoriously claims that *bread-sellers* only reached Rome in the aftermath of the defeat of Macedon (167 BCE: *Natural History* 18.107, taken in good faith by Moritz [1958] 69–70). This happens to be the only *oenopolium* (200) in surviving Latin, and presumably works as catachresis deploring degenerate Greekness. Only an imaginary Rome could live "before capital."

19. Would "120" be a significant number (= "2 talents")? Do we assessors reckon

"6 year's worth" gets you the girl for keeps, because that's a whore's expected shelf-life? (Propertius ready-reckons Cynthia's hold on him as a quinquennium, 3.25.3: from *c* 29 BCE, say, through *c* 23?) Naturally, there are 20 mentions of the 20 minae in *Asinaria*. (In Slater [1985] 66, a typo makes it "80 minae" in the end.)

Chapter 3. Funny Money

1. His part (in driving the plot) starts here (249): *nunc . . .*—or rather it does when he cues Two on stage (265; 267): *nunc. . . .* Or rather it does when this White Rabbit's "running on the spot" party-piece is done to death (291, *loquens lacerat diem*), as contact and hello's are curtailed (295–308, *ibo aduersum atque electabo quicquid est . . . quid istuc est negoti?*), and the business of divulging the message staggers its ever-so-gradual exhausting-inexorable-traditional way toward the turnaround of delay caused by the *receiver's* urgent pleas for urgency (317, 325, 328, 331, 334–5, 346, 350): *quicquid est eloquere* → *quin rem actutum edisseris?* → *age age mansero . . .* → *quod affers aures expectant meae* → *quid tum postea?* → *quid tum postea?* → *quid tum?* ↔ *ausculta ergo, scies!*

2. One's cunning plan (358) is just to send Two off to master (367): nunc *tu abi*, while "meantime" he holds the fort, stalls the Courier (370, *interea*, 379, *interea*). Two even tells *him* what to do (379).

3. One's wordy first words here underscore the comic equation (= *atque*) of waking up a while = dreaming up a scheme (249–50): *expergiscier* | ~ *fingere fallaciam* |.

4. Contrast with this fun caring-sharing (*pariter* ~ *partiam*) ex-*pers* at 44, 506 (p. **229 n.1**).

5. Typical, Two, that is, for One to have one's cake and eat it: Whizzkid still pops the expected question for Brains, since he has found the solution before he knew the problem (358) *quid nunc consili captandum censes? dice.*

6. Konstan (1983) 53.

7. The long scene of the "reception/interception party" is well signposted: Courier's arrival (392, *sed quid uenis? quid quaeritas?*), Pseudo-Steward's arrival (403). The hot number take-off method-acts "Red Mist" (407–47), until closed "at length" when it has proved self-defeating (447, *quiesco.* ↔ *tandem, opinor, conticuit. nunc adeam . . .* ↔ *ehem opportune. quam dudum tu aduenisti? . . .*). The request for pater is repeated—he's still not at home (392–03, *Demaenetum uolebam.* ↔ *si sit domi, dicam tibi* ~ 452, *si domi est, Demaenetum uolebam.* ↔ *negat esse intus*). Persuasion and more Red Mist turned on Courier self-destruct—running into the sand "eventually" (486–7, *i nunciam ad erum quo uocas,* iam dudum *quo uolebas.* | ↔ *nunc demum*). Abortive? No—deconstructive.

8. Slater (1985) 62. The play's slogan of "cash-for-asses" is first bruited here (396–7: p. **193**).

9. Quintessential Plautus: Fraenkel (1960) esp. 119–20.

10. This will be quintessential Plautus: Fraenkel (1960) esp. 206–8; Lowe (1992) 165–70.

11. This image of "pregnant weals" sparks off a searing chain of sexual violence imagery: 281–3, occ*asionem* opprimere . . . , op*imitates* . . . effertissimas . . . pariet, 292, p*atronam* comprimat.

12. "Military" talk: *optionem*, 101, *insidias* . . . , *hostes*, 106; cf. esp. 269, *triumphum* . . . *aduentu*, 552–3, *legiones, copiae exercitusque eorum* | *ui pugnando*, etc., 559, *domi duellique*, etc.: p. **219 n.4**). Master's real-*man*-of-a-father turns out to be named "Army Man" (*Strato*, 344).

13. Cf. Fraenkel (1960) 136.

14. Libanus, however, thinks he is holding his own, verbal tittle for verbal tattle (377, *hostire*, cf. 172, *hostimentum*, p. **139**).

15. The attack on the door preludes more verboten touches of touching (sexual assault: 384–7, *nostras sic frangit* fores; tetigit; attigisse . . . nolo ego fores conseruas | meas a te *uerberari*. The personification continues with Ms Portal's "rape alarm" at 390–1).

16. NB: Plautus does *not* deploy a (Graeco-Latin) pun which would make "20 *minae*" enough to buy a score of "menaces."

17. What little we know about classical barbers: Nicolson (1891), Kaufman (1932) 145–8.

18. Metadramaturgically speaking, "it's a gas" when One and Two conspire to fake it that "The Brains" has been so slow in turning up at the mall that he held up "Slave in a 'Urry" until he lost patience, and now gets on with his part, in the guise of mock Steward (413–15, *hic me moratus est* . . . , *detinuisse*). One shifting the blame for this onto Courier as part of the con is also part of the attempt to intimidate *him*.

19. The Steward talks like a cash-register—of banker, jingling coins, and metal goblets (438, 440, 444).

20. The deictics written into the text here, here, and here, (*hoc* . . . *hinc*, . . . *has*) exhort any production to ham for all the player is worth: the slave playing actor must play the slave playing up the slave in a stew as he uses his big stick as mock shovel, broom, and duster. In this quicktime parody skit that summarizes the combined operation of a household invested in continual self-care, pantomime captures in one action-packed instant both how the job should be done, and how it's not been or being done, as usual, never does get done: so it's a (self-enacting) challenge to get right, not to get wrong. What the play's about.

21. In terms of stagecraft, "it's a gas" for this actor acting another actor's part to prevent the over-hearer coming out of his bubble, by *keeping* him aside, deliberately unacknowledged, to con him, work him over. To indoctrinate and prompt him.

22. Unlike the other names on the list, *Exaerambus* is opaque to us: *sounds like* a satirical twist on ἐξ-αιρετός, "select, special;" it's not clear whether we should pay attention to "information" such as Dio Chrysostom 4 (p. 172 Reiske): Δρόμωνα μὲν καὶ Σάραβον, ὅτι ἐν Ἀθήναις καπηλεύουσι ὑπ᾽ Ἀθηναίων τοῦτο ἀκούουσι τοὔνομα, δικαίως φαμὲν ἀκούειν. Cf. Schmidt (1902) 368.

23. *Dromo* is a common name for comedy and other slaves: their pace is dictated to them—forced either to race or else to freeze (but see last note).

24. Just as telling Courier "Don't be afraid" (*ne formida,* 462) metatheatrically sums up his role, so "Don't be a bore" (*molestus ne sis,* 469) accurately nails his part in the play. He is here to tantalize, block, spoil the comedy: he does, however, save *us* from "Saurea's world," as it gets too much of a good thing going. And he gets to whisper *Asinaria's* last word on this stand-out episode, too (p. **209**).

25. "High Profile": a common—blank—name in Plautus, though actually—conspicuously—unattested in Greek (Schmidt [1902] 377).

26. *Our* father refuses to be "as other fathers" (50), but this limp wrist will never live up to *his* swashbuckling Father, that idolized dare-devil who *can't have been* married into money by *his* father, but left the textosterone imprint of his scrapes out on the town playing pirate Bluebeard (52–7): *uolo me patris mei similem . . .* | *eos me decretumst persequi mores patris.* No daring raids down at the brothel from our pale shadow, *his* wimp idea of winning *his* son will be to divert income from Ma, not kidnap his tart. So the best Wilt will manage is to play his own son's clone, and inflict the performance on the boy. Narcissism. Exhibitionism. Infantilism. You-name it-ism. Fun, really.

Chapter 4. American Beauty

1. With 517–18, cf. Prologue's word of advice to his p.a. man: "mind you get paid for both performances: speaking and . . . sitting down" (5).

2. The pair swapped couplets of counter-expostulation (504–5 ~ 506–7), then the Llass's eloquent line of exculpation is recognized and negated in the same breath (511): *satis* dicacula *es* amatrix, and her one line of self-vindication earns the put-down (513): tu mihi *aduersatrix ades.* The first soundbite implodes ma's bark, with a brash flourish of pious Personification: matris *expers* imperiis → piem Pietatem . . . more moratam . . . | postŭlem plăcerĕ, mater, mĭhĭ quo pacto praecĭpis? |. (To which ma merely retaliates—cut down to size: "pietatem" . . . matri imperium minuere.) The second flash of rhetoric is a honey, real poise and grace: | nĕquĕ quae recte făcĭunt culpo nĕquĕ quae delinquunt ămo. (Cf. 514, | neque . . . accuso neque . . . existimo. |.) But the third—the third packs the complete anatomy of erotic self-portraiture in one demure slip of a daughterly damsel's hookline verse (and sinker).

| linguă poscit, corpus quaerĭt, ănĭmŭs orat, res mŏnet. |.

A psychedelic perfectly formed loose-limbed fourfold dipody which has the lot (i.e., calls for overacting), this is poetry in motion. And this bit part embodying the oldest profession (*is mihi quaestus est*) proves meretricious courtroom oratory as lubricious as the delicious bedroom muse of courting is judicious. There's a person inside this cyborg? (p. **239 n.10**)

Chapter 5. Beating the System

1. Cf. 270–1, *pariter potant, pariter scortari solent,* | *. . . praedam pariter . . . partiam,* 317, *magna est praeda cum magno malo;* cf. p. **192:** this is the word-noise that defines and animates Leonida's plosive part—and persuades Libanus to flag him down: *properans . . . pedibus* (290) boils up (*[patronam comprimat . . . pro illo peiierat]* |) to *approperabo-praedae-praesidium-parem* (294), and *that does it* ("*praeda,*" 295).

2. Sutton (1998) 94, cf. Sherberg (1992) 144–5. This is, for example, how that comic turn Cicero's *Pro Caelio* plays Rome, and how its commentary replays the classroom (Henderson [2002] 205–34).

3. His slaves' honorary mate is fêted by them as Comic Genius / Figure For Comedy, but we *miss* his biggest, his only, laugh when he stuck to the script so well . . . off-stage (580–4): *edepol . . . Demaenetum* lepidum *fuisse nobis:* | *ut* assimulabat . . . *quam facete.* | *nimis aegre* risum contini . . . , | *ut memoriter . . .*

4. For "*suprema* 'end of the day's session' announced by the *praetor* to the people in the *comitium*": Zagagi (1980) 117–18, at n. 40.

5. Talk about silly (591, 594, 597, 604, 606, 632, cur me retentas?; domum ire iussit; quo nunc abis? quin tu hic manes?; abire; quo properas?; ex aedibus deiecit). See Fraenkel (1960), 206–8, on 597–602. Who cares about *her,* if her Romeo manages to Juliet his hooker and pimp his Juliet throughout, whereas her horizon is having him for special, on the side, for free? That's all she can say. Call it comic parody and deal with it that way, if that's the way you feel about it (p. **228 n.2**).

6. I.e. *Plautine,* not Demophilus' dramaturgy: Lowe (1992) 166, cf. **167,** and (1999), p. **185.**

7. ". . . your eyes they are watering. Hence my question."

8. My "Moses" here is Plautus' *Solon,* legendary law-giver of Athens.

9. The convoluted and invaginated staging of the scene with these two couples calls for a welter of "him's" and "her's," as all *jockey for positions* (cf. Franko [2004] esp. 44–5 on this "ensemble scene"). And the three guys lapse into othering the She (604, 631, 631, 631, 635, 679, 725, 736). But this herd are here to model *her* ass (you heard) as the play's concentrate of money and sex: hanc . . . hanc (662, cf. 676; fused in the fun pun *haec,* 739).

10. The Boy just agreed to stay for one last night (597, *nox*). But Pa has already booked her for tonight (736, *noctem huius et cenam sibi*). The Peeping Tom Slaves know this all along (esp. 602, *dies noctesque potent*).

11. Schmidt (1902) 356–7. Gratwick (2001) 47 n.8 has "*Argyrippus*" dub for the (real) gold of "*Chrysippus.*"

12. Cf. Sutton (1993) 89.

13. Segal (1968) 105–9, finds thirteen verbs for "beseeching" between 662 and 699. Cf. 783; 917; 926.

14. In Greek this kiss was called "the pitcher" (χύτρα, Pollux 10.100: specially for kissing a "kid": ὁπότε τὰ παιδία φιλοίη, τῶν ὤτων ἐπιλαμβανόμενα).

15. Both contrived tonguing and contrived kisses would be banned by Diabolus' contract (794–5; 796–8). Kissing and naming in a toast will bring down on pater the wrath of wife: also outlawed by the contract (891–5; 904–6, cf. 780).

16. This twinning is aptly celebrated by Segal (105–9). Indeed: "It is hardly possible to differentiate the characters of the two slaves or their roles in this scene so as to assign each speech to one or the other with confidence" (Lowe [2000] 167 n. 87).

17. Note Slater (1985) 63 n. 6: "Note all the -*ludo* compounds in this scene: 677, 679, 711, 730, 731."

18. Our Babes in the Wood meet the $£aves and a $ackfu£ of Farce where up-market Theatre would have laid on a centre-stage *altar* for refugee waifs and prayers to soften the will of higher powers (esp. 712, *aram*).

Chapter 6. Stick to the Script

1. As in *Bacchides* 14–15.

2. Slater (1985) 64. Diabolus' Pal is not called *parasitus* in the text, but he fits the bill: Damon (1997) 37–40, Antonsen-Resch (2005).

3. The pun *leges* / -*lego* sloganizes terms and conditions for the whole play-script (*translego* is ἅπαξ). Ledgerdemain, bang to writes: so many false quantities to offend the ear. For such contracts, and the subjugations and anxieties they obsess on, see Scafuro (2003) and James (2003) 280 n. 19, and esp. (2006).

Logos—

4. Slater (1985) 64. No hitches or glitches: so let's add, "The parasite and Diabolus" *wield* "the power of art to shape the life of the viewer." You can't be too careful, not when you're writing and word-painting, as is Diabolus.

5. The dynamics and logic of this *Ars Amatoria* are expertly explored by James (2006).

6. Gowers (1993) esp. 87–9 serves up our fishy play as basted into a loverly broth*el*—first "turned" (11, *uertit*, from Greek), then (preferably fresh) "seasoned any which way, as in pan-fry or bakeria, . . . turn 'em which way you like," ready for us to enjoy (179–80, . . . *condias* . . . | *uel patinarium uel assum, uerses* . . .), and for cocked-up Pa to pay for, host and miss (935–6).

Chapter 7. Rotten Rhetorics

1. Hear comedy laugh at laughter, watch theatre denounce acting (840–2): *ne sic fueris* . . .—*em aspecta: rideo.*—*utinam male qui uolunt* sic rideant. Both actors need to bat this personable smile to and fro between them—convincing-and-fake / brave-and-pitiful.

2. Lowe (1992) 170–5, at 170–1, "Plautine alterations . . . , a pair of eavesdroppers carries on a dialogue commenting on another dialogue."

3. The opening dialogue *insists* that the well of "fear" driving this hen-run of a plot is gynephobia: *per illam quam tu metuis uxorem tuam* (19 ~ *ne uxor resciscat metuit*, 743–4—where Son interrupts—*heia*—before Slave Two can name the

dreaded deed she'll—...). Not, therefore, into cowing the slaves, unlike most comedies out of ten (see 44–50, *dono te ... ut expers sis metu ... | patres ut faciunt ceteri* → 111–13, p. 133).

4. Konstan (1983) 48.

5. Slater (1985) 65.

6. Sutton (1993) 96.

7. Cf. 927, *odium, non uxor, eram.*

8. For the range within the Plautine *senex amator* type, see Ryder (1984) esp. 181–2 on Demaenetus.

9. First One leads Two in swapping dumb insults, locked two to a line (297–8), before Two emphasises for our sake that *he's* the one in the know, and launches off on more of his plosives with his elaborate weighing of syllables of flesh by the foot (300–5, *e*xpendi → pondo ... pendes per pedes, pedes *centum*pondium ... *de*pendes ... propendes.) One does get to label the scene—and cut it (307, uerbiuelitationem *fieri com*pendi *uolo*).

10. This "straightahead" play just keeps on keepin' on, straight on through, out of the hutch and straight back home (54, cf. 115): *pergam quo occepi ...*

11. Line 33 must be deleted. The slave made up two thunderously nightmare words to avoid putting his hell [the ✶✶ll] on the map: *fustitudinus* and *ferricrepinus* never reappear in all the Latin we have. On the other hand, whereas mythical isles promised utopia (cf. Romm [1992] esp. 156–171), Roman *insulae* were always (in) the neighbourhood, in the shape of the *"island"* blocks (of flats), where the poor lived (pun in e.g. *Appendix Vergiliana, Catalepta* 10.7).

12. Her wares feature: posh "gold doubloons" from Macedon and "Cupid's nail"; a splendid line (giving it all she's got) to introduce image and gloss in equipoise (153–6; 157): | *remigio ueloque* → *quantum poteris* ← *festina et fuge* |; and a crafted verse of wave + backwash psychodrama to cash the round voyage out (158):

quam *magis* te in *a*ltum *capessis*
tam aestus te in *portum refert.*

Enough, all this, to provoke the Boy to land his first face-to-face threat. Loud and clear (159): *ego pol istum* portito*rem* priu*abo* portorio.

But they *should* be talking portals, not ports (241): portitorum *simillimae sunt ianuae lenoniae.* "Money opens doors / money disappears indoors" is this playwrong's cardinal principle—daylight robbery (271–2: i.e. stage money, in a bag ~ stage houses, no interior ~ comic script, in/out of performance).

13. Unnamed until her part is over, madam duets with the customer in (stale) imagery from *Athens on Sea* (Vanoyeke [1990] 99–101, "Le pouvoir des prostituées").

14. Then our resident expert on love-birds and love-words finds "lovers in plovers," amator*es* (221). For hooking johns as bird-catching in Plautin: *Bacchides* 50, *Poenulus* 679, *Truculentus* 951.

15. *uult ... | uult ... uult, ... uult, | uult ... uult ... ;* and by running down the

status ladder she ends up wagging his tail/shaking her tail-feathers for him: "play-mate → me → lady's page → slaves of the house → maids → my pup gets sweet talk from the brand new lover, so *he's* overjoyed to see him!" An invitation, in most anyone's language, to Mae West your lapdog—cradle and rock—then wiggle your ass—bump and grind—on Bawdway.

16. *in-lex* is here the lure of in-*licio* (cf. 133, *perlecebrae*, 206, *illiciebas*), but out-lawing in-*lex* from *in+lex* is as illegitimate as the Plautin sous-entendre that reads the—a, any—*lectus* as necessarily a dilectable *diva's* divine "divan": so 151–2, *illece-bra . . . non licitum est.*

17. The ex-pert sexpert *mimes* the come-on routine of master-baiting (222–3): cued by the punter's accusation (206, *illiciebas me ad te blande ac benedice*) this bébé dollop lip-glosses like -l through *bene* ↔ bland*iter* and *salut*ando con- ↔ com*pell*ando ↔ os*cul*ando. Kissing the airwaves in *cons"escunt*, she opens wide to "mouth" (*os*) all these orgasm omegas: → os*culando*, *oratione*; and whinnies her way through a double-pout of ooh-la-la-Latin climax: uinnula uenustula (explained by Nonius [p. 519 Lindsay], reporting a gloss reading out of the context in *Asinaria* (?): *dicitur molliter se gerens et minime quid uiriliter faciens*; cf. Krostenko [2000]).

18. Our rheterotic mistress' body, at-*and*-past her best, serves as her own man-nikin as she turns from moving words to crawling flesh (224–5): | *si papillam per-tractauit*, | *sauium sumpsit, sumere*. The "stage-direction" pointer | *haecine* (226) comes and sums up the full-on fondling she just gave at least one palpably aroused nipple. Plus the all-consuming swoon she's faked, in take-me-in-your-arms, take-me, take-me, pulsation. In *this* necking of the woods, a kiss is still a kiss (p. **163**).

19. Madame's terminal terms are "open-and-shut," and leave the desperado to wave at her either/or's in repeating them louder; and in re-doubling his termi-nal determination to go under (241–8): si . . . , *tum* patent, si non . . . , non pat-ent. | ↔ | interii si non . . . , | et profecto nisi . . . , pereundum est mihi. | . . . | nam si . . . non . . . , certum est sumam . . . ; *pergam-atque experiar*, opi*bus*-*omni* copia, *suppl*ic*abo*-*exobsec*rabo, dignos-indignos, a*dire*-*atque*-*expe*riri.

20. The verse 260 *does this*, surrounding the speaker with his own words, in the line-dissecting aural chiasmus "to left and to right," *p*- . . . *c*- ↔ *c*- *p*-. Four lots of birds with one quadrant—and every bush filled with spectators, he points (us) out, "in every direction" (259, *quouis*). The augury is either spot on citation of law or else a perfect take-off of lore: see Horace, *Odes* 3.27.1–16, *parrae . . . auis . . . coruum . . . cornix*, with Nisbet and Rudd (2004) 324 on ib. 11–12.

21. Libanus' travesty of augury finds the curate's egg: the prediction is that life swoops between good and bad, and it does, at once (260 ~ 317; cf. Gulick (1896) 240–1). He is good as telling us, if we can read the signs, that his feud with the Steward runs deep (264).

22. *nudus* for the slave means a back stripped for a whipping, where to us it means "in your stockinged feet," for accurate weighing minus clothes: why else would either party strip, as *pendeo* plays between "weighed" and "strung up for

torture"? (p. 134) The wordgames work us through this hell: if strung up tight to a beam, then weightless—hanging without dangling.

23. Scandalized Courier will, or can, stand no more after One's scandal of a badmouthing, which "badmouths" *him* as a "scandal" himself, while under the guise of obeying compulsory orders, the voice in his ear mutters for him to submit and escape more scandalous badmouthing (from Two)—for *the verse itself* is agape, a "scandal" of "badmouthing" (473): *flăgĭtĭŭm | hŏmĭnis. {dᵃ, obsĕcrᵒ, argentᵘᵐ huic, ne mălĕ lŏquatur.}*

24. Philaenium's "eloquence" amounts to an unyielding barrage of appeals to "mother" (507, 511, 535, 537, 540, 544, p. 170). Argyrippus' equivalent barrage with "pater" studs *his* "devotion" scene (828, 831, 833, 842, 843; cf., at the "party," 882, 889, 899, 904, 938. The girl might've won if she could get madam to reciprocate: father's game is to trade binding togetherness with "[that's] my boy": *mi nate . . . nate mi,* 829–30, 836, 882. Her son crawls to *his* "mater": 911, 931; she isn't fooled: *bellum filium,* 931: ironic, or not: *you* decide, p. 182).

25. In the starkest terms, the scene polarizes Madame's treatment of her Girl against her treatment of the Boy: 543, intro abi ~ 228, *nunc* abi (cf. p. 225 n.12).

26. Repetition of repetitions of repetition, no less (551, 560, 564 ~567, 571, 574): *saepe, memorari multa possunt, saepe ~ iterari multa et uero possunt, saepe, saepe* (cf. *infidelis-peiieras-in furto ubi sis-prehensus ~ fideli infidus-ubi prensus in furto sies-peiieras-fidelis*). The "amoebaean" duet-duel goes out with a Big Bang (564–5 ~ 574–5): *ubi saepe . . . octo | artutos, audacis uiros, ualentis uirgatores ~ ubi saepe . . . octo | ualidos lictores, ulmeis affectos lentis uirgis. |.*

27. "In a particularly obscene passage," Habinek explains: "*uerbero, -are* 'to flog,' can be a metaphor for assuming the penetrative position in sexual intercourse. The master uses the noun, *uerbero,* scoundrel, as an insult, The first slave puns on the noun *uerbero* as the verb *uerberare* to propose that if the *meretrix* is off limits he'll gladly have his way with his fellow slave. And the second slave points out that, as a *cinaedus,* the first couldn't have his way, even with a willing partner, because his preference is the receptive role, especially, it would seem, during oral sex" (see Habinek [2005] 183). What wallopping whoppers (416, 569, 589 → 625–8, *uerbum caue faxis, uerbero*). Cf. Willcock (1997).

28. The stand-out scene shouts aloud its excrescence to mere plot: contact and greetings (619–24, *ere, salue; Philaenium, salue*) key in self-pity, despair (629–30, . . . *hodie numquam ad uesperum uiuam*), before we learn there's no time to lose (633–8, *hodie . . . daturus dixit*)—but plenty of time to play (638, *iam dedit . . . ? non dedit*). After this, it's time-out/brinkmanship for tantalizing torment all the way (646, 677–9, 730–1, *uin erum deludi?; etiam me delusisti? . . . delude; cur ludatis . . . | satis iam delusum censeo*). It's gottabe a scream when the "Back to the plot" formula leads straight to "In the nick of time" thanksgiving (731, 733, nunc *rem ut est eloquamur → ut tempori opportuneque attulistis.*). Finally: "Back inside, the pair of you" (745, *ite intro cito*).

29. "By the time" Plautus' Pal "is finished with *amor*, there is no primal authenticity left to the sexual scene of the" Republican "world" (Henderson [forthcoming] on Ovid, *Ars Amatoria*). The contract in *Asinaria* was explicitly introduced, in triplicate, as a fantasy engine: *si tu uoles ::* ... *ut uoles* ... | *ut uoles, ut tibi libebit* (237–9).

30. In particular, 238, syngraphum *facito afferas* is fulfilled at 746, *ostende* ... syngraphum.

31. The contract starts with a dose of hiatuses and pomposities. It plays a joke on Diabolus, which washes over his head (772–3: *sapiat:*): "*She must toast you, you must drink;* | *she must not have less or more taste than you*" :: "Approved." And it makes a leggy joke, en passant, when it orders the girl (779: *talos* ... *homini admoueo* = "press her ankle on a guy" + "pass the ankle-bone dice to someone"): "*Not to make advances during the betting.*"

32. See Franko (2004) esp. 45 for this all-in finale.

33. Plautus' plays update urbanity for Rome—awash in alcohol: Miniconi (1964).

Chapter 8. "It's a gas"

1. Compare most helpfully Havet and Freté (1925), 8–11, "Sommaire des Actes." On the play's "dramatic architecture," see Danese (1999).

2. Attribution of lines at 104–26 is (tellingly) uncertain. See López (1970).

3. Where the music strikes up / where the play starts up: Moore (1998) 253.

4. On this *locus conclamatus,* see esp. Lowe (1992) 171–3, and (1995) esp. 27.

5. See Beare (1964), "The *Angiportum* and Roman Drama," 256–63, esp. 259–60 on our passage.

6. *Pace* Lowe (1992) 164, "Only the phrase *trudetur foras,* rather than *excludetur,* suggests that Argyrippus is at present in the house; the sentence as a whole suggests the opposite."

7. *Pace* Lowe (1992) 164, "Is it likely that the two women would have come out leaving him inside?"

8. As the Loeb edition puts it: Nixon (1916) 1:149, "Act II."

9. Slater (1985) 60, "Libanus conclusively loses control to a ghost-writer" (= Leonida, from 265)—but this is far from "conclusive," since teamwork must win out between the double-act of comics (pp. 143–4). The yoke's on them (288).

10. "His complaint of wasted time is a common trick to emphasize the passage of dramatic time" (Hough [1937] 23, citing seven passages from Plautin at n. 7). And the point of this emphasis is to warn that the situation just moved on ("so have your wit and fun about you; watch out—LISTEN!"). This answers the key question: "But how does Libanus have this information?" (Lowe [1992] 164).

11. Thus madam and girl told their client they loved just him like an only son: *unice unum* (208 ~ *unicum natum*, 16).

Chapter 9. Beastly Lives

1. Not counting one parable ("Ox and Ass," *Aulularia* 229–35, with Plautus' only *asellus;* cf. Brind'Amour [1976], Konstan [1983] 42–3) and one proverbial quip ("Profit?—Kick-back, more like," *Poenulus* 684: *quorsum asinus caedit calcibus* = Otto [1890/1971] 42, s.v. *asinus* §13). The "asses" of *Pseudolus* 136 = "stubbornness," whereas all three "asses" in Terence = "stupidity" (opined Lilja [1965] 33). Our "sanctuaries" maintain the "slave" image matrix; when it comes to real donkeys, nous sommes d'une ânerie: Svendse (1986), www.lovelongears.com.

2. A comedy name: Schmidt (1902) 179–80.

3. Havet-Freté (1925) xxxii–iii. The infinite differences a title can make: cf. Bertini (1968) 44–7 and p. **211**. How many asses do make a *pace*? According to Cicero's sneer, Pompey's great theatre opened in 55 BCE with "600 mules" on-stage in a Broadway *Clytemnestra* (*Ad Familiares* 7.1.2). Cf. Horace, *Epistles* 2.1.187–92 for such extravaganzas—and "Know-It-All" Jacobs (2005) 325: "In the nineteenth century, theaters featured a genre called 'the racing drama,' where live horses galloped on treadmills set into the stage floor. The chariot race from *Ben Hur* was staged this way in 1899. Too bad this was discontinued. Even I'd go to the theater to see that."

4. The whole world of the play is contained within, so when the agents fear they are "shut out" of the moneybag by the recalcitrant courier they show how meretrix, madam, and the joint run by madam are the equivalents of cash (*exclusi,* 361 ~ *excludetur,* 533).

5. As the play winds up (by) reminding us (p. **213**), *both* master and slave were roles for slaves simply because they are roles: but the recapture of the runaway husband who dared cut the apron's strings loose casts him figuratively as another slave domestic, part of the furniture. When the play showcases the "loyal" slaves successfully mauling the Jezebel and taking Mama's precious boy for a ride as the price of releasing funds siphoned off from Her accounts, this precisely prequels, pre-figures, hams up, the Master's briefer, speeded-up, failed party-piece (pp. **170, 180–1**). Pater undertook to carry the can for his agents, but no one can do that for him (91). No one but us (946–7, p. **215**).

6. "Arcadian asses" are said to be "the original exports—big tall ones" (Isidore 12.1.40, cf. Varro, *De Re Rustica* 2.1.14, quoted by Pliny, *Natural History* 8.167). *Pella,* imperial capital of the Philips and Alexander of Macedon, *might* conceivably be selected for a translingual hint of *pello,* "drive (a herd)," as when Argyrippus' costly *amores* are imaged as if cattle: *dispulsos compulit* (738).

7. See McCarthy (2000), esp. 211–13, "The slave's image in the master's mind," Fitzgerald (2000) 40.

8. See Bradley (2000), esp. 120–1, "the reality that all slave-owners have always had to face, that all slaves cannot be reduced to a condition of total subservience and compliance all the time, that the human will cannot always be completely

suppressed. . . . The slave-owner could never count on converting the slave into a tamed animal."

9. E.g. Apuleius, *Metamorphoses* 8.25, *non asinum uides. . . . nec calcitronem,* Pliny, *Natural Histories* 30.149, *mulas non calcitrare, cum uinum biberint.*

10. Cf. Labeo *in libris quos ad duodecim tabulas conscripsit* (fr. 25, cited by Gellius 20.1.13, on the law *SI INIVRIAM ALTERI FAXSIT, XXV AERIS POENAE SVNTO*): *L. Veratius fuit egregie homo improbus atque immani uecordia. is pro delectamento habebat os hominis liberi manus suae palma uerberare. eum seruus sequebatur ferens crumenam plenam assium; ut quemque depalmauerat, numerari statim secundum duodecim tabulas quinque et uiginti asses iubebat* (with Holford-Strevens [1988] 90–1).

11. These slaves share their role(s) to the point of each fighting the other to outpraise each other (558–9 ~ 576): *uirtutes qui tuas non possis* collaudare | *sicut ego possim* ~ *num male relata est gratia, ut collegam* collaudauui |. The set-piece is marked as such (575, *ut meque teque maxime atque ingenio nostro decuit*)—and the striking pos . . . turings declared over (578): *iam omitte* haec . . .

12. NB: *Assterisks*. At no ~~other~~ point can we ascribe to *Asinaria* any hint of the ghost of any shadow of the ~~otherwise~~ unattested pun assibilating between Roman coinage and Roman donkeys: *as, assis,* and *asinus, -i.*

On the other hand, the derivation of *pecunia,* "money," from *pecus,* "cow," carries with it the diminutive form, *peculium,* the saved-up "stash" which is all a "proper" slave ever saw of cash. A neat line links the whore's plea for just one sheep to be her very own—*peculiarem,* 541—to the boy's imaging of their affair as *amores, dispulsos* and *compuls[os]* like a herd of *pecudes* (738). Plautus' choice of *Phil-hippeioi* for his cash (152) underlines the cardinal role of hip *Argyr-ippus*' hippie *name* in the ~~plot~~ (p. 161).

13. Here the verbal puncepts *patior-pater* and *faciet-facile* underline the assmilation of *meretrix* to money in the indicative-deictic pun *haec* (p. 229 n.9, cf. p. 232 n.18).

14. "There is ~~perhaps~~ no better example in Roman Comedy of sheer Saturnalian perversity, the elevation of the slave and humiliation of the master." (Konstan [1983] 55) More needs saying than just "They force embraces from the girl, piggyback rides from her lover" (ibid.), or "The scene ends in boysterous slapstick, as Libanus rides horseback on his master Argyrippus. The tragic tone is banished by triumphant (visual) demonstration" (Slater [1985] 63).

15. For *libet* as logo of this please-yourself theatre: Leadbeater (1987).

16. Cf. Scullard (1981) 91–2.

17. For this Plautin puncept—the slave's "lumbared"—cf. *Epidicus* 360.

18. Slaves catch it in the "back and legs": *tergo-et-cruribus* (409), cf. *crura hercle diffringentur* (474).

19. Of course, the verb *fero* carries any script: words for money. But for the record, where "[. . .]" means *not* directly fetching *cash,* cf.: *adfero,* 231, 238, 240, 242,

269, 331, 337, 361, 369, 532, 733, [761]; *aufero*, 97, 154, 163, [424], [469], [816]; *defero*, 852, [885]; *fero*, [323], 347, 355, 487, 503, 670, [672], 699, 700, 732, [803]; *offero*, [593]; *profero*, 651; *refero*, [158], [164], [398], 441, 444, [576]; *suffero*, [557]; cf. *furcifer*, [484+485], [677]. Contrast: *baiulo*, 660; *porto*, 690, *deporto*, 524 (perhaps 159 and 241 pun between *portitor* = "toll-gatherer at a port [*portus*]" / = "carrier [*porto*]"); *ueho*, [343], 699, 700, 701, *subuecto*, [342].

20. Moritz (1958) 67–73, "Mills and millers in Plautus' comedies," at 68; cf. 74, "In Italy the donkey-mill was soon to become the grain-mill par excellence" (*mola asinaria*: Cato *De Agri Cultura* 10.4, 11.4); and 97–102, "Animal-mills and slave-mills," esp. 100, "the commonest mill-animal was undoubtedly the ass which was notoriously cheap to keep, and if horses were used they were horses unfit for any other purpose."

21. Normally, we could put it, the boy would ride the pederast cock-horse, as in Petronius 64.11–12, where Lord Trimalchio takes slave-pet Croesus aboard, *basiauit puerum ac iussit supra dorsum ascendere suum. non moratus ille usus est equo manuque plena scapulas eius subinde uerberauit.* Who's taking whom for a ride of course itself includes the pleasures of . . . perverse inversion, as well as of . . . transverse game-and-reality conversion. Cf. Rimell (2002) 50–2.

22. The scene parodies scenes such as Menander, *Samia* 366–4, 390–8.

23. *Salus* (*Publica, Romana*, etc.) did receive temple and cult (cf. Cicero, *De Natura Deorum* 2.61), but most references are just S.O.S. appeals (cf. *Oxford Latin Dictionary s.v.* §7).

Fortuna Obsequens has cult attested in inscription and on coin, but is more a locution here than a divinity (as in Pseudo-Seneca, *Octavia* 452; cf. *Oxford Latin Dictionary s.v. Obsequens* §2b).

Plautus' slaves are messing with Hellenizing convulsions in Rome along a path from linguistic abstraction to cultic reification: see Axtell (1907). "Statue + altar" define cult status: Stewart (2003) 24.

24. Contrast *illic hanc mihi seruandam* (676), where *haec* is the bag of money (p. 198).

25. Cf. 515, where Philaenium laments: *meas queror fortunas.*

26. *Supplico*: cf. 150, 246, in the exchanges between madam and client; 467, in the assault on the courier.

27. Cf. *illic homo socium ad malam rem quaerit quem* adiungat *sibi* (288), as One geared up to being joined by, and to, Two.

28. Besides the opportunity for some stage antics of mutual revulsion, this by-play intimates that the slaves are interested in a bigger prize than humiliation through sexual manhandling: power of and through money impresses them more.

29. The rest of the play will choreograph ugly proxemics, touched off by the lovers' hug for dear life (615, *complectere*). The couple of slaves encompass the couple of lovers in a memorably self-reflexive chiasmus (618): | *circumsistamus* → alter hinc ↔ hinc alter ← *appelle*mus. |; then put distance between themselves and

their victims-to-be (639, 646, *secede huc, concedite istuc*). "Hugs between lovers, and between lovers and louts," they insist, "*not* between louts" (640–7, 668–9, 679, 692, 696–7, *complexos . . . complexos . . . complexum . . . amplexetur; amplexare;* | *prehende auriculis, compara labella cum labellis* |, | *circumda . . . bracchiis, . . . circumplecte* | *. . . circumplectatur*). "Kissings" abut "lashings and chippings of them" (670, *osculetur, uerbero,* 697, *circumplectatur, carnifex;* cf. 687). All to forestaste Father's saucy sandwich, between the pair of young things on heat (739, *patrem hanc amplexari,* p. **195**).

30. Cf. *me emere natum suum,* 72, *tun redimes me . . .*—*redimam,* 106–7 ~ *redime . . . te . . . et tibi eme hunc,* 673. We have a nightmère expert on "buying" and "borrowing" in Madam: *diem aquam solem lunam noctem, haec argento non emo* (198). But she must be joking (*noctem . . . ?*). She *was* joking when she added (199): "The rest we want to use, we purchase on Greek credit" (p. **127**).

31. Sutton (1993) 92–4 aptly expounds the Oedipality of our under-assertive kid's "dejected passivity," for him the mainspring of the drama—not the structure of power within the *domus.*

32. The opposition, equid-distant from the ox, is worked hard in Aesopica: 181, 357, 565, 571 Perry. Cf. Drake (1968–9).

33. The girl's rhapsody at 664–5 is run-of-the-mill; the slave's special request at 666–8 is laughable (Dickey [2002] 156–7). Diabolus' comic contract would restrict her to pure Attic diction—"not one single word of aporia" (792–3: *perplexabilis* is ἅπαξ, so *is* it Latin?).

Chapter 10. A Right Earful

1. All of Plautus' scripts are shot through with insistence on the phonic materiality of language—Plautin verse *uses* the body, *does* utterance: e.g. esp. *mala-male-malo,* 129–30, *blande ac benedice,* 206, | *faciebatis* ~ | *fugiebatis,* 212, 213, and *of-*ficium facis *ac . . . fugis,* 380, *ianuae lenoniae,* 241, *quod des aedes,* 242, facio facetum *me atque magnificum uirum,* 351, *tibi ero praesente reddam.* | *. . . ero huic praesente reddam* |, 455–6, *facere fas,* 514, *lacrimantem lacinia tenet lacrimans,* 587, *labore liberas . . . baiulabo,* 660, *dispulsos compulit,* 738, *faenerato funditat,* 902.

2. Father's sermon encloses the elision and resolution flurry of its meat (66–72) within the ring between his clarion call to order (64): *omnes—parent—es* | Liban—e lib -eris—suis, and its closing asseveration at 73 (p. **182**):*eos me—decre—tum ᵉst per—sequi—mores—patris.* Notice that a key set piece is on its way, and comes where it belongs, at 65.

3. Theatre people, drama queens and critics in the round, obsass over visuality (kinetics). But acting styles (choreographies) work (with) *words,* for all they are worth (p. **171**). So *the* miracle of public drama must be the bond of mass silence which founds an auditorium. Hence *Asinaria*'s sound check (4).

4. Here, as you have heard (pp. **136–7**), we are to listen *hard* to the Graeco-Latin play between *consilia+exordiar and Archi-bulum,* which tells us that the play will

go with the money, straight inside madame's next door, where all the action is coming from.

5. At 327–8, One quells Two with traffic-calming verse: with *mansero* abiding at verse end, and the deferential "in your own time" turning into an instant surprise prick of irritation, at having to wait sooo looong: *uel . . . adeo . . . usque . . . dum—peris.* One invites Two to pop his soooo impoooortant question all in a rush *at verse end*, a tactic which injects extra "drama" into the frantic crawl towards the urgent news release held up between 267 and 333: *non uides* | → *ag^e age mansero* | → *ubinamst erus?* | → *iam satis est mihi* | → *mitte ridicularia* | (326–30, touching off the "ridiculous emission" of parodic pomposity in 331) → *. . . haec scias :: taceo :: beas* | (332: and they're off).

6. Listen: hear Plautus make fun of, as well as with, the formulae for cooking plot information into the semblance of dialogue. Don't forget (cf. p. **193**), the crucial début of the "asses" in *Asinaria* is in the guise of a "memory," and the theme livens up lame narration:

meministine? :: memini ~ teneo . . . memor es (333–4 ~ 342)

~

quid tum postea? | → *quid tum postea?* | → *quid tum? :: ausculta ergo, scies.* | (334+335, 346, 350; cf. *postea,* 357 ~ *interea,* 370).

Sending Slave in a 'Urry racing off to tell Master at the mall spares us hearing the script recapped: *narra haec ut nos acturi sumus* (367); until we get it, anyway, "memoriously" recounted by One to Two as the "memorious" triumph of Master's comic wit, unfortunately spared us today, but for this five line narration (580–4).

7. The Courier (*really,* "The Trader," and Very Much His Own Man, but not *dynamically*) has his own agent, a slave/boy to do the door knocking for him; but *this* agent remains instrumental, granted significance, though neither voice, nor agency (382–3).

8. Courier picks up on Libanus' placatory attempts to understate his financial reportage to the ogre: *tandem opinor* |, 448 ~ *fecisse satis opinor* |, 436, *dimidio minus opinor* |, 441.

9. Libanus' "double role within the scene": Slater (1985) 61–2.

10. Having figured herself as shepherd of an owner's flock, keeping just one favourite for their own (539–40), this sheepish lamb is whistled back to the fold at just one word from mama. But she *has* picked up on ma's accusation (505) *an ita tu es* animata . . . ? Whores (she proves) have a heart, mind (513, *animus orat*), and it can get in the way, professionally speaking (537, *animus occupatus est*), unless allowed one little pen in the fold for its own (542, *animi causa*). This *person* does manage to infiltrate "hope," "consolation" and "one true love," into the play's palette of *amor.* Just barely.

11. Schmidt (1902) 178–9.

12. Cf. Fontaine (2005)—in support, however, of the reading Ὄναγρος, "Wild Ass," "according to the best MSS" and Danese (2004).

13. The sight of husband nesting with a cuddly bird will be a blow, too, only to matrona: *em tibi hominem* (880).

14. "Argyrippus" answer is revealing (= 849+850). The father who sold his right to respect now relies on the naked—bespoken—power of cash to bend his son to his will. Thematically, then, this scene recapitulates the movement of the drama as a whole." (Konstan (1983) 54). Off his stroke for the nonce, Slater (1985) 65 translaters "Yes, you've *conquered* me with that stroke."

Epilogue

1. For a start, this is where we came in (came *on*): *si uultis*, 946 ~ *s ᶦᵘultis*, 1.

2. Tying up the play, as *Demaenetus'* psychodrama: cf. 113, *omnem animum* ostendisti *tuum*, p. **221 n.13.**

3. Slater (1985) 67–9, at 69 n. 10.

4. Rose (1984) 29, 35–6.

Bibliography

Scholarship on *Asinaria* is in bold

Anderson, W. S. 1993. "Guilty Elderly Love Balked: *Asinaria.*" In *Barbarian Play: Plautus' Roman Comedy,* 79–82. Toronto.
Antonsen-Resch, A. 2005. *Von Gnathon zu Saturio: Die Parasitenfigur und das Verhältnis der römischen Komödie zur griechischen.* Berlin.
Axtell, H. L. 1907 = 1987. *The Deification of Abstract Ideas in Roman Literature and Inscriptions.* New York.
Beare, W. 1964. *The Roman Stage.* 3rd. ed. London.
Bertini, F., ed. 1968. *Plauti, Asinaria cum Commentario Exegetico.* Genoa.
Bertschinger, J. 1921. *Volkstümliche Elemente in der Sprache des Phädrus.* Bern.
Borghini, A. 1999. "Logica e continuità della stirpe: Una proiezione comica: nota a Plauto, *Asin.* 68 sgg." In Raffaelli and Tontini, 115–20.
Bradley, K. 2000. "Animalizing the Slave: The Truth of Fiction." *Journal of Roman Studies* 90: 110–25.
Brind'Amour, P. 1976. "Des ânes et des boeufs dans l'*Aululaire:* Commentaire des vers 226 à 235." *Maia* 28: 25–7.
Brown, P. G. McC. 2002. "Actors and Actor-managers at Rome in the Time of Plautus and Terence." In *Greek and Roman Actors: Aspects of an Ancient Profession,* ed. P. Easterling and E. Hall, 225–37. Cambridge.
Corte, F. della. 1961. "Contaminatio e retractatio nell'*Asinaria.*" *Dioniso* 35: 30–52.
Damon, C. 1997. *The Mask of the Parasite: A Pathology of Roman Patronage.* Ann Arbor.
Danese, R. M. 1999. "I meccanismi scenici dell'«Asinaria»." In Raffaelli and Tontini, 49–95.
———, ed. 2004. *Titus Maccius Plautus: Asinaria.* Editio Plautina Sarsinatia II. Sarsina/Urbino.
Dickey, E. 2002. *Latin Forms of Address from Plautus to Apuleius.* Oxford.

Drake, G. C. 1968–9. "Candidus: A Unifying Theme in Apuleius' *Metamorphoses.*" *Classical Journal* 64: 102–9.

Ernout, A., ed. 1932. *Plaute. Tome I. Amphitryon—Asinaria—Aulularia.* Paris.

Fitzgerald, W. 2000. *Slavery and the Roman Literary Imagination.* Cambridge.

Fontaine, M. 2005. Review of Danese (2004). *Bryn Mawr Classical Review* 7.

Fraenkel, E. 1960. *Elementi Plautini in Plauto.* Florence.

Franko. G. F. 2004. "Ensemble Scenes in Plautus." *American Journal of Philology* 125: 27–59.

Freyburger, G. 1986. *Fides: Étude sémantique et religieuse depuis les Origines jusqu'à l'Époque augustéenne.* Paris.

Gibson, B. 2001. "*Argutia Nilotici calami:* A Theocritean Reed?" In Kahane and Laird, 67–76.

Gilula, D. 1993. "The Crier's Routine (Plaut. *Asin,* 4–5; *Poen.* 11–15)." *Athenaeum* 81: 283–7.

Goetz, G., and G. Loewe, eds. 1889; 1881. *T. Macci Plauti Comoediae, Asinaria,* 1. Leipzig.

Gowers, E. 1993. *The Loaded Table: Representations of Food in Roman Literature.* Oxford.

———. 2001. "Apuleius and Persius." In Kahane and Laird, 77–87.

Gratwick, A. S. 1973. "Titus Maccius Plautus." *Classical Quarterly* 23: 78–84.

———, ed. 1993. *Plautus, Menaechmi.* Cambridge.

———. 2001. "Paternal *obsequelia:* Some Passages of Plautus, Nonius, and Terence." *Hermes* 129: 45–62.

Gratwick, A. S., and S. J. Lightley. 1982. "Light and Heavy Syllables in Plautus and Others." *Classical Quarterly* 32: 124–33.

Gray, J. H., ed. 1894. *T. Macci Plauti Asinaria.* Cambridge.

Gulick, C. B. 1896. "Omens and Augury in Plautus." *Harvard Studies in Classical Philology* 7: 235–47.

Habinek, T. 2005. *The World of Roman Song: From Ritualized Speech to Social Order.* Baltimore.

Havet, L. 1905. "Études sur Plaute, *Asinaria* I—La seconde et la troisième scènes et la composition générale." *Révue de Philologie* 29: 94–103.

Havet, L., with A. Freté, eds. 1925. *Pseudo-Plaute, Le Prix des Ânes* (Asinaria*).* Paris.

Henderson, J. 1992. "Wrapping Up the Case: Reading Ovid, *Amores,* 2, 7 (+ 8). II." *Materiali e Discussioni* 28: 27–83.

———. 1999. *Writing Down Rome: Satire, Comedy, and Other Offences in Latin Poetry.* Oxford.

———. 2001a. "From Megalopolis to Cosmopolis: Polybius, or There and Back Again." In *Being Greek under Rome: Cultural Identity, the Second Sophistic and the Development of Empire,* ed. S. Goldhill, 29–49. Cambridge.

———. 2001b. "In Ya Pre(face) . . ." In Kahane and Laird, 188–97.

———. 2002. "The Way We Were: R. G. Austin, *In Caelianam.*" In *The Classical Commentary: Histories, Practices, Theory,* ed. R. K. Gibson and C. S. Kraus, 205–34. Mnemosyne Supplement 232. Leiden.

———. Forthcoming. "In Ovid with Bed (*Ars* II and III)." In *Ars 2K,* ed. R. K. Gibson and A. R. Sharrock.

Holford-Strevens, L. 1988. *Aulus Gellius.* London.

Hough, J. N. 1937. "The Structure of the *Asinaria.*" *American Journal of Philology* 58: 19–37.

Hunter, R. L. 1980. "Philemon, Plautus and the *Trinummus.*" *Museum Helveticum* 37: 216–30.

Jacobs, A. J. 2005. *The Know-It-All: One Man's Humble Quest to Become the Smartest Person in the World.* London.

James, S. L. 2003. *Learned Girls and Male Persuasion: Gender and Reading in Roman Love Elegy.* Berkeley, Los Angeles, and London.

———. 2006. "A Courtesan's Choreography: Female Liberty and Male Anxiety at the Roman Dinner Party" In *Prostitutes and Courtesans in the Ancient World,* ed. C. A. Faraone and L. K. McClure, 224–51. Madison.

Jory, E. J. 1966. "*Dominus gregis.*" *Classical Philology* 61: 102–05.

Kahane, A., and A. Laird, eds. 2001. *A Companion to the Prologue of Apuleius' Metamorphoses.* Oxford.

Kaufman, D. B. 1932. "Roman Barbers." *Classical Weekly* 25: 145–8.

Konstan, D. 1983. "*Asinaria:* The family." In *Roman Comedy,* 47–56. Ithaca and London.

Krostenko, B. A. 2000. "Latin *vinnus, vinnulus.*" *Glotta* 76: 66–74.

Leadbeater, L. W. 1987. "Lubet and the Principle of Pleasure in the Plays of Plautus." *Classical Bulletin* 63: 5–11.

Leo, F., ed. 1895. *Plauti Comoediae,* 1. Berlin.

Lilja, S. 1965. *Terms of Abuse in Roman Comedy.* Annales Academiae Scientiarum Fennicae 141. Helsinki.

Lindsay, W. M., ed. 1904. *T. Macci Plauti Comoediae,* 1. Oxford.

Lombardi, L. 1961. *Dalla «fides» alla «bona fides».* Milan.

López, G. 1970. "Sui vv. 104–126 dell'*Asinaria.*" *Giornale Italiano di Filologia* 22: 82–5.

Lowe, J. C. B. 1992. "Aspects of Plautus' Originality in the *Asinaria.*" *Classical Quarterly* 42: 152–75.

———. 1995. "Plautus' 'Indoor Scenes' and Improvised Drama." In *Plautus und die Tradition des Stegreifspiels: Festgabe für Eckard Lefèvre zum 60, Geburtstag,* ed. L. Benz, E. Stärk, and G. Vogt-Spira, 23–31. ScriptOralia 75. Tübingen.

———. 1999. "l'«*Asinaria*» e il suo modello Greco." In Raffaelli and Tontini, 13–24.

Lowe, N. J. 2000. *The Classical Plot and the Invention of Western Narrative.* Cambridge.

MacCary, W. T., and M. M. Willcock, eds. 1976. *Plautus, Casina.* Cambridge.

Maltby, R. 1991. *A Lexikon of Ancient Latin Etymologies.* Leeds.

McCarthy, K. 2000. *Slaves, Masters and the Art of Plautine Comedy.* Princeton.

McGinn, T. A. J. 1998. *Prostitution, Sexuality, and the Law in Ancient Rome.* Oxford.

Miniconi, P. 1964. "Le vocabulaire plautinien de la boisson et de l'ivresse." In *Hommages à J. Bayet,* ed. M. Renard and R. Schilling, 495–508. Collection Latomus 70. Brussels.

Moore, T. J. 1998. "Music and Structure in Roman Comedy." *American Journal of Philology* 119: 245–73.

Moritz, L. A. 1958. *Grain-Mills and Flour in Classical Antiquity.* Oxford.

Nicolson, F. W. 1891. "Greek and Roman Barbers." *Harvard Studies in Classical Philology* 2: 41–61.

Nisbet, R. G. M., and N. Rudd. 2004. *A Commentary on Horace, Odes, Book III.* Oxford.

Nixon, P., trans. 1916. *Plautus: In Four Volumes.* Cambridge, Mass.

Otto, A. 1890 = 1971. *Die Sprichwörter der Römer.* Leipzig = Hildesheim and New York.

Parker, H. 1989. "Crucially Funny, or Tranio on the Couch: The *seruus callidus* and Jokes about Torture." *Transactions of the American Philological Association* 119: 233–46.

Phillimore, J. S. 1926. "The Budé *Asinaria.*" *Classical Review* 40: 129–30.

Putnam, M. C. J. 2003. "Horace *epi.* 1. 13: Compliments to Augustus." In *Gestures: Essays in Ancient History, Literature, and Philosophy Presented to Alan L. Boegehold,* ed. G. W. Bakewell and J. P. Sickinger, 100–12. Oxford.

Raccanelli, R. 1998. *l'Amicitia nelle Comedie di Plauto: Un'Indagine Antropologica.* Bari.

Raffaelli, R., and A. Tontini, eds. 1999. *Asinaria: Sarsina, 12 Settembre 1998.* Urbino.

Rei, A. 1998. "Villains, Wives, and Slaves in the Comedies of Plautus." In *Women and Slaves in Greco-Roman Culture: Differential Equations,* ed. S. Murnaghan and S. R. Joshel, 92–108. London and New York.

Ribbeck, O., ed. 1873. *Comicorum Romanorum Fragmenta.* Leipzig.

Rimell, V. 2002. *Petronius and the Anatomy of Fiction.* Cambridge.

Robbins, B. 1993. *The Servant's Hand: English Fiction from Below.* Durham and London.

Romm, J. S. 1992. *The Edges of the Earth in Ancient Thought.* Princeton.

Rose, J. 1984. *The Case of Peter Pan, or The Impossibility of Children's Fiction.* London and Basingstoke.

Rosivach, V. J. 1998. *When a Young Man Falls in Love: The Sexual Exploitation of Women in New Comedy.* London and New York.

Ryder, K. C. 1984. "The *senex amator* in Plautus." *Greece & Rome* 31: 181–9.

Scafuro, A.C. 1997. *The Forensic Stage: Settling Disputes in Graeco-Roman New Comedy.* Cambridge.

———. 2003. "The Rigmarole of the Parasite's Contract for a Prostitute in *Asinaria*: Legal Documents in Plautus and Terence." *Leeds International Classical Studies* 3.4.

Schauwecker, Y. 2002. "Zum Sprechverhalten der Frauentypen bei Plautus." *Gymnasium* 109: 191–211.

Schmidt, K. 1902. "Die griechischen Personnamen bei Plautus." *Hermes* 37: 173–211, 353–90, 608–26.

Schuhmann, E. 1977. "Der Typ der *uxor dotata* in den Komödie des Plautus." *Philologus* 121: 45–65.

Scullard, H.H. 1981. *Festivals and Ceremonies of the Roman Republic.* London.

Segal, E. 1968. *Roman Laughter: The Comedy of Plautus.* Cambridge, Mass.

Sherberg, B. 1992. *Das Vater-Sohn-Verhältnis in der griechischen und römischen Komödie.* Tübingen.

Shershow, S.C. 1986. *Laughing Matters: The Paradox of Comedy.* Amherst, Mass.

Slater, N. 1985. "*Asinaria* as Guerrilla Theatre." In *Plautus in Performance: The Theatre of the Mind,* 55–69. Princeton.

Solin, H. 2003. *Die griechischen Personnamen in Rom: Ein Namenbuch,* 1–3. 2nd ed. Berlin.

Stewart, P. 2003. *Statues in Roman Society: Representation and Response.* Oxford.

Sutton, D.F. 1993. "*Asinaria.*" In *Ancient Comedy: The War of the Generations,* 86–95. New York and Ontario.

Svendse, E.D. 1986. *The Professional Handbook of the Donkey.* New York.

Trapp, M.B. 2001. "Tickling the Ears: Apuleius' Prologue and the Anxieties of Philosophers." In Kahane and Laird, 39–46.

Treggiari, S. 1991. *Roman Marriage: Iusti Coniuges from the Time of Cicero to the Time of Ulpian.* Oxford.

Ussing, J.L., ed. 1875. *T. Macci Plauti, Comoediae,* 1: 347–435. Copenhagen.

Vanoyeke, V. 1990. *La Prostitution en Grèce et à Rome.* Paris.

Vogt-Spira, G. 1991. "*Asinaria oder Maccus vortit barbare.*" In *Plautus barbarus: Sechs Kapiteln zur Originalität des Plautus,* ed. E. Lefèvre, E. Stärk, and G. Vogt-Spira, 11–69. ScriptOralia 25. Tübingen.

Walker, J. 2005. Review of Danese (2004). *Bryn Mawr Classical Review* 7.

Willcock, M.M. 1997. Review of *Cantica,* ed. C. Questa (1995). *Classical Review* 47: 296–8.

Wright, J. 1974. *Dancing in Chains: The Stylistic Unity of the Comoedia Palliata.* Papers and Monographs of the American Academy in Rome 25. Rome.

Zagagi, N. 1980. *Tradition and Originality in Plautus: Studies of the Amatory Motifs in Plautine Comedy.* Hypomnemata 62. Göttingen.

Indexes

1. *Asinaria*

accipio/do (take/pay dough), 140, 145, 150

Aeacides = Achilles, 148

aequus, 141

alley, rear entrance (*angiportum*), 187, 189

anger, 133, 148–49, 222, 226

artutus, 112

aside, 169, 207, 210, 227
  overheard, 159, 209, 229–30

asinaria, -ius, 211, 219

asses, 191, 235
  Arcadian, 193, 235
  beaten, 191, 193–94
  bray, vii, 177, 194
  ears and texts, vii, 220, and *passim*
  grex, xii, 219
  and horses, 206, 238
  and oxen, 203, 235
  stubborn (not stupid), 235
  worn out, 193, 197–98
  See also calcitro; mill

assonance, 172, 200
  See also sigmatism

Athens, 126–27, 139

audience (hearing/heeding,), 207–15

gynephobic, 133, 170, 180, 196, 230–31
  of (leading) men, 159, 213–15
  = silence, xii, 208, 219, 238
  trap for, 137, 223

authorship, 224

bag of cash/asses/comedy (*crumina*), 176–77, 192–94, 198, 226

bear (load, *baiiulo, fero, adfero,* etc., *porto, ueho*), 196–97, 200–202, 236–37
  See also suffer

beg, beseech (*obsecro, oro, exoro*), 134, 163, 229

"brothel," hires out girl, for a day/ party/year, 140–41, 180, 229
  -keeping, *as* bird-catching/fishing/ port, 139–40, 171–72, 231
  mirrors bourgeoisie, 136
  raided for girl, 159, 228

calcitro, 193, 236

carry. *See* bear; suffer

celox, 173

2. Other

WISCONSIN STUDIES IN CLASSICS

WILLIAM AYLWARD, NICHOLAS D. CAHILL,
AND PATRICIA A. ROSENMEYER, *General Editors*

E. A. THOMPSON
Romans and Barbarians: The Decline of the Western Empire

JENNIFER TOLBERT ROBERTS
Accountability in Athenian Government

H. I. MARROU
A History of Education in Antiquity
Histoire de l'Education dans l'Antiquité, translated by George Lamb

ERIKA SIMON
Festivals of Attica: An Archaeological Commentary

G. MICHAEL WOLOCH
Roman Cities: Les villes romaines by Pierre Grimal, translated and
edited by G. Michael Woloch, together with A Descriptive Catalogue of
Roman Cities by G. Michael Woloch

WARREN G. MOON, editor
Ancient Greek Art and Iconography

KATHERINE DOHAN MORROW
Greek Footwear and the Dating of Sculpture

JOHN KEVIN NEWMAN
The Classical Epic Tradition

JEANNY VORYS CANBY, EDITH PORADA,
BRUNILDE SISMONDO RIDGWAY, and TAMARA STECH, editors
Ancient Anatolia: Aspects of Change and Cultural Development

ANN NORRIS MICHELINI
Euripides and the Tragic Tradition

WENDY J. RASCHKE, editor
*The Archaeology of the Olympics: The Olympics and
Other Festivals in Antiquity*

PAUL PLASS
*Wit and the Writing of History:
The Rhetoric of Historiography in Imperial Rome*

BARBARA HUGHES FOWLER
The Hellenistic Aesthetic

F. M. CLOVER and R. S. HUMPHREYS, editors
Tradition and Innovation in Late Antiquity

BRUNILDE SISMONDO RIDGWAY
Hellenistic Sculpture I: The Styles of ca. 331–200 B.C.

BARBARA HUGHES FOWLER, editor and translator
Hellenistic Poetry: An Anthology

KATHRYN J. GUTZWILLER
Theocritus' Pastoral Analogies: The Formation of a Genre

VIMALA BEGLEY and RICHARD DANIEL DE PUMA, editors
Rome and India: The Ancient Sea Trade

RUDOLF BLUM and HANS H. WELLISCH, translators
Kallimachos: The Alexandrian Library and the Origins of Bibliography

DAVID CASTRIOTA
Myth, Ethos, and Actuality: Official Art in Fifth Century B.C. Athens

BARBARA HUGHES FOWLER, editor and translator
Archaic Greek Poetry: An Anthology

JOHN H. OAKLEY and REBECCA H. SINOS
The Wedding in Ancient Athens

CHRISTOPHER A. FARAONE and LAURA K. McCLURE, editors
Prostitutes and Courtesans in the Ancient World

Plautus
JOHN HENDERSON, translator and commentator
Asinaria: The One about the Asses

PATRICE RANKINE
Ulysses in Black: Ralph Ellison, Classicism, and African American Literature

Paul Rehak
JOHN G. YOUNGER, editor
Imperium and Cosmos: Augustus and the Northern Campus Martius